PRACTICAL ACCOUNTING SYSTEMS AND PROCEDURES

PRACTICAL ACCOUNTING SYSTEMS AND PROCEDURES

Martin F. Towles, CPA

Prentice-Hall, Inc. / Englewood Cliffs, NJ

Prentice-Hall International, Inc., *London*
Prentice-Hall of Australia, Pty. Ltd., *Sydney*
Prentice-Hall of Canada, Ltd., *Toronto*
Prentice-Hall of India Private Ltd., *New Delhi*
Prentice-Hall of Japan, Inc., *Tokyo*
Prentice-Hall of Southeast Asia Pte. Ltd., *Singapore*
Whitehall Books, Ltd., *Wellington, New Zealand*

Library of Congress Cataloging in Publication Data

Towles, Martin F
Practical accounting systems and procedures.

Includes index.
1. Accounting. I. Title.
HF5635.T67 657 77-9383
ISBN 0-13-689208-6

This publication is designed to provide accurate and authoritative information in regard to the subject matter covered. It is sold with the understanding that the publisher is not engaged in rendering legal, accounting or other professional service. If legal advice or other expert assistance is required, the services of a competent professional person should be sought.

—From a Declaration of Principles jointly adopted by a Committee of the American Bar Association and a Committee of Publishers and Associations

Printed in the United States of America

ABOUT THE AUTHOR

Martin F. Towles is a CPA and has a degree in accounting from Johns Hopkins University. He began his accounting career as a junior accountant with Ernst & Ernst and in 1954, after having worked for Haskins & Sells and several local CPA firms, he joined the staff of Wooden & Benson, one of the largest accounting firms in Maryland.

His extensive practical experience includes organizing and supervising audits of governmental entities, banks, savings and loan associations, investment bankers, insurance companies, hospitals, charitable organizations, radio broadcasting companies, mechanical and construction contractors, real estate firms, housing developers and a wide range of companies engaged in manufacturing, wholesale, and retail enterprise.

He has supervised and conducted federal and multi-state income tax service, where applicable, for all types of organizations listed above.

In 1970 he declined an offer of a partnership in Wooden & Benson and joined the staff of Lower, McClean, Berndt and Taylor, a local firm in Towson, Maryland. In 1972 he rejoined Wooden & Benson and is charged with the responsibility for reviewing audit reports and related workpapers. Since that time, in addition to reviewing reports, he has organized and conducted audits, made systems analyses, prepared feasibility studies, implemented LIFO valuation systems, and contributed articles to national accounting periodicals.

He is a member of the American Institute of Certified Public Accountants, the American Accounting Association, and the Maryland Association of Certified Public Accountants.

A WORD FROM THE AUTHOR

The purpose of this book is to analyze typical accounting problems that have developed from recently changed conditions and to demonstrate practical techniques for solutions that conform to generally accepted accounting principles.

The broadly cross-representative accounting subjects in such areas that have been selected for exposition in this book are: the present value of leases, computation of imputed interest for receivables and payables, conversion of conventional statements for reporting in units of general purchasing power, implementation and operation of LIFO inventory valuation systems, establishment of collateral bad debt reserves, dual accounting, accounting for the consummation of business combinations, the equity method of accounting for investments, essentials of statistical sampling, and the design and application of flowcharts and decision tables.

In each chapter typical accounting problems are constructed and step-by-step techniques for their solution are given in such a manner that the reader is able to project the factors of a similar problem of his own into the format provided and arrive at a satisfactory conclusion by completing the steps outlined in the model. Consider the following examples:

- In the chapter on statistical sampling, cross-referenced charts are used to provide a step-by-step demonstration of a methodological routine that permits the reader to set up mathematically valid attribute, discovery, variable, and stratified sampling tests and evaluate their results without any reference to the abstruse mathematical concepts involved in the statistical process.
- In the chapter on flowcharting, standard symbols are illustrated and described for the basic functions of input/output, processing, flow direction, and annotation, as well as a variety of specialized input/output and processing symbols. The chapter contains detailed charts to illustrate both program flowcharts and systems flowcharts, and displays examples of both striped and departmental flowcharts used to highlight features of internal control.

- The chapter on decision tables contains diagrams showing the basic structure of decision tables and provides illustrations of limited entry tables, extended entry tables, mixed entry tables, open tables, closed tables, and action tables. Examples are used to demonstrate application of decision tables to actual decision-making with reference to such problems as feasibility studies, internal control procedures, and multiple tables for detailed instructions.

In summary, this reference work will provide explicit techniques for the practical solution of newly developed accounting problems that are beginning to continually confront professionals in their day-to-day operations; it will be equally useful to those who seek procedures, systems, and tools that will enable them to cope with new requirements and improve the quality of their work.

Martin F. Towles

CONTENTS

3 LIFO INVENTORY VALUATION: Implementation and Techniques for Computation of Values (cont.)

5 SYSTEMS OF DUAL ACCOUNTING: Establishing Collateral Bad Debt Reserves for Financial Institutions (cont.)

PRACTICAL ACCOUNTING SYSTEMS AND PROCEDURES

1

ACCOUNTING FOR LEASES

Prior to 1964, accounting for leases generally was an uneventful operation. Leases were almost always considered to be simple executory contracts and periodic rent was reported as current revenue by the lessor and as current cost by the lessee; and depreciation and maintenance expenses were charged to operations by the lessor in accordance with what were then generally accepted accounting principles.

However, with the issuance of Opinion No. 5 by its Accounting Principles Board in September 1964, the American Institute of Certified Public Accountants sanctioned deviation from what formerly were generally accepted accounting principles in two major areas. The Opinion decreed that henceforth, in certain lease transactions, substance was to be considered more important than legal formality: assets were to be recorded without passage of title, and discounted present value, rather than historic cost, was to be the accounting basis for recording the transaction.

Subsequent to the publication of Opinion No. 5 the Accounting Principles Board, prior to its demise on June 30, 1973, issued Opinions Nos. 7, 27, and 31. The overall effect of the new accounting principles promulgated in these directives was to require separate accounting treatment for leases treated as executory contracts and those treated as purchases and sales of capital assets. The following categories of accounting methods for leases is set up in the Opinions:

Lessees
- Ordinary leases treated as executory contracts.
- Leases treated as purchases.

Lessors
- Ordinary leases treated as executory contracts.
- Leases treated as financing devices.

Manufacturers and Dealers
- Ordinary leases treated as executory contracts.
- Leases treated as sales.

Since discounted present values normally are conceptually illusive to accountants indoctrinated in the historic cost basis of accounting, many accountants have not bothered with the concept unless they were actually confronted by it. Leasing is becoming a major financing device, however, and the practice is likely to continue to expand in volume and increase in complexity; eventually all accountants will become involved in the processes. This chapter gives a synopsis of the applicable Opinions of the Accounting Principles Board, simplified computational methods for present values, and the application thereof to selected accounting problems.[1]

[1] At this writing the Financial Accounting Standards Board has issued a discussion memorandum concerning an analysis of issues related to accounting for leases. It is certainly reasonable to anticipate that there might be some slight change in the criteria for determining which method should be used in accounting for leases, but the methods themselves, as illustrated in this chapter, will remain valid.

LESSEES

LEASE TREATED AS A PURCHASE

Since leases covering merely the right to use property in exchange for future rental payments are nothing more than executory contracts and involve no accounting problems, Opinion No. 5 is concerned only with accounting for noncancelable leases (or leases cancelable only upon the occurrence of some remote contingency) which are clearly in substance installment purchases of property; and the Opinion provides that the property and the related obligation should be included as an asset and liability in the balance sheet if the terms of the lease result in the creation of a material equity in the property. The criteria for determining the accounting treatment of leases are found in the conditions within, and the circumstances surrounding, the lease agreement. The Board decided that any one criterion listed below will tend to indicate that the lease is in substance a purchase, and should be accounted for as such.

Conditions contained in the lease:

1. The initial term is materially less than the useful life of the property, and the lessee has the option to renew the lease for the remaining useful life of the property at substantially less than the fair rental value; or
2. The lessee has the right, during or at the expiration of the lease, to acquire the property at a price which at the inception of the lease appears to be substantially less than the probable fair value of the property at the time or times of permitted acquisition by the lessee.

Circumstances surrounding the lease agreement:

1. The property was acquired by the lessor to meet the special needs of the lessee and will probably be usable only for that purpose and only by the lessee.
2. The term of the lease corresponds substantially to the estimated useful life of the property, and the lessee is obligated to pay costs such as taxes, insurance, and maintenance, which are usually considered incidental to ownership.
3. The lessee has guaranteed the obligations of the lessor with respect to the property leased.
4. The lessee has treated the lease as a purchase for tax purposes.

RELATED PARTIES

The Opinion further states that in cases where the lessee and lessor are related, leases should be treated as purchases even though they do not meet the criteria set forth above if a primary purpose of ownership of the property by the lessor is to lease it to the lessee and (a) the lease payments are pledged to secure the debts of the lessor or (b) the lessee is able, directly or indirectly, to control or influence significantly the actions of the lessor with respect to the lease.

SALE AND LEASEBACK

In a sale and leaseback arrangement the criteria outlined above apply to the agreement covering the leaseback as though no concurrent sale were involved. However, the Opinion states that material gains or losses resulting from the sale of properties that are the subject of sale and leaseback transactions, together with the related tax effect, should not be shown as revenue, but should be amortized over the life of the lease as an adjustment of the rental cost (or, if the leased property is capitalized, as an adjustment of depreciation).

ACCOUNTING FOR LEASES AS PURCHASES

Accounting for leases determined to be purchases on the basis of the criteria in Opinion No. 5 requires a departure from the historic cost basis of accounting. The aggregate payments to the lessor, reduced to present values by an appropriate discount factor, should be recorded as the cost of the asset and a similar amount should be set up to represent the liability under the lease. The difference between the aggregate rental payments and the liability set up on the books represents interest expense that will be amortized over the period of the payments. Also, it is appropriate to depreciate the amount capitalized as property over the estimated life of the asset, rather than over the period of the lease.

ILLUSTRATIVE PROBLEM No. 1

A lease arrangement fitting the criteria for a purchase requires annual rentals of $10,000 over a six-year period at a time when current interest rates are 8-¾% per annum.

Since the first payment of $10,000 has a present value of 1, we consult the table in the Appendix and find that the present value of five annual payments of $10,000 is $39,150.10. Therefore, the present value of the aggregate lease payments is $49,150.10, and this amount should be recorded both as the cost of the asset and as the liability for future lease payments. Since future annual payments of $10,000 will be charged proportionately to interest expense and to the liability account, the accountant should prepare a schedule similar to the one shown below.

AMORTIZATION SCHEDULE

Payment Number	Amount of Payment	Payments Applied to: Interest Expense	Payments Applied to: Reduction of Liability	Balance of Liability (Unamortized Present Value)
1	10,000	–	10,000	39,150
2	10,000	3,426	6,574	32,576
3	10,000	2,850	7,150	25,426
4	10,000	2,225	7,775	17,651
5	10,000	1,544	8,456	9,195
6	10,000	805	9,195	–

It will be noted that the interest charge is computed at 8¾% on the balance of the unamortized present value before the concurrent payment is made. Also, the interest charges shown above are for twelve-month periods, and interest expense at the end of a fiscal period must be accrued or deferred in relation to the date of the payment of the periodic rent.

LESSORS

ACCOUNTING METHODS

Accounting Principles Board Opinion No. 7 states that the principal accounting problems of lessors concern the allocation of revenue and expense to the accounting periods covered by the lease, and the Opinion outlines the following two methods designed to accomplish appropriate allocation of such income.

Operating Method

This is the conventional method of accounting for periodic rent. Aggregate rentals are reported as revenue over the life of the lease and expenses and depreciation are recognized in each accounting period as determined by methods that are conventionally used for such expenses when incurred in activities other than leasing.

Financing Method

Under the financing method, the excess of aggregate rentals over the cost (reduced by estimated residual value at the termination of the lease) of the leased property is generally designed to compensate the lessor for the use of the funds invested. Since this excess is in the nature of interest, it is recognized as revenue during the term of the lease in decreasing amounts related to the declining balance of the unrecovered investment or, in other words, as an approximately level rate of the return on funds not yet recovered.

BASIS OF SELECTION OF ACCOUNTING METHOD

The financing method is generally appropriate for leases designed to pass all or most of the usual ownership risks or rewards to the lessee, and to assure the lessor of, and generally limit him to, a full recovery of his investment plus a reasonable return on the use of funds invested. The operating method is appropriate for companies that retain the usual risks or rewards of ownership in connection with their leasing activities.

INITIAL DIRECT COSTS

When initial direct costs of negotiating and closing leases are reasonably expected to be recovered from revenues, these costs should be deferred and allocated to future periods by a method of allocation consistent with that used to recognize revenue under the financing or operating method.

ACCOUNTING FOR LEASES AS FINANCING DEVICES

There are no unusual problems involved in accounting for leases under the operating method. However, since under the financing method the excess of aggregate rentals over the cost of the asset must be recognized as revenue during the term of the lease in decreasing amounts related to the declining balance of the unrecovered investment, the concept of discounted present value must be utilized in computing the amount of the income to be amortized.

ILLUSTRATIVE PROBLEM No. 2

A machine that has an expected useful life of six years costs you $60,000. You want to lease it for six years at an annual rental that will yield 8 ¾%, compounded annually, on your investment.

The six required payments form an ordinary annuity whose present value is $60,000. If the payments were to be made at the end of each year, the formula for computing the required annual payment would be:

$$R = 60{,}000 \, \frac{1}{4.51955}$$

However, since the payments are made at the beginning of the year, and no interest is allocable to the first payment, the result found from the above formula must be divided by 1.0875 (1 + i) in order to arrive at the correct required annual payment. In short, you compute a reciprocal of the present value of 60,000 for six periods at 8.75% as shown in the table in the Appendix by dividing the present value ratio into 1, multiplying it by 60,000, and dividing the result by 1.0875, as follows:

$$\frac{1}{4.51955} = .22126 \qquad .22126 \times 60{,}000 = 13{,}275.60$$

$$13{,}275.60 \div 1.0875 = \$12{,}207.44$$

Annual payments must be made in the amount of $12,207.44, and will amount to $73,244.64 over the six-payment period. This will result in interest income of $13,244.64. The aggregate rental of $73,244.64 less the unrecovered finance charge of $13,244.64 should be set up as a receivable. Since future annual receipts of $12,207.44 will be charged proportionately to interest income and to the receivable account, the accountant should prepare a schedule similar to the one shown below.

AMORTIZATION SCHEDULE

		Receipts Applied to		
Payment Number	Amount of Payment	Interest Income	Reduction in Unrecovered Cost	Balance of Unrecovered Cost (Account Receivable)
–				60,000
1	12,207	–	12,207	47,793
2	12,207	4,182	8,025	39,768
3	12,208	3,479	8,729	31,039
4	12,207	2,716	9,491	21,548
5	12,207	1,885	10,322	11,226
6	12,208	982	11,226	–

The interest income is computed at 8-¾% of the balance of unrecovered cost before the payment is received. The interest income shown above covers 12 months for each period. Therefore, interest income at the end of each fiscal period must be accrued or deferred in relation to the date of the date of the receipt of the periodic rent.

MANUFACTURER AND DEALER LESSORS

In leasing activities there is, generally, a significant difference between the objectives of financial or similar institutions and those of manufacturers or dealers. Financial entities usually are satisfied with a reasonable return, in the nature of interest, based on the cost of the investment. Manufacturers and dealers, on the other hand, seek to make a profit on the transaction and to receive interest at an appropriate rate on the uncollected lease payments. Therefore, in many cases, the lease of a manufacturer or dealer lessor will be equivalent to a sale of the property with the sales price collectible over a period of time. In such cases the gain or loss on the sale should be recognized currently, and the interest income inherent in the transaction should be amortized over the period of the payments on the lease.

CRITERIA FOR DETERMINING THAT A LEASE IS IN SUBSTANCE A SALE

The accounting for leases of manufacturer and dealer lessors was covered in Accounting Principles Board Opinion No. 7. However, the interpretation and application in practice of the Opinion raised so many questions that the Board issued Opinion No. 27 in November 1972 to provide more specific criteria to determine when a manufacturer or dealer lessor should recognize a lease transaction as if it were a sale.

The Opinion provides that a manufacturer or dealer lessor should account for a lease transaction with an independent lessee as a sale if:

(a) collectibility of the payments required from the lessee is reasonably assured,

(b) no excessive commitments are made to the lessee to guarantee performance, and

(c) any one of the following conditions is present:

  (i) the lease transfers title to the lessee by the end of its term; or

  (ii) the lease gives the lessee the option to obtain title without cost or at a nominal cost by the end of the term of the lease; or

  (iii) the leased property, or like property, is available for sale; and the sum of (1) the present value of the required rental payments and (2) any related investment tax credit retained by the lessor is equal to or greater than the normal selling price or, in the absence thereof, the fair value (either of which may be less than cost) of the leased property or like property; or

  (iv) the term of the lease is substantially equal to the remaining economic life of the property.

PARTICIPATION BY THIRD PARTIES (LEVERAGED LEASES) AND TRANSACTIONS WITH RELATED COMPANIES

The sale or assignment by a manufacturer or dealer to an independent financing institution, or to a company related to the lessor, of a lease, or property subject to a lease, that meets the criteria set forth above does not negate the original determination that the lease transaction should be accounted for as a sale. Profit or loss, if any, on the transaction with the financing institution should be recognized at the time of sale or assignment to the financing institution. Any profit or loss on the transaction with the related company should be recognized following the principles of consolidation, or the equity method of accounting for investments in common stock, whichever is appropriate.

ACCOUNTING FOR LEASES AS SALES

Opinion No. 27 provides that when a lease transaction by a manufacturer or dealer lessor is recorded as a sale:

(a) revenue should be recognized in the period of the sale in an amount equal to the present value of the required rental payments, and

(b) the cost of the property (not reduced by residual value) and the estimated related future costs (other than interest) should be charged against income in that period.

In order to compute the present value of the future payments on the lease a discount factor must be used. Opinion No. 27 does not provide any guidance on how to select an appropriate interest rate to be used in the discount factor but does refer, by footnote, to Opinion No. 21, "Interest on Receivables and Payables." The selection of an interest rate is discussed in chapter 2 of this volume.

ILLUSTRATIVE PROBLEM No. 3

You are a manufacturer and have constructed a machine at a cost of $29,617.83. You also have entered into a lease agreement, the conditions of which indicate the transaction to be in substance a sale. The lease required eight annual payments of $6,500 each at a time when the lessee could have financed the purchase of a similar machine at an annual interest rate of 8-¾%.

It is necessary first to compute the present value of the payments required under the lease. Since the first payment has a value of 1, we consult the tables in the Appendix and find that the present value of seven annual payments of $6,500 each is $32,990.43. Therefore, the present value of the aggregate lease payments is $39,490.43.

The gain on the transaction to be recognized at the time of the lease is as follows:

Present Value of Aggregate Lease Payments, (Accounts Receivable)	39,490.43
Less Cost (Cost of Goods Sold)	29,617.83
Net Gain on Transaction	9,872.60

The interest income to be amortized over the life of the lease is.

Aggregate Lease payments	52,000.00
Less Present Value of Aggregate Lease Payments	39,490.00
	12,510.00

Since the future annual receipts of $6,500 will be distributed proportionately to interest income and to accounts receivable, the accountant should prepare a schedule similar to the one shown below:

AMORTIZATION SCHEDULE

		Receipts Applied to		
Payment Number	Amount of Payment	Interest Income	Reduction in Accounts Receivable	Balance of Accounts Receivable
—				39,490
1	6,500	—	6,500	32,990
2	6,500	2,887	3,613	29,377
3	6,500	2,570	3,930	25,447
4	6,500	2,227	4,273	21,174
5	6,500	1,853	4,647	16,527
6	6,500	1,446	5,054	11,473
7	6,500	1,004	5,496	5,977
8	6,500	523	5,977	—

The interest income is computed at 8-¾% on the balance of the unrecovered present value of future lease payments. As in other cases, the interest income shown above covers twelve-month periods. Therefore, interest income at the end of each fiscal period must be accrued or deferred in relation to the date of the receipt of the periodic rent.

INCOME TAX CONSIDERATIONS

Generally, the Internal Revenue Service requirements concerning treatment of leases for income tax purposes coincides with generally accepted accounting principles as outlined in this chapter. However, when lease revenues or expenses are recognized for tax purposes in a period other than the one in which they are recognized for financial reporting, appropriate consideration should be given to allocation of income taxes among accounting periods.

REQUIRED DISCLOSURE IN FINANCIAL STATEMENTS

CAPITALIZED LEASES

In addition to an appropriate description in the balance sheet of the items capitalized under the lease agreement, notes to the financial statements should disclose the significant provisions of the leasing transactions.

NONCAPITALIZED LEASES

In June 1973 the Accounting Principles Board released Opinion No. 31 in which the Board declared that it believes that the financial statements of lessees should disclose sufficient information regarding noncapitalized lease commitments to enable users of the statements to assess the present and prospective effect of those commitments upon the financial position, results of operations, and changes in financial position of the lessee, and accordingly, it specified, in detail, the information concerning total rental expenses, minimum rental commitments, and other general data that must be disclosed as an integral part of the financial statements.

2

PROCEDURES FOR IMPUTATION OF INTEREST ON RECEIVABLES AND PAYABLES

In 1971 the Accounting Principles Board of the American Institute of Certified Public Accountants published Opinion No. 21 which set forth the Board's views regarding appropriate accounting methods where the face amount of a note[1] did not reasonably represent the present value of the consideration given or received in exchange. The primary objective of the Opinion was to refine existing accounting procedures rather than to create new accounting principles. Nevertheless, the Opinion did, in fact, introduce new accounting principles: it compelled yet another departure from the historic cost concept in that it required that a computed present value be substituted for the cost basis of certain notes. The Opinion describes the conditions within the contracts and the circumstances surrounding the transactions that form the criteria for determining whether or not imputation of interest and conversion to present value should be applied to a particular note.

This chapter explains the provisions of the Opinion and provides illustrations of procedures and techniques for computing present values and accounting for imputed interest.

PRESENT VALUE CONCEPTS

APB Opinion No. 21, in a footnote, defines present value as "... the sum of the future payments discounted to the present date at an appropriate rate of interest." There are two basic concepts involved in present value as applied to imputed interest on receivables and payables:

(a) the present value of a series of future payments to be made at uniform intervals, which is technically known as the present value of an annuity; and,

(b) the present value of a single future payment.

The application of both these concepts is illustrated in the examples that follow in this chapter.

IMPUTED INTEREST

In ideal circumstances, the face amount of a note represents the value of the consideration given or received in exchange, and the interest rate stipulated in the note represents appropriate compensation to the lender for the use of funds he would have received in a cash transaction. In such circumstances, the cost of the consideration is recorded in an amount equivalent to the face value of the note, and the interest is accounted for as income or expense over its life.

In many instances the value of the consideration does not, in fact, correspond to the face value of the note. In such cases, when the stipulated interest rate is reasonable, the note is valued and accounted for at the value of the consideration exchanged, and the difference between the face value of the note and the value of the consideration is accounted for as premium or discount and amortized over the life of the note as an adjustment to interest income or expense.

[1] In the Opinion, and also in this chapter, "note" refers to a receivable or payable whether or not the obligation is an open account or secured by a formal note.

However, situations arise where a note is non-interest bearing, or it has a stated interest rate different from the rate of interest appropriate for the debt on the date of the transaction. Generally, in such circumstances, the note should be recorded at its present value. The value assigned to the consideration given or received, and the amount of interest income or expense to be amortized, should be based on the present value of such note. To do otherwise would result in a misstatement of the seller's sales price and profit and of the buyer's purchase price and cost in the year of the transaction, and an inaccuracy in recording interest income and expense in subsequent years.

If the exchange price of a note such as that described in the preceding paragraph could be established, both the present value of the note and its effective interest rate could be determined from the exchange price. However, if an exchange price cannot be established, then the present value of the note must be estimated.

To estimate the present value of a note, a discount factor, which may be different from the stipulated interest rate, must be used. In such cases an appropriate interest rate is approximated from available facts and this rate is ascribed to the note. This process of approximation is called *imputation,* and the resulting rate is called an *imputed interest rate.*

THE PURPOSE OF APB OPINION No. 21

The purpose of APB Opinion No. 21 is to prescribe appropriate accounting procedures where the face value of a note does not reasonably represent the present value of the consideration given or received in exchange.

The Opinion did not disrupt the established procedure for accounting for notes where either the market value of the note or the fair value of the consideration could be determined. For example, it had long been a practice to record the purchase of a bond at cost. The cost of the bond represented its market value and, consequently, its present value. The difference between the purchase price and the face value of the bond was set up as a discount or premium and amortized over the remaining life of the bond as an adjustment to interest income. The Opinion did not require a change in this procedure.

The major impact of the Opinion on accounting practices current at the time of its issue derived from its provision for the imputation, in certain situations, of an interest rate that differed from the rate stipulated in the transaction.

However, imputation of an interest rate is necessary only where *both* of the following conditions exist:

(a) the established exchange price of the note cannot be determined; and,

(b) the cash sales price of property, goods, or service acquired or sold in consideration for the note cannot be determined.

If either or both of the above values can be determined, both the present value of the note and the fair value of the consideration can be determined, and no imputation of interest is necessary. The following situations illustrate the determination of present value if either the exchange price of the note or the cash sales price of the goods or services is known.

Sale of a Machine in Exchange for a Note

In this example a machine is sold in exchange for a $100,000 note, payable in ten years with interest at 10% per annum.

1. *Where the Cash Sales Price of the Consideration Is Determinable.* If the exchange price of the note cannot be established but it can be determined that the cash sales price of the machine is, for example, $80,000, then the present value of both the machine and the note becomes $80,000. The difference of $20,000 between the face value of the note and its present value would be discount or premium and amortized by the interest method over the life of the note as an adjustment to interest income by the seller and as an adjustment to interest expense by the purchaser.

2. *Where the Exchange Price of the Note Is Determinable.* If the cash sales price of

the machine cannot be determined but an exchange price for the note can be established at, for example, $90,000, then the present value of both the machine and the note becomes $90,000. The difference of $10,000 between the $100,000 face value of the note and its present value of $90,000 would be accounted for in the same manner as described in the preceding paragraph.

3. *Where Both the Sales Price of the Consideration and the Exchange Price of the Note Is Determinable.* This example assumes that it can be reasonably determined that the cash sale price of the machine is $80,000 and that the exchange price of the note is $90,000. In this case the present value of the machine becomes $90,000 instead of $80,000, and the seller has made a profit of $10,000 in addition to the profit he would have made in a normal cash sale. In this instance the seller would credit sales with $90,000, premium on notes receivable with $10,000 and set up $100,000 as notes receivable. The purchaser would set up an asset for $90,000, discount on notes payable for $10,000, and record the note for $100,000. The premium and discount would be amortized over the life of the note by the interest method as an adjustment of interest income and interest expense by the seller and purchaser, respectively. No imputation of an interest rate need be made.

If an established exchange price for the note is not determinable, and the cash sales price of goods, property, or service is not known, it becomes necessary to determine the present value of the note by ascribing to it an approximated interest rate in accordance with the provisions of APB Opinion No. 21.

PROVISIONS OF APB OPINION No. 21

The following sections of this chapter outline the provisions of APB Opinion No. 21. The discussion covers the general types of transactions to which the Opinion applies and the ones to which it does not; the three categories of receivables and payables specifically described and illustrated in the Opinion; income tax allocation; determination of an appropriate interest rate; and statement presentation of discount and premium. The discussion also demonstrates appropriate accounting procedures for each of the three categories of notes described in the Opinion.

APPLICABILITY

The Opinion states that the principles discussed therein are applicable to receivables and payables that represent contractual rights to receive money or contractual obligations to pay money on fixed or determinable dates, whether or not there is any stated provision for interest, except for such transactions as are specifically exempted in the Opinion. By definition of the applicability, the Opinion does not apply to receivables or payables that will be payable in property, goods, or services instead of money, nor does it apply to notes payable on demand or at some indeterminate future date.

TYPES OF RECEIVABLES AND PAYABLES COVERED BY THE OPINION

The Opinion lists the following as examples of receivables and payables to which its provisions apply:

1. Secured notes.
2. Unsecured notes.
3. Debentures.
4. Bonds.
5. Mortgages.
6. Certain specified types of accounts receivable and payable.

TYPES OF RECEIVABLES AND PAYABLES SPECIFICALLY EXEMPTED FROM THE PROVISIONS OF THE OPINION

The Opinion states that its provisions are not intended to apply to the following types of transactions. It is important to note, however, that statement presentation of discount and premium, prescribed in paragraph 16 of the Opinion and discussed later in this chapter, is applicable in all circumstances.

(a) Receivables and payables arising from transactions with customers or suppliers in the normal course of business which are due in customary trade terms not exceeding approximately one year.
(b) Amounts that do not require repayment in the future, but rather will be applied to the purchase price of the property, goods, or service involved; e.g., deposits or progress payments on construction contracts, advance payments for acquisition of resources and raw materials, advances to encourage exploration in the extractive industries.
(c) Amounts intended to provide security for one party to an agreement; e.g., security deposits, retainages on contracts.
(d) The customary cash-lending activities and demand or savings deposit activities of financial institutions whose primary business is lending money.
(e) Transactions where interest rates are affected by the tax attributes or legal restrictions prescribed by a governmental agency; e.g., industrial revenue bonds, tax-exempt obligations, government-guaranteed obligations, income tax settlements.
(f) Transactions between parent and subsidiary companies and between subsidiaries of a common parent.
(g) Obligations assumed in connection with sales of property, goods, or services; e.g., a warranty for product performance.
(h) Convertible debt securities, described in APB Opinion No. 14, "Accounting for Convertible Debt and Debt Issued with Stock Purchase Warrants."

THREE CARDINAL GROUPS OF RECEIVABLES AND PAYABLES

The Opinion discusses and illustrates the following three fundamental groups of receivables and payables (referred to as "notes") and outlines appropriate accounting treatment for each group.

1. Note received or issued solely for cash.
2. Note exchanged for cash and some other rights or privileges.
3. Note exchanged solely for property, goods, or services.

The explanation in the paragraphs that follow concerning the three categories of receivables and payables includes solutions of problems that demonstrate the accounting procedures prescribed in the Opinion.

NOTE RECEIVED OR ISSUED SOLELY FOR CASH

Where a note is received or issued solely for cash, it is presumed to have a present value at issuance measured by the cash proceeds exchanged, and the total amount of interest during the entire period of a cash loan is generally measured by the difference between the actual amount of cash received by the borrower and the total amount agreed to be repaid to the lender. The difference between the face amount and the proceeds upon issuance is considered to be discount or premium, and is amortized over the life of the note. The effective interest rate for such notes is the rate stipulated in the note, adjusted by the discount or premium to be amortized. No imputation of interest need be made.

The following examples illustrate the accounting treatment for notes exchanged solely for cash.

Noninterest-Bearing Note

A five-year, noninterest-bearing note with a face value of $5,000 is issued in exchange for $5,000 in cash.

In this case, no imputation of interest is required, and no discount or premium is involved. The lender and borrower record $5,000 as a receivable and payable, respectively, and maintain the accounts intact on their books until the debt is paid.

Interest-Bearing Note—Proceeds at Par

A five-year note, with interest payable annually at 10% per annum, is issued in exchange for $5,000 in cash.

No imputation of interest is necessary in this transaction, and no discount or premium is entailed. The lender and borrower record $5,000 as a receivable and payable, respectively, and maintain the accounts intact on their books until the debt is paid. Annual interest payments are credited and charged to current operations as interest by the lender and borrower, respectively.

Interest-Bearing Note Issued at a Discount

A five-year note having a face value of $5,000, with interest payable annually at 10% per annum, is exchanged for $4,500 in cash.

No imputation of interest is necessary in this case. However, the $500 discount must be accounted for by both the lender and the borrower.

The lender records the note receivable at $5,000 and the discount at $500. The annual entry for interest received and discount amortized is summarized in the following journal entry:

	Debit	Credit
Cash	500.00	
Discount on Notes Receivable	100.00	
Interest Income		600.00

The borrower records the note payable at $5,000 and the discount at $500. The annual entry for interest paid and discount amortized is summarized in the following journal entry:

Interest Expense	600.00	
Discount on Notes Payable		100.00
Cash		500.00

Installment Note Issued at a Discount

A lender agrees to lend $3,000 in cash as proceeds of a discounted note to be repaid in twelve monthly installments so that each installment includes interest at the rate of 12% per annum, computed on the unpaid principal balance at the date of the installment.

No imputation of interest is necessary in this situation. However, the face amount of the note and the amount of the required monthly installments must be computed, and the difference between $3,000 and the total amount to be repaid must be recorded as discount.

To compute the required monthly installments. By referring to the table of present values of annuities, it is found that the present value of 1 at 1% interest for twelve periods is 11.25507. This present value ratio of 11.25507 divided into the amount of cash proceeds of $3,000 gives $266.54 as a dividend. Therefore, the monthly payments would be $266.54, and the face of the note would be twelve times that amount, or $3,198.48.

Proof of computation of monthly payments and face value of note. The following schedule proves that monthly installments of $266.54 would fulfill the requirements of the lender.

Amortization Schedule

Payment Number	Total Payment: Applied to Note	Applied to Interest	Applied to Principal	Remaining Principal Balance	Remaining Balance Due on Note
—	—	—	—	3,000.00	3,198.48
1	266.54	30.00	236.54	2,763.46	2,931.94
2	266.54	27.63	238.91	2,524.55	2,665.40
3	266.54	25.25	241.29	2,283.26	2,398.86
4	266.54	22.83	243.71	2,039.55	2,132.32
5	266.54	20.40	246.14	1,793.41	1,865.78
6	266.54	17.93	248.61	1,544.80	1,599.24
7	266.54	15.45	251.09	1,293.71	1,332.70
8	266.54	12.94	253.60	1,040.11	1,066.16
9	266.54	10.40	256.14	783.97	799.62
10	266.54	7.84	258.70	525.27	533.08
11	266.54	5.25	261.29	263.98	266.54
12	266.54	2.56*	263.98	—	—
	3,198.48	198.48	3,000.00		

*Adjusted for pennies.

Both the lender and the borrower would set up the note at its face value of $3,198.48, and would then set up the discount on the note in the amount of $198.48. The monthly payments of $266.54 would reduce the balance in the account for the note, and if monthly amortization of discount were desired, a collateral entry to interest income or expense could be made in the amounts shown in the schedule, so that at the end of the twelve months all nominal accounts would have a zero balance.

Another accepted method would be to set up the receivable and liability in the amount of $3,000 and reduce this balance each month by the amount indicated on the schedule as being applicable to principal. The remainder of the payment, indicated in the schedule as being applied to interest, would be credited to interest income by the lender and to interest expense by the borrower.

Whichever method is used, it must be remembered, as explained later in this chapter, APB Opinion No. 21 requires that in all circumstances the premium or discount be added or deducted from the face amount of the note for presentation in the financial statements.

Comparison of the Interest Method and the Rule of 78ths Method

The "interest method" of amortizing premium and discount is recommended by APB Opinion No. 21. The interest method applies interest, computed on the unpaid principal balance at the date of the payment, using the applicable rate of interest. This method is illustrated in the above example of an installment note issued at a discount.

An alternative method for amortizing premium and discount, recognized in the Opinion, is the "rule of 78ths method." This method is simply a sum-of-the-digits method, and gets its name from the fact that 78 is the sum of the digits of a twelve-month period.

A comparison of the two methods, as applied to amortization of discount on an installment note issued at a discount, is set forth in the schedule displayed in the following subsection of this chapter.

Comparative Schedule of Amortization—Sum-of-the-digits and Interest Methods

The amounts for amortization under the interest method are the same amounts that appear in the foregoing schedule for amortization of discount on an installment note issued at a discount.

The amounts for amortization under the sum-of-the-digits method are computed as follows:

Discount to be amortized: $198.48
Period: 12 months

Sum of the digits: $\frac{12^2 + 12}{2} = 78$

Discount to be amortized divided by sum of the digits:
$198.48 \div 78 = 2.5446$

Comparative Amortization Schedule

Payment Number	Computation of the Sum of the Digits	Amount of Amortization by the Sum-of-the-digits Method	Amount of Amortization by the Interest Method
1	12 x 2.5446	30.54	30.00
2	11 x 2.5446	27.99	27.63
3	10 x 2.5446	25.45	25.25
4	9 x 2.5446	22.90	22.83
5	8 x 2.5446	20.36	20.40
6	7 x 2.5446	17.81	17.93
7	6 x 2.5446	15.27	15.45
8	5 x 2.5446	12.72	12.94
9	4 x 2.5446	10.18	10.40
10	3 x 2.5446	7.63	7.84
11	2 x 2.5446	5.09	5.25
12	1 x 2.5446	2.54*	2.56*
		198.48	198.48

*Adjusted for pennies.

NOTE EXCHANGED FOR CASH AND SOME OTHER RIGHTS OR PRIVILEGES

A note issued for cash equal to its face amount is presumed to earn the stated rate of interest, and the face value of the note coincides with its present value. However, in some cases the parties may also exchange stated or unstated rights or privileges in connection with the cash consideration. In such cases these rights and privileges must be evaluated in connection with the interest stated in the note. If the rights or privileges have a determinable value, the effective interest rate will differ from the stated rate. In some cases the present value of the attendant rights or privileges can be determined to be the difference between the present value of the note at the stipulated interest rate and the present value of the note computed at the currently prevailing rate applicable to similar notes. Accounting recognition should be given to the rights and privileges connected with the transaction by imputing an appropriate interest rate and calculating the present value of the note on the basis of the imputed discount factor.

The following example is given in the Opinion:

Problem

A corporation lends a supplier cash that is to be repaid at the end of five years without interest. It is assumed that the loan is partial consideration under a purchase contract for supplier's products at lower than prevailing market prices. In this circumstance, the difference between the present value of the receivable and the cash loaned to the supplier is appropriately regarded as an addition to the cost of products purchased during the contract term. The note discount is amortized as interest income over the five-year life of the note.

Additional Assumptions

The Opinion does not offer any numerical values in citing the example. In order to demonstrate the complete development and solution of the problem the following further assumptions are made:

Face value of note	$50,000
Current prevailing interest rate applicable to such notes	8%

Present Value of Note

The prevailing interest rate of 8% for such loans is the imputed interest rate, and is used as a discount factor in computing the present value of the note, as follows:

> Line 5 in the 8% column of the table of present values of 1 at compound interest indicates that the present value ratio is .68058. Multiplying this ratio by the face value of the note, $50,000, gives a present value of $34,029. The unamortized discount would be $15,971, which is the difference between the face value and the present value of the note.

Method of Recording the Note

To record the note and the attendant discount, the lender and the supplier should make the following entries, respectively:

	Debit	Credit
Lender		
Note Receivable	50,000	
Deferred Charges	15,971	
Cash		50,000
Discount on Note Receivable		15,971
Supplier		
Cash	50,000	
Discount on Note Payable	15,971	
Note Payable		50,000
Deferred Income		15,971

Amortization Schedule

Both the lender and the supplier should prepare the following schedule for the purpose of recording annual amortization of discount:

Amortization Schedule

End of Annual Period	Face Amount of Loan	Annual Amortization of Discount	Unamortized Discount	Principal Balance
—	50,000	—	15,971	34,029
1	50,000	2,722	13,249	36,751
2	50,000	2,940	10,309	39,691
3	50,000	3,175	7,134	42,866
4	50,000	3,429	3,705	46,295
5	50,000	3,705	—	50,000
		15,971		

The annual discount is computed at the rate of 8% per annum on the principal balance at year end.

Recording Amortization of Discount

The purpose of imputing interest to this particular note is to account for the constructive interest income realized by the lender, and to increase the cost of goods sold by an equivalent amount; and to account for the constructive interest expense incurred by the supplier and to increase his income from sales by a like amount.

The discount should be amortized annually as an adjustment to interest by both parties in the amount shown on the above schedule for each respective year. The deferred charge and deferred income should be reduced by the lender and supplier based on the percentage of completion of the purchase contract.

Assuming that one-fifth of the total purchases contracted for were made during the first year, the entries at the end of the year for each respective party would be:

Lender	Debit	Credit
Cost of Goods Sold (Purchases)	3,194	
Discount on Note Receivable	2,722	
Deferred Charge		3,194
Interest Income		2,722
Supplier		
Deferred Income	3,194	
Interest Expense	2,722	
Sales		3,194
Discount on Note Payable		2,722

The above entries would amortize the discount by the interest method, and amortize deferred charges and deferred income on the basis of the percentage of completion of the purchase contract.

NOTE EXCHANGED SOLELY FOR PROPERTY, GOODS, OR SERVICES

The Opinion states that when a note is exchanged for property, goods, or services in a bargained transaction entered into at arm's length, there should be a general presumption that the rate of interest stipulated by the parties to the transaction represents fair and adequate compensation to the supplier for the use of the related funds. That presumption, however, must not permit the form of the transaction to prevail over its economic substance and thus would not apply if:

(a) interest is not stated, or
(b) the stated interest rate is unreasonable, or
(c) the stated face amount of the note is materially different from the current cash sales price for the same or similar items or from the market value of the note at the date of transaction.

Where the presumption that the rate of interest stipulated by the parties to the transaction is not overcome by any one of the above three conditions, no imputation of interest is necessary, and the stated interest rate should be used in accounting for the transaction.

Where any of the three indicated conditions do exist, however, the note, the sales price, and the cost of the property, goods, or services exchanged for the note should be recorded at the fair market value of the property, goods, or services, or at an amount that reasonably approximates the market value of the note, whichever is more clearly determinable. That amount may or may not be the same as the face value of the note, and any resulting discount or premium should be accounted for as an element of interest over the life of the note.

Following are two illustrations that demonstrate the method of imputing an interest rate. The first example concerns a noninterest-bearing note to which interest is imputed at an appropriate rate, and the second example shows the accounting treatment for an interest-bearing note to which a higher and more suitable interest rate is imputed.

Problem—Imputing Interest to a Noninterest-Bearing Note

A company manufactured a custom-made machine for a purchaser at a cost of $60,000. The machine was exchanged for a $100,000 ten-year, noninterest-bearing note to be paid in ten annual installments of $10,000 each.

The cash sale price of the machine could not be established, but it was determined that the purchaser could obtain financing for this type of transaction at an interest rate of 8% per annum.

The present value of the note was computed, using a discount factor of 8%, compounded annually; the present value of the note was used as the basis of the machine; and resulting discount was amortized over the life of the note by the interest method. The development of this case is outlined below.

Present Value of Note

Line 10 in the 8% column of the table of values of an annuity of 1 reveals the present value ratio to be 6.71008. Multiplying this factor by $10,000, the amount of the annual installments, gives a present value of $67,101. The unamortized discount is $32,899, which is the difference between the face value of the note and its present value.

Recording the Transaction

To record the purchase, the sale, the note, and the unamortized discount, the following entries were made by the seller and the purchaser, respectively:

Seller	Debit	Credit
Note Receivable	100,000	
Sales		67,101
Discount on Note Receivable		32,899
Purchaser		
Property	67,101	
Discount on Note Payable	32,899	
Note Payable		100,000

Amortization Schedule

Both the seller and the purchaser should prepare the following schedule for the purpose of recording annual amortization of discount.

Amortization Schedule

End of Annual Period	Total Payment	Payment Applied to Unamortized Discount	Payment Applied to Principal	Principal Balance
—	—	—	—	67,101
1	10,000	5,368	4,632	62,469
2	10,000	4,998	5,002	57,467
3	10,000	4,597	5,403	52,064
4	10,000	4,165	5,835	46,229
5	10,000	3,698	6,302	39,927
6	10,000	3,194	6,806	33,121
7	10,000	2,650	7,350	25,771
8	10,000	2,062	7,938	17,833
9	10,000	1,427	8,573	9,260
10	10,000	740	9,260	—
	100,000	32,899	67,101	

Recording Amortization of Discount

The purpose of imputing interest in this case is to set up the note at its present value and thereby value the consideration at its fair value. The difference between the face value of the note and its present value computed by an appropriate discount factor of 8% represents return to the seller for use of funds that he would have received in a cash sale, and interest expense to the buyer that he would have incurred had he borrowed the money to pay cash for the machine. Had interest not been imputed, the cost to the purchaser and the sales revenue of the seller would have been overstated by $32,899 in the year of the transaction, and interest expense and interest income of the purchaser and seller, respectively, would have been misstated by $32,899 over the following ten years.

At the end of the first year the following entries would be made by the respective parties.

Seller	Debit	Credit
Discount on Note Receivable	5,368	
Interest Income		5,368

Purchaser		
Interest Expense	5,368	
Discount on Note Payable		5,368

Similar entries would be made at the end of the next nine years, in the amounts indicated as amortization of discount on the above amortization schedule.

Problem—Imputing a Higher Interest Rate to an Interest-Bearing Note

This example is based on the preceding problem. A company manufactured a custom-made machine for a purchaser at a cost of $60,000. The machine was exchanged for a $100,000 ten-year note, bearing interest at the rate of 5% per annum. The note is to be paid in ten annual installments of $10,000 each. Each annual installment will include $10,000 principal plus interest on the unpaid principal balance at 5% per annum.

As in the preceding example, the cash sales price of the machine could not be established, but it was determined that the rate of interest appropriate for the debt on the date of the transaction was 8%.

Therefore, the present value of the note was computed, using a discount factor of 8%, compounded annually; the present value of the note was considered to be the cost of the machine; and resulting discount was amortized over the life of the note by the interest method.

Present Value of Note

The present value of this note, based on an 8% discount factor, was computed by the following steps:

1. determine what the total of each payment will be, including both principal and interest;
2. determine the present value of each future installment at 8% interest, compounded annually; and
3. take the sum of the present values of the future installments to obtain the present value of the note at 8% interest.

These three sets of computations are illustrated below.

1. The total payments to be made are shown in the Schedule of Actual Payments to Be Made by Purchaser.
2. The present value of each payment to be received can be computed by referring to the tables for present values of 1 at compound interest. The value of each payment will be found in the 8% column on a line that corresponds with the number of years between now and the date it is due.

   This computation is illustrated in the Schedule of Present Value of Future Payments.
3. The sum of the present value of the future payments is $87,662. Therefore, the present value of the note is $87,662 and the unamortized discount is $39,838.

Schedule of Actual Cash Payments to Be Made by Purchaser

Annual Period	Principal Balance at Beginning of Year	Payments at End of Year: Interest Computed at 5%	Principal	Total Payment
1	100,000	5,000	10,000	15,000
2	90,000	4,500	10,000	14,500
3	80,000	4,000	10,000	14,000
4	70,000	3,500	10,000	13,500
5	60,000	3,000	10,000	13,000
6	50,000	2,500	10,000	12,500
7	40,000	2,000	10,000	12,000
8	30,000	1,500	10,000	11,500
9	20,000	1,000	10,000	11,000
10	10,000	500	10,000	10,500
		27,500	100,000	127,500

Schedule of Present Value of Future Payments

Annual Period	Total Payment to Be Received	Present Value Ratio Shown in Tables	Present Value of Each Payment
1	15,000	.92593	13,889
2	14,500	.85734	12,431
3	14,000	.79383	11,114
4	13,500	.73503	9,923
5	13,000	.68058	8,847
6	12,500	.63017	7,877
7	12,000	.58349	7,002
8	11,500	.54027	6,213
9	11,000	.50025	5,503
10	10,500	.46319	4,863
	127,500		87,662

Recording the Transaction

The entries for setting up the note and related discount should be made in the same manner as that shown in the preceding illustration for recording the transaction involving a noninterest-bearing note.

Amortization Schedule

The following schedule should be prepared for the purpose of recording annual amortization of discount.

Amortization Schedule

End of Annual Period	Total Payment	Payment Applied to Unamortized Discount	Payment Applied to Principal	Principal Balance
—	—	—	—	87,662
1	15,000	7,013	7,987	79,675
2	14,500	6,374	8,126	71,549
3	14,000	5,724	8,276	63,273
4	13,500	5,062	8,438	54,835
5	13,000	4,387	8,613	46,222
6	12,500	3,698	8,802	37,420
7	12,000	2,994	9,006	28,414
8	11,500	2,273	9,227	19,187
9	11,000	1,535	9,465	9,722
10	10,500	778	9,722	—
	127,500	39,838	87,662	

Recording Amortization of Discount

The fact that a portion of each annual payment represents interest at the stipulated rate of 5% per annum should be disregarded in making annual entries for amortization of discount. The *total* payment should be considered, and the payment should be distributed in accordance with the amount applicable to interest and principal, as indicated for each annual payment, respectively, in the foregoing schedule.

For example, at the end of the first year the following entries would be made by the respective parties:

	Debit	Credit
Seller		
Cash	15,000	
Discount on Note Receivable		7,013
Note Receivable		7,987
Purchaser		
Note Payable	7,987	
Discount on Note Payable	7,013	
Cash		15,000

Similar entries would be made at the end of each of the nine subsequent years in the amounts indicated in the above amortization schedule.

INCOME TAX ALLOCATION

Differences between the recognition for financial accounting purposes and income tax purposes of discount or premium resulting from the determination of the present value of a note should be treated as a timing difference, and appropriate provision for income taxes should be made by setting up a deferred income tax debit or credit account.

For the sake of clarity in the exposition of the principles of imputed interest, the income tax effects have been omitted from consideration in the problems discussed in this chapter.

DETERMINING AN APPROPRIATE INTEREST RATE

If the present value of the consideration for a note can be established, the present value of the note will coincide with the present value of the consideration, and any necessary imputed interest rate can be calculated on the basis of the difference between the present value of the note and its face value, giving appropriate effect to the amounts and intervals of payments made on the note.

However, if such present value of the consideration cannot be determined, and it is necessary to impute interest to the note, an appropriate discount factor, or interest rate, must be used to compute the present value of the note. There are so many considerations that may affect the selection of an appropriate interest rate that it is not feasible to cover all of them in this chapter. However, in any event, the rate used for valuation purposes should be equal to the rate at which a debtor can obtain financing of a similar nature from other sources at the date of the transaction.

STATEMENT PRESENTATION OF DISCOUNT AND PREMIUM

APB Opinion No. 21 states that the discount or premium resulting from the determination of present value is not an asset or liability separable from the note that gives rise to it. Therefore, the discount or premium should be reported in the balance sheet as a direct deduction from or addition to the face amount of the note. It should not be classified as a deferred charge or deferred credit.

3

LIFO INVENTORY VALUATION:

Implementation and Techniques for Computation of Values

The operation of a business enterprise generally requires a continuing investment in inventory. Theoretically this investment should represent the residue of costs not applied against sales revenues. However, an inventory is composed of two distinct qualities: quantity and value. The *quantitative* attribute is objective, factual, and irrefutable, whereas the *values* assigned to the inventory are subjective and require the exercise of judgment. Since there are optional generally accepted methods of valuing inventories, the discretionary action taken in selecting the method used to apply such values will have a direct effect on residual costs and, correlatively, on net earnings.

FEASIBILITY OF CONVERSION TO LIFO

METHODS OF INVENTORY VALUATION—FIFO AND LIFO

There are two basic methods for applying inventory costs to operations: first-in-first-out (FIFO) and last-in-first-out (LIFO).

The FIFO method is based on the flow of inventory goods and assumes that the earliest acquired inventory items are applied to operations first; and that the resulting flow of inventory cost factors follows a strict chronological order related to the date of acquisition of the inventory goods.

The LIFO method is based on the flow of costs rather than goods, and insofar as quantities are concerned is the exact converse of FIFO. LIFO seeks to apply the latest acquired inventory costs to current operations. Under this method the flow of inventory cost factors is maintained on a current basis. If the demands of current operations exceed the quantity of current inventory acquisitions, the investment in inventory is assumed to be liquidated to the extent of such excess. In such cases the flow of inventory cost factors would follow an inverse chronological order in relation to the date of acquisition of inventory items.

COMPARISON OF FIFO AND LIFO

In times of relative economic stability, the historic cost, or FIFO method of valuing residual costs in inventory, provides for a flow of cost factors that satisfactorily matches them against related revenues. However, during periods of accelerated economic activity, or during an inflationary spiral, the FIFO method will not match revenues derived from high selling prices with current high costs of sales but, instead, will inflate the value of residual costs in inventory and produce paper profits that are not a true reflection of income. On the other hand, during such an inflationary period, the LIFO method of accounting for residual costs in inventory will direct the flow of cost factors so that current sales will be matched with costs most recently incurred. This method will tend to maintain inventory as an investment rather than as a cost factor itself and will result in a more accurate accounting for current income.

THE ADVANTAGES OF LIFO DURING INFLATION

Generally, during a period of rising prices, LIFO valuation of inventories is preferable to any other method for three important reasons:

(a) current income is more accurately reflected in financial statements;
(b) the elimination of inflated profits produces an immediate tax savings; and,
(c) the reduction in tax liability reduces the demand on cash funds at a time when they are of maximum utility.

A LIFO DISADVANTAGE

Normally, the LIFO method of inventory valuation matches current sales with costs most recently incurred and, if inventories are maintained at near normal requirement levels, the character of the flow of cost factors induced by LIFO persists through both inflationary and deflationary trends in the economy.

However, if during an inflationary period there is a significant decline in inventory quantities, and a partial liquidation of the LIFO base occurs, current sales will then be charged with old, lower costs, and the gross profit percentage will be distorted for the year in which the base was invaded. Subsequent maintenance of the inventories at normal requirement levels will reinstate the gross profit ratio as a valid measurement.

A decline in inventory quantities can be brought about involuntarily, as in a case where strikes prevent replenishment, or voluntarily, as in a situation where overall fiscal policies at a particular time require a reduction in the inventory investment. In any event, the contingency of liquidating the LIFO base should be given consideration in any decision to adopt the LIFO method of inventory valuation.

FEASIBILITY OF CONVERSION TO LIFO

The LIFO method of inventory valuation is acceptable to both the American Institute of Certified Public Accountants for financial accounting purposes and to the Internal Revenue Service for use in the determination of taxable income. Other than the procedures necessary to comply with certain technical requirements imposed by the American Institute of Certified Public Accountants and by the Internal Revenue Service, the change to LIFO generally is an uneventful transition. For tax purposes, the change may be made at any time during the fiscal year up to the due date of the corporate income tax return for the year of change, including any approved extensions of time for filing.

Since LIFO inventory valuation involves only residual costs, the change to the LIFO method generally can be accomplished without making any changes in the method already in use for inventory accounting. The required LIFO adjustments at the end of each month, and at the end of the fiscal year, can be calculated from the costs that are accumulated through normal accounting operations.

From an accounting standpoint, the conversion to LIFO can be easily and successfully accomplished. Generally, however, the public accountant is not in a position to make a definite recommendation as to whether or not such an election should be made. He cannot forecast future price levels and he does not know what the future inventory volume and turnover will be. In addition, normally he does not have an adequate conception of many intangibles that should be considered such as the attitude of stockholders, relations with employee personnel, and commitments to others. A proper decision can be made only by management, which has the necessary intimate knowledge of operations and intuitive feeling for future developments that derive only from experience in running the company. The accountant can, however, submit facts and figures that might aid management in arriving at a decision.

TIMING OF LIFO ELECTION

The prediction of future costs should be the prime factor involved in the decision to adopt LIFO. However, the timing of the election should be subject to consideration of the quantity of the inventory and of the predictable future volume changes. The ideal time to make the election generally is when prices have increased substantially during the fiscal year and are expected to continue to rise; and inventory quantities are, and are expected to continue to be, near normal requirement levels.

SPECIAL CONSIDERATIONS

a. Financial Reporting

The primary reason for adopting LIFO is to reduce both reportable and taxable income during a period of rising prices, and to take advantage of the resulting conservation of cash funds. However, this very desirable situation, if it occurs, will have the effect of reducing net income and earnings per share reported on the income statements furnished stockholders. The Internal Revenue Service financial requirements, described below in the section "Technical Requirements of the Internal Revenue Service," limits the disclosure that may be presented in the financial statements and specifically forbids the presentation of earnings per share computed on any basis other than LIFO for comparison purposes. In a publically held company this can be a major disadvantage in the use of LIFO. In the case of a closely held company the effect on stockholders of reduced earnings per share may not be significant, but it is a consideration that must be taken into account in a decision to make the election to use LIFO.

b. Nondiscretionary Adjustments

A major consideration in a decision whether or not to convert to LIFO must be the effect of such election on whatever nondiscretionary adjustments are required to be made to reportable income. The provisions of a profit-sharing plan, any possible union involvement, the possibility of disgruntled employees, the impact of possible reduction of income of executives, etc., should all be reviewed and evaluated prior to making a decision.

c. Dividends

The LIFO reserve represents a reduction in retained earnings available for dividend distributions.

d. State Laws

Consideration should be given to the effect of state statutory requirements, such as whether or not LIFO is recognized by the state for income tax purposes, for franchise tax reporting, and for personal property tax valuations.

TECHNICAL REQUIREMENTS OF THE INTERNAL REVENUE SERVICE

The following review concerns Internal Revenue Service technical rules, restrictions, and limitations pertaining to the adoption and use of the LIFO method.

a. Financial Reporting Requirement

The LIFO method of inventory valuation is authorized by Section 472 of the Internal Revenue Code. Paragraphs 472(c) and 472(e) (2) prohibit the taxpayer from using any method other than a LIFO inventory valuation in any of its reports to shareholders or creditors except for the following:

Dollar amounts of the beginning and ending LIFO reserves, and the per-share amount of each, may be shown as footnotes in the statements. However, the footnote should make no mention of the per-share increase in the reserve for the year.

(a) Revenue Ruling 73-66-1973 permits the following footnote: "If the first-in-first-out (FIFO) method of inventory accounting had been used by the company, inventories would have been $_____ and $_____ higher than reported on December 31, 19____ and December 31, 19____."

(b) Revenue Procedure 73-37, 1973 provides that disclosures required by Accounting Principles Board Opinion No. 20 will not terminate the election to use LIFO.

b. LIFO Election Must Be Timely

1. LIFO may be adopted and used only if the taxpayer files Form 970 in triplicate with his return for the year of adoption.
2. The taxpayer must attach to his income tax return for the first taxable year for which an index is used a statement describing the index. Also, a copy of the statement must be filed with the Commissioner of Internal Revenue, Attention: T:I:C:, Washington, DC 20224.

c. Opening LIFO Inventory Must Be at Cost

1. *Ascertainment of Actual Costs.* Regulations Paragraph 1.472-2(c) provide that the actual cost of aggregate opening LIFO inventory shall be determined pursuant to the inventory method employed by the taxpayer under the regulations applicable to the prior taxable year with the exception that restoration shall be made with respect to any write-down to market values resulting from the pricing of former inventories.

2. *Preceding Closing Inventory.* The opening inventory for the LIFO election year and the closing inventory for the preceding year are one and the same inventory. Therefore, any increase in cost of sales for the first LIFO year (by raising the opening inventory to cost) must be "paid for" by a corresponding decrease in cost of sales for the preceding year, which is accomplished by increasing the value of the ending inventory for the preceding year. This will result in a deficiency that must be paid with interest from the due date of the returns for the year preceding the first LIFO year.

d. Determination of Cost

The taxpayer should indicate on Form 970 the method of computing total year-end costs under the dollar-value LIFO method. Any increment over the base inventory can be valued at the following optional methods: earliest, latest, average, or any other proper method which in the opinion of the Commissioner clearly reflects income.

e. Products Included in LIFO

The taxpayer may select the class or classes of products to which the LIFO method will apply. However, this is subject to the Commissioner's regulatory authority to require that LIFO be used for products other than those specified in the statement of election if necessary to clearly reflect income.

f. Election Irrevocable by Taxpayer

The LIFO election is irrevocable by the taxpayer. The Commissioner may authorize a change pursuant to a written request to discontinue LIFO filed by the taxpayer within the first 90 days of the taxable year of change.

g. Election Subject to Commissioner Approval

Form 970 must be approved by the Commissioner in connection with the examination of the taxpayer's return.

h. Pools for Wholesalers, Retailers, etc.

Regulations Paragraph 1.472-8(c) states that items of inventory in the hands of wholesalers, retailers, jobbers, and distributors shall be placed in pools by major lines, types, or classes of goods.

i. Lower of Cost or Market

Under the LIFO method of inventory accounting, there will be no write-downs to market value permitted for reporting taxable income.

COMPLIANCE WITH GENERALLY ACCEPTED ACCOUNTING PRINCIPLES

LIFO inventory valuation is affirmed as a generally accepted accounting principle in Statement No. 4, Chapter 4, of Accounting Research Bulletin No. 43, published by the American Institute of Accountants in 1953.

In making a *change* to LIFO there are other official accounting directives that must be considered. In most cases the tax benefits to be derived are major considerations in an election to use LIFO inventory valuation. The Accounting Principles Board has stated that an accounting change is appropriate only if the enterprise can justify the use of an alternative principle on the basis that it is preferable. In addition, the Financial Accounting Standards Board states that preferability among accounting principles shall be determined on the basis of whether the new principle constitutes an improvement in financial reporting and not on the basis of income tax effects alone. However, in times of rising prices it should not be difficult to demonstrate that LIFO is preferable for reporting purposes, no matter what considerations triggered the change.

Some problems arise in making required full disclosure on the financial statements because of the restrictions in the Internal Revenue Service financial reporting requirements, but it appears that adequate disclosure will be made if the financial statements include the following notes:

a. Statement of the change from FIFO to LIFO, and the justification for such change.
b. The effect on inventory at the end of the year of change.
c. The amount of the inventory reserve at the end of the year of change.
d. A statement that there is no cumulative effect of the change on retained earnings of prior years.
e. The per-share value of the inventory reserve at the end of the year of change.
f. The excess of replacement costs over stated LIFO values resulting from base inventory liquidations, whenever this situation occurs.

TECHNIQUES FOR COMPUTATION OF VALUES

LIFO may be adopted on either a quantity basis or an aggregate dollar basis. The quantity basis is called "specific identification" and the aggregate dollar basis is referred to as "dollar-value LIFO."

SPECIFIC IDENTIFICATION

Specific identification valuation conforms to traditional inventory methods insofar as quantities are concerned. The LIFO concept involved is readily perceived. It assumes that individual inventory items acquired will be added to inventory at their respective purchase prices in strict chronological order, and that they will be removed from inventory at the same price in strict *inverse* chronological order.

This method is seldom used by business enterprises because of the enormous amount of detail work involved. Generally, some sort of perpetual inventory records are required in order to identify the items added to and deducted from the physical inventory.

DOLLAR-VALUE LIFO

The assumption in LIFO inventory valuation concerns the flow of costs rather than the flow of goods. This flow of cost factors is clearly evident when LIFO inventories are maintained on the specific identification basis. However, as stated previously, the specific identification basis is impractical and seldom used. Therefore, the dollar-value LIFO method has been developed in order to demonstrate the flow of inventory cost factors and at the same time obviate the necessity for specific identification and pricing of individual items.

Basically, the dollar-value method of pricing LIFO inventories permits inventories to be stated in terms of dollars adjusted for price-level changes. Under this method, currency rather than the physical unit of measure is used as a common denominator.

There are three basic systems for computing the value of LIFO inventories:

a. the base-year double-extension method;
b. the link-chain method; and,
c. the price-index method.

Techniques for computation of LIFO inventory values in connection with the three methods listed above are discussed in the paragraphs that follow.

BASE-YEAR DOUBLE-EXTENSION METHOD

The year in which LIFO is adopted is known as the "base year" and the prices at which the inventory items were extended at the *beginning* of the base year are referred to as "base-year costs." The object of dollar-value LIFO is to convert the value of the inventory recorded at current costs to the value that would be developed if the inventory items were priced and extended at base-year costs. Under the base-year double-extension method, the current inventory is extended twice; once at current prices and once at base-year prices. The value of the inventory at current costs is then divided by the value of the inventory at base costs to arrive at a ratio of current costs to base costs. This ratio, when multiplied by 100, is referred to as an index number to the base year. The index developed from double extension can be used to value the current inventory at base-year costs; to determine whether there has been any change in the quantity of the inventory in terms of base-year costs; and to value any increase at current prices.

INDEX NUMBERS AS CONVERSION FACTORS

In working with index numbers it is important to remember the following conversion techniques:

(a) to convert current values to base values, current values must be multiplied by a fraction, the denominator of which is the current index and the numerator the base index.

(b) to convert base values to current values, the base values must be multiplied by a fraction, the denominator of which is the base index and the numerator the current index.

INCREMENTS AND LAYERS

The original LIFO inventory is established at the beginning of the year LIFO is adopted. At the end of the first LIFO year, and for each successive year thereafter, the year-end inventory computed at base prices must be compared to the beginning-of-year inventory computed at base prices. If the ending inventory at base costs exceeds the beginning inventory at base costs, quantities in the inventory have increased. This increment must be valued at current costs and added to the beginning-of-year LIFO inventory to arrive at the value of the ending LIFO inventory. Current costs used for the purpose of valuing increments may be computed on any one of the following bases:

(a) cost of most recent acquisitions during the year;

(b) cost of earliest acquisitions during the year;

(c) average cost of all acquisitions during the year; or,

(d) current-year index to base year.

LIQUIDATIONS

Whenever the current inventory priced at base costs is less than the beginning-of-year inventory priced at base costs, a liquidation has occurred and LIFO inventory must be reduced by the amount of the difference. However, in addition to being reduced by the difference in *base-year costs,* LIFO must also be reduced by the adjustments for *current value* that were made on an equivalent amount of increment at base cost in prior years, beginning with the most recent additions to LIFO.

ADDITIONS TO BASE

When new and different types of items enter the inventory subsequent to the base year, equivalent base-year costs must be established for purposes of double extension. In many cases, however, specific base-year costs will not be available. In such cases the base-year costs can be approximated by use of base-year and current-year *price* indexes. The use of price indexes is discussed later in this chapter.

LIFO ADJUSTMENT

At the end of each year the existence of a difference between the LIFO inventory and the book inventory at current prices requires that an adjustment be made to cost of goods sold. The amount and nature of the necessary adjustment can be determined by comparing end-of-year LIFO with book inventory. The difference developed will represent the amount of all LIFO adjustments from the year of LIFO adoption to the present year. Therefore, this difference must be reduced by the net amount of all prior LIFO adjustments to arrive at the adjustment to operations that must be made in the current year.

LIFO RESERVE

The LIFO adjustment may be made directly to inventory and to cost of operations if the accounting records are organized to assimilate this type of entry. In most cases, however, adjusting the book inventory to LIFO would wreak havoc in the accounting system. Therefore, the generally accepted method for accommodating the adjustment is the use of a device referred to as the "LIFO Reserve." A LIFO Reserve account can be set up on the books to accumulate all LIFO adjustments, so that accounting for inventory at cost need not be disturbed. The balance in the LIFO reserve account at all times will be equivalent to the difference between LIFO and book inventory. When statements are prepared, only LIFO inventory values appear on the balance sheet, and the LIFO reserve is disclosed in notes to the financial statements.

ILLUSTRATION OF BASE-YEAR DOUBLE EXTENSION METHOD

Baker Company elected to adopt LIFO valuation of inventories at the end of 19X5. Perpetual inventory records are maintained by electronic data processing on a FIFO basis.

Year-end inventories recorded on the books of Baker Company were as follows:

19X4—$13,650
19X5— 16,890
19X6— 17,053

The book inventory at the end of 19X4 is the beginning LIFO inventory and the prices at which it was extended are the base-year costs.

19X5 OPERATIONS

DOUBLE EXTENSION

At the end of 19X5 Baker Company selected a representative sample of its inventory and double extended the items at both base costs and current costs. This double extension is shown in the schedule below:

Product Catalog Number	Current Inventory Quantities	Current Inventory at Current Year-End Prices		Current Inventory at Base-Year Prices	
		Price	Amount	Price	Amount
862	18	$12	$ 216	$10	$ 180
864	36	13	468	10	360
869	92	11	1,012	10	920
871	84	20	1,680	16	1,344
872	10	19	190	18	180
894	11	24	264	21	231
901	21	18	378	15	315
904	32	9	288	9	288
906	14	10	140	8	112
908	17	11	187	9	153
			$4,823		$4,083

INDEX NUMBERS

Index numbers computed from the above data are:

Base Year: 4,083 ÷ 4,083 = 1 x 100 = 100.00

Current Year: 4,823 ÷ 4,083 = 1.1812 x 100 = 118.12

Applying the index to the book value of current inventory:

16,890 x 100 = 1,689,000 ÷ 118.12 = 14,299

Therefore the current inventory at base price is $14,299.

INCREMENT AND LAYER

The increase in inventory at base prices is:

Ending inventory at base prices	$14,299
Less: Beginning inventory at base prices	13,650
Increase at base prices	$ 649

The current value of the increment is found by applying index numbers as follows:

$$649 \times 118.12 = 76{,}659.88 \div 100 = 767$$

Therefore $767 is the LIFO value of the increment and represents the LIFO layer for 19X5. The ending LIFO inventory is computed as follows:

Beginning LIFO inventory	$13,650
Add: Value of increment	767
Ending LIFO inventory	$14,417

LIFO ADJUSTMENT

The LIFO adjustment is:

Book inventory	$16,890
Less: Ending LIFO inventory	14,417
LIFO adjustment	$ 2,473

Since this is the first year of LIFO and no prior LIFO adjustments have been made, this $2,473 is the adjustment required for the current year.

LIFO RESERVE

Baker Company charged current operations with $2,473 and set up a credit in a LIFO reserve account for an equivalent amount.

19X6 OPERATIONS

At the end of 19X6 Baker Company double extended a representative sample of its current inventory at both base and current costs in the same manner as that used in 19X5. The computed index number for 19X6 was 124.02.

LIQUIDATION

Applying the index number to current inventory:

$$17{,}053 \times 100 = 1{,}705{,}300 \div 124.02 = 13{,}750$$

Therefore the current inventory at base prices is $13,750.

The decrease in inventory at base prices during the year is:

Beginning inventory at base prices	$14,299
Less: Ending inventory at base prices	13,750
Decrease in inventory at base prices	$ 549

Since the increase at base prices of $649 in 19X5 exceeds the decrease of $549 at base prices in 19X6, the total amount of the decrease must be converted to the same values that were used in the 19X5 increment in order to arrive at the LIFO value of the 19X6 liquidation.

To accomplish this, the 19X5 index is applied to the 19X6 decrease at base cost of $549.

$$549 \times 118.12 = 64{,}847.88 \div 100 = 648$$

Therefore, $648 is the LIFO value of the liquidation occurring in 19X6, and the LIFO inventory is computed as follows:

Beginning LIFO inventory	$14,417
Less: LIFO value of liquidation	648
Ending LIFO inventory	$13,769

LIFO ADJUSTMENT

Calculation of the LIFO adjustment is performed as follows:

Book inventory	$17,053
Less: Ending LIFO inventory	13,769
Excess of book inventory over LIFO inventory	3,284
Less: Prior LIFO adjustments	2,473
Current adjustment to be made to LIFO reserve	$ 811

LIFO RESERVE

Baker Company charged current operations with $811 and credited the LIFO reserve account with $811. The LIFO reserve account at December 31, 19X6 was as follows:

Additions for 19X5 adjustment	$ 2,473
Additions for 19X6 adjustment	811
Total reserve	$ 3,284

THE LINK-CHAIN METHOD

The link-chain method of LIFO valuation of inventories is simply a variation of the base-year double-extension method. The theory is exactly the same, and there is only a slight change in the method of making the required computations. Under the link-chain method, current inventory costs are double extended with the previous year costs rather than with base costs. The value of the inventory at current costs is divided by the value of the inventory at previous-year costs to develop a current-year index. A cumulative index from the base year is maintained and is computed by multiplying it each year with the current-year index computed by the link-chain double-extension method. This cumulative index is used to value current inventory at base-year costs, to determine changes in quantity in terms of base-year costs, and to value increases at current prices.

IDEAL CONDITIONS FOR USE OF LINK-CHAIN METHOD

As the base year recedes into the past, it becomes increasingly difficult to identify specific items in the current inventory with similar items in the base-year inventory. Therefore, the base-year double-extension method is appropriate only for simple inventories that remain fairly stable from year to year. Where the components of the inventory undergo substantial change, or where there are continuous significant changes in its composition, the link-chain method is preferable and far more practical than the base-year double-extension method.

ILLUSTRATION OF LINK-CHAIN METHOD

This example is based on the one used to illustrate the base-year double-extension method. The facts are the same, except that the example is extended for two years to include 19X7 and 19X8.

A schedule of required computations for the years from 19X5 to 19X8 is shown in the following table of the first LIFO year.

If the reader follows the schedule step by step and compares the computations shown thereon with those described in the example of the base-year double-extension method, he will find that there is no difference in effect. The only differences in computations are:

(a) current-year index is computed by double extension of the current inventory with previous-year prices rather than base-year prices; and

(b) a cumulative index is used to convert current values to base-year values rather than using a base-year index.

The principles of double extension, index numbers, increments, layers, liquidations, LIFO adjustment, and LIFO reserve are the same under both methods.

PRICE-INDEX METHOD

The price-index method of computing the value of LIFO inventories is the simplest, most economical, and fastest method yet devised. The only difference between the price-index method and the link-chain method is that the link-chain method requires double extension of inventory items to develop indexes and the price-index method uses the indexes prepared by the federal government.

OBVIATION OF DOUBLE EXTENSION

Since the price-index method uses the prefabricated indexes of the federal government, double extension is not necessary. The price-index method is not necessarily the most accurate method, however. Unless prepared indexes can be found that reasonably coincide with components of the inventory, it is not appropriate to use such indexes in lieu of preparing indexes by double extension.

PRICE INDEXES

The Bureau of Labor Statistics of the Department of Labor prepares periodic indexes on prices, using a base year of its own selection. The indexes cover a wide range in general, but some of the particular classifications in the indexes are extremely limited in their application. The major indexes published by the Bureau of Labor Statistics are:

Consumer price indexes
Commodity price indexes
Wholesale price indexes
Retail price indexes

ATTITUDE OF INTERNAL REVENUE SERVICE

The Internal Revenue Service has taken the position that, except for department stores, BLS indexes will not be accepted by the Service in connection with the use of the LIFO method unless the taxpayer can independently demonstrate the accuracy, reliability, and suitability of the use of such indexes to the satisfaction of the district director.

RATIOS PROVIDED BY PRICE INDEXES

Price indexes provide the current-year index that is developed by double extension under the link-chain method. As in the link-chain method, the price-index method requires the annual computation of a cumulative index that can be used to convert current values to base-year values. The difference in the cumulative index of the link-chain method and that of the price-index method is that under the former the index is accumulated from 100 at the beginning of the base year, and under the latter it starts with whatever index was published by BLS at the beginning of the first year of LIFO.

Therefore, the cumulative index for the link-chain method is computed by simply multiplying

	First LIFO Year (Base) 19X5	19X6	19X7	19X8
1. Ending inventory at year-end prices (book inventory)	16,890	17,053	19,610	22,552
2. Index for year computed by double extension	118.12	104.99	108.22	110.08
3. Cumulative index—(line 2 x line 3, last year) : 100	118.12	124.02	134.21	147.73
4. Ending inventory at base costs—(line 1 : line 3) x 100	14,299	13,750	14,611	15,266
5. Beginning inventory at base costs—line 4, last year	13,650	14,299	13,750	14,611
6. Increase (decrease) at base costs	649	(549)	861	655
LIFO VALUE OF INCREMENT				
7. Inventory increase at base costs—line 6	649		861	655
8. Inventory increase at end-of-year costs—(line 7 x (line 3 – 100)] : 100	118		295	313
LIFO VALUE OF LIQUIDATION				
9. Inventory decrease at base costs—line 6		(549)		
10. Decrease applied to increase, 19X5—[line 9 x (line 3, last year – 100)] : 100		(99)		
11. Total increase (decrease) in LIFO inventory	767	(648)	1,156	968
12. LIFO inventory at beginning of year—line 13, last year	13,650	14,417	13,769	14,925
13. LIFO inventory—end of year	14,417	13,769	14,925	15,893
COMPUTATION OF LIFO ADJUSTMENT				
14. Inventory per books—line 1	16,890	17,053	19,610	22,552
15. LIFO inventory—end of year—line 13	14,417	13,769	14,925	15,893
16. LIFO Reserve	2,473	3,284	4,685	6,659
17. Less prior additions to reserve—line 16, last year	–	2,473	3,284	4,685
18. Current increase in LIFO reserve	2,473	811	1,401	1,974

the previous-year cumulative index by the current-year index, while under the price-index method the cumulative index is computed by first dividing the current year BLS index by the BLS index of the first year of LIFO and multiplying the result by the previous-year cumulative index.

ILLUSTRATION OF PRICE-INDEX METHOD

The following example is again based on the one used for the base-year double-extension method, as expanded in the section discussing the link-chain method.

	First LIFO Year (Base)			
	19X5	19X6	19X7	19X8
1. Ending inventory at year-end prices (book inventory)	16,890	17,053	19,610	22,552
2. Price index—end of year	132.39	117,67	121.29	123,38
*3. Cumulative price index——(line 2 ÷ 112.08) x line 3, last year	118.12	124.02	134.21	147.73
4. Ending inventory at base costs——(line 1 ÷ line 3) x 100	14,299	13,750	14,611	15,266
5. Beginning inventory at base costs——line 4, last year	13,650	14,299	13,750	14,611
6. Increase (decrease) at base costs	649	(549)	861	655

*This computation is made on the assumption that 112.08 was the index published for 19X4, and was used to value beginning LIFO for 19X5.

The reader will note that the only differences in the six steps outlined above between the link-chain method and the price-index method are the following:

(a) current indexes are computed by double extension under the link-chain method, but are taken from published indexes under the price-index method; and,

(b) the cumulative index is based on 100 in the link-chain method, but is based on the published index in the year of adoption of LIFO under the price-index method (in the case above, 112.08).

The last twelve steps shown in the example for the link-chain method have not been reproduced in the above example because they are exactly the same in both instances.

All of the principles of index numbers, increments, layers, liquidations, LIFO adjustment, and the LIFO reserve are identical under all methods described in this chapter.

RETAIL INVENTORY METHOD

The principles for establishing and maintaining LIFO valuation of inventories accounted for by the retail inventory method are exactly the same as those that apply to the price-index method. There are, however, some differences in the computational techniques required by each respective method. The retail inventory method differs from other methods in its use of retail sales values rather than cost in accounting for inventory. However, markup percentages are used in the retail industry to convert inventory from retail value to cost. After the cost of the retail inventory has been established, the procedures for converting current costs to base costs, adding layers and increments, deducting liquidations, and computing the LIFO adjustment are exactly the same as those under the price-index method.

RETAIL PRICE INDEX

Section 1.472-8(e)(1) of the Internal Revenue Regulations provides that a taxpayer entitled to use the retail method of pricing LIFO inventories may use the retail price indexes prepared by the Bureau of Labor Statistics. These indexes are published semiannually in the Internal Revenue Cumulative Bulletin.

DIFFERENCES IN MARKUP PERCENTAGES

In order to arrive at a ratio between cost and retail sales price with which to deflate the value of retail priced inventory to cost, retail establishments perform two operations for conventional retail that are not appropriate for LIFO retail:

(1) beginning inventory is included in both the cost and the retail value computations; and,

(2) markdowns are sometimes considered as pertaining totally to goods sold, and are not restored to items remaining in the ending inventory.

The computations for the LIFO value of inventories accounted for by the retail method omits the beginning inventory in computing the total of both the retail and cost values. Also, the LIFO computations require that the effect of markdowns pertaining to inventory items be recognized in the computations.

Following are two schedules, Restatement of Markup Percentages for Inventory and Computation of Markup Percentages for Inventory, that show the restatement of markup percentages for the beginning inventory in the first year of LIFO, and the computation of LIFO markup percentages at the end of that year. The reader should note that the beginning inventories are included in the LIFO computations for the *first* year of LIFO, but are omitted in the LIFO calculations in subsequent years.

RESTATEMENT OF MARKUP PERCENTAGES FOR INVENTORY
BEGINNING OF FIRST LIFO YEAR

	Conventional Retail			LIFO Retail		
	Retail	Cost	Markup %	Retail	Cost	Markup %
Beginning Inventory	150,000	94,575	36.95	150,000	94,575	36.95
Purchases	680,000	420,920	38.10	680,000	420,920	38.10
Freight In		4,000			4,000	
Additional Markups	15,000			15,000		
Markdowns				(48,000)		
	845,000	519,495	38.52	797,000	519,495	34.82

Computation of Markup Percentages

845,000 - 519,495 = 325,505 ÷ 845,000 = 38.52%
797,000 - 519,495 = 277,505 ÷ 797,000 = 34.82%

COMPUTATION OF MARKUP PERCENTAGES FOR INVENTORY
END OF FIRST LIFO YEAR

	Conventional Retail			LIFO Retail		
	Retail	Cost	Markup %	Retail	Cost	Markup %
Beginning Inventory	190,000	116,812	38.52	—	—	—
Purchases	794,000	460,000	42.06	794,000	460,000	42.06
Freight In		5,000			5,000	
Additional Markups	14,000			14,000		
Markdowns				(46,000)		
	998,000	581,812	41.70	762,000	465,000	38.98

RESTATEMENT FOR GENERAL PRICE-LEVEL CHANGES

The effect of LIFO valuation of inventories on statements restated for general price-level changes is discussed in chapter 4. However, it might be appropriate to state here that the LIFO computational techniques described in this chapter are not in any way affected by the requirement to prepare statements in units of general purchasing power.

FULL-ABSORPTION COSTING OF INVENTORIES

The adoption in 1973 by the Internal Revenue Service of the concept of full-absorption costing of inventories by manufacturers creates problems in the allocation of certain indirect production costs to inventory, but has no effect on the principles of valuation discussed in this chapter.

STANDARD COSTS

All of the principles of LIFO inventory valuation outlined in this chapter are applicable to LIFO inventories that are accounted for by the standard cost method.

However, an important principle concerning standard costs in connection with LIFO inventory valuation is that significant variations between standard and actual costs must be appropriately reallocated to inventory. Immaterial net variances need not be restored to inventory, but the treatment of over and short variances should be consistent.

LIFO POOLS

The term "LIFO pool" refers to the grouping of dollar-value inventory components into a theoretical single unit, to which a separate LIFO valuation is applied. Regulations 1.472-8(b) and (c) define pools and describe the nature of pools that can be established. Generally, manufacturers and processors may use a single pool for a natural business unit, consisting of all items entering into the inventory; or they may elect to establish multiple pools, consisting of various groups of inventory items, where each group is ordinarily composed of items that are substantially similar. Items of inventory in the hands of wholesalers, retailers, jobbers, and distributors are required to be placed into pools by major lines, types, or classes of goods.

A prudent selection of pools will maximize the benefits of LIFO. In a single pool, quantity decreases in individual items could be offset by increases in other items so that lower cost items would be less likely to be removed from the inventory. In certain cases, however, benefits could be derived from selecting multiple pools. The choice of multiple pools might be beneficial under the following conditions:

(a) there is a large quantity of slow-moving items on hand; or,

(b) prices are expected to affect certain products more than others; or,

(c) there are anticipated changes in production techniques and production technology.

Separate LIFO pools may be selected for raw materials, labor, and manufacturing overhead. In such a case, care should be taken to set up procedures that will ensure that no change in the cost assigned to an inventory will result from the movement of goods from a raw materials state to a finished goods state, and that a shift in proportion of these three pools does not, of itself, result in the recognition of income.

The examples of computational methods described in this chapter are all based on the assumption that the inventory consists of a single pool. If the inventory consisted of multiple pools, the same computational methods are applicable, but they would be applied to each individual pool separately.

CHANGE IN LIFO METHODS

The change to dollar-value LIFO from another method of LIFO is an accounting change for tax purposes and the taxpayer must first secure permission from the Commissioner for the change. When such a change is made, the base year will be the first year for which LIFO was adopted. There will be no adjustment to the LIFO value of the beginning inventory for the year of change. However, the inventory should be restated in terms that will accommodate computations required under the dollar-value method.

While this type of change is an accounting change for tax purposes, it is not a change in accounting principle for purposes of financial reporting. The cost elements of inventory remain the same under the dollar-value method, and only the mechanics of computation have changed.

TERMINATION OF LIFO

Once adopted, LIFO valuation of inventories must continue to be used by a taxpayer unless involuntarily terminated by the Commissioner. Termination by the taxpayer must be approved in advance by the Commissioner.

For the first taxable year affected by the termination, and for each taxable year thereafter, inventory shall be taken:

(a) in conformity with the method used by the taxpayer in inventorying goods not included in his LIFO inventory computations; or

(b) if *all* goods were under LIFO, then in conformity with the inventory method used by the taxpayer prior to his adoption of LIFO; or

(c) if the taxpayer had not used inventories prior to his adoption of LIFO, then in conformity with such inventory methods as may be selected by the taxpayer and approved by the Commissioner as resulting in a clear reflection of income.

Similarly, the taxpayer must seek approval from the Commissioner for changes in LIFO procedures such as methods of pooling, method of LIFO computations (double-extension, link-chain, etc.), and the method of valuing increments.

For purposes of financial reporting, termination of LIFO is an accounting change and must be reported in accordance with the provisions of Accounting Principles Board Opinion No. 20 and in compliance with Financial Accounting Standards Board Interpretation No. 1 which states that a ". . . change in composition of the elements of cost included in inventory is an accounting change."

INTERIM STATEMENTS

Many problems are encountered in computing LIFO valuation of inventories for interim statements. Where monthly statements are prepared, the fairness of the LIFO adjustment will depend upon the conditions on which it was calculated. Normally, it is not feasible to make double extensions each month, and, if a Bureau of Labor Statistics price index is applied to book value each month, there may be extensive variations in inventory during the year as a result of the variable influences of changes in quantities and fluctuations in the index. If a fixed inventory valuation is determined and used to calculate the reserve by application of a price index, the effects of changes in quantity will be eliminated, but the influence of index fluctuations will remain.

Variations in monthly inventories could be minimized by preparing a twelve-interval graduated index based on the estimated price change for the year and applying it to a predetermined fixed inventory valuation each month to calculate the required reserve adjustment. Methods may also be devised basing the LIFO adjustment calculation on a cost-of-goods-sold factor, standard cost assumptions, etc. However, to make no LIFO adjustment at all would defeat the whole purpose of LIFO valuation.

Determination of a method to calculate the LIFO adjustment generally is a matter of judgment. Since there are many accepted methods to choose from, the final selection should be the one that most clearly reflects income for the period involved.

Paragraph 14b of Accounting Principles Board Opinion No. 28 states that companies using the LIFO method may encounter a liquidation of base-period inventories at an interim date that is expected to be replaced by the end of the annual period, and that, in such cases, the inventory at the interim reporting date should not give effect to the LIFO liquidation, but cost of sales for the interim reporting period should include the expected cost of replacement of the liquidated LIFO base.

When LIFO is *adopted* at an interim period, Financial Accounting Standards Board Statement No. 3 requires the following disclosures:

(a) *LIFO adopted in first interim period.*
  1. nature of, and justification for, the change; and
  2. the effect of the change on income before extraordinary items, net income, and related per-share amounts for the period of change.

(b) *LIFO adopted in other than the first interim period.*
  1. the information described in 1 and 2 above; and,
  2. when financial information for the prechange interim periods of that fiscal year is presented it shall be restated by applying the newly adopted accounting principles to those prechange interim periods.

The Internal Revenue Service is not concerned with the financial reporting for interim periods. Regulation 1.472-1 permits the taxpayer to use market value or another method in interim reporting without violating the provisions for the use of LIFO valuation of inventories.

4

FINANCIAL REPORTING IN UNITS OF GENERAL PURCHASING POWER

Restating financial statements for general price-level changes is a simple and direct approach to inflation accounting which requires that financial statements based on units of general purchasing power be reported concurrent with the presentation of financial statements based on units of money.

The method of restatement in general use is based on concepts developed in *Accounting Research Study No. 6,* "Reporting the Financial Effect of Price-Level Changes,"[1] and on procedures outlined in *Statement of the Accounting Principles Board No. 3,* "Financial Statements Restated for General Price-Level Changes."[2] In December 1974 the Financial Accounting Standards Board published an exposure draft of a proposed Statement of Financial Standards[3] which sanctioned the concepts and procedures contained in the two publications referred to above. The proposed statement was intended to *require* every business entity to report certain information based on units of general purchasing power. However, the exposure draft was withdrawn in 1976 because the FASB concluded that it could not justify imposing the cost of implementation upon all preparers of financial statements at that time.

This chapter contains explanations and illustrations of the procedures, computational systems, and conversion techniques disclosed in the aforementioned publications; and provides a model case that demonstrates a step-by-step process for converting conventional financial statements to financial statements based on units of general purchasing power.

UNITS OF GENERAL PURCHASING POWER (UGPP)

A unit of general purchasing power represents the quantity of goods and services demanded in exchange for one dollar at a given point in time. Thus, the unit of purchasing power coincides with the *value* of a dollar. Since the value of a dollar varies significantly over a period of time, the changes in the unit of purchasing power representing this value indicate general price-level changes.

MEASURING CHANGES IN UNITS OF GENERAL PURCHASING POWER

The quantity of goods and services that can be purchased with a dollar is of great practical importance, but the unit of general purchasing power that represents the *value* of a dollar is meaningless as an abstraction. However, if the unit of purchasing power of one period is compared with a unit of

[1] "Reporting the Financial Effects of Price-Level Changes," *Accounting Research Study No. 6* (New York, NY: American Institute of Certified Public Accountants, 1963).

[2] "Financial Statements Restated for General Price-Level Changes," *Statement of the Accounting Principles Board No. 3* (New York, NY: American Institute of Certified Public Accounts, 1969).

[3] "Financial Reporting in Units of General Purchasing Power," *Exposure Draft of Proposed Statement of Financial Accounting Standards* (Stamford, CT: Financial Accounting Standards Board, 1974).

purchasing power of another period, a measurement of change is produced, and all sorts of analyses can be built on that measurement.

INDEX NUMBERS

Government agencies continuously make statistical analyses of prices, and from these analyses they compile and publish indices that indicate current price levels in relation to price levels determined in a prior base year. The indices are constructed by designating the price level in the base year as 100, and expressing price levels in other years as a percentage of 100. For example, if the price of a product in the base year was $75, this $75 would have an index number of 100. If subsequently the price increased to $90, the index number of that product at that time would be 120, which represents a 20% increase in the base-year price.

RESTATEMENT IN UNITS OF GENERAL PURCHASING POWER

Restating financial statements for general price-level changes, or, in other words, financial reporting in units of general purchasing power, is a precise procedure based on the conversion of historic costs to units of *general* purchasing power. The objective of such restatement is to disclose the effects of changes in *general* price levels on the financial statements of the business entity.

The balance sheet and income statement should be presented in terms of units of general purchasing power at the date of the balance sheet. Where conventional statements are presented for both the current period and prior periods, statements expressed in terms of the general purchasing power of the dollar at the latest balance sheet date should be presented for all periods reported in the conventional statements.

Generally accepted accounting principles are applicable to statements in units of general purchasing power on the same basis, and in the same manner, as they are to historic cost-basis statements.

The general price levels used in such restatment are not meant to, and normally will not, coincide with current values, selling prices, replacement costs, or present values of asset and liability components of the balance sheet.

Since restatement of financial statements is made for *general* price-level changes, a price index that is compiled to measure changes in the entire economy should be used for the conversion process. All of the publications on price-level accounting referred to previously in this chapter recommend use of the Gross National Product Implicit Price Deflator (GNP Deflator).

CONVERSION TECHNIQUES

All index numbers indicate a relationship to a base year and consequently they are convenient tools for converting dollar amount values from one year to another.

Conversion Formula

The basic conversion formula is very simple. The procedure is to multiply the dollar amount by a fraction having as a *numerator* the index number of the year *to* which the conversion is to be carried, and as a *denominator* the index number of the year *from* which the conversion is to be made.

For example, assume the following index numbers for the years indicated:

19X0	120
19X5	150

(a) Convert a 19X5 cost of $2,500 to 19X0 dollar values:
The numerator of the fraction is the 19X0 index, and its denominator is the index number of the year 19X5:

$$\$2{,}500 \text{ x} \frac{120}{150} = \$2{,}000$$

(b) Convert a 19X0 cost of $2,500 to 19X5 dollar values:
The numerator is the index for the year 19X5, and the denominator is the index for the year 19X0:

$$\$2{,}500 \text{ x} \frac{150}{120} = \$3{,}125$$

Restatement Formula

The latest balance sheet date is used to prepare statements adjusted for general price-level changes. Therefore, the procedure requires that costs incurred in prior years be valued at the date of the latest balance sheet, and the computation under (b) above should be used for the purpose of such restatement. This procedure may be difficult to comprehend if one thinks in terms of an erosion in purchasing power occurring over the years. However, what restatement does is to value prior-year dollars upward, rather than value current-year dollars downward. The results indicate what the prior cost *would be* if it were incurred currently. For example, illustration (b) above indicates that a product that cost $2,500 in 19X0 would cost $3,125 in 19X5. Therefore, in restatement, the 19X0 cost of $2,500 is restated in a 19X5 cost of $3,125.

The formula for restating assets and liabilities to current units of general purchasing power, therefore, is as follows:

$$\text{Cost of Asset or Amount of Liability} \times \frac{\text{Index at End of Current Period}}{\text{Index at Date Asset Was Acquired or Liability Incurred}} = \text{Restated Amount in Units of General Purchasing Power (Current Dollars)}$$

For example, using the foregoing list of index numbers, a machine that cost $5,000 in 19X0 would be shown on the 19X5 balance sheet restated in units of general purchasing power as $6,250, computed as follows:

$$\$5{,}000 \times \frac{150}{120} = \$6{,}250$$

Conversion Factors

Where assets have been acquired over a long period of time it is usually convenient to prepare a table of conversion factors for each of the years in which the assets were purchased. With such a table at hand, restatement can be accomplished by multiplication and the division process obviated.

For example, assume the following index numbers:

19X0	120
19X1	125
19X2	130
19X3	140
19X4	145
19X5	150

Conversion factors for 19X5 can be computed simply by dividing the index number of each respective year into 150, the index number for the year 19X5, as follows:

$$\begin{aligned} 19X0 &= 150 \div 120 = 1.2500 \\ 19X1 &= 150 \div 125 = 1.2000 \\ 19X2 &= 150 \div 130 = 1.1538 \\ 19X3 &= 150 \div 140 = 1.0714 \\ 19X4 &= 150 \div 145 = 1.0345 \end{aligned}$$

A comparison of restatement by conversion factor and by the restatement formula is as follows:

A machine acquired for $7,500 in 19X2 is to be restated in units of general purchasing power in 19X5:

By restatement formula:

$$\$7{,}500 \times \frac{150}{130} = \$8{,}654$$

By conversion factor:

$$\$7{,}500 \times 1.1538 = \$8{,}654$$

Quarterly Indices

The GNP Deflator indices are compiled quarterly, based on an averaging of prices during the respective quarters. A yearly index is computed, based on the arithmetical average of the four quarterly indices compiled during the year.

Applying the Appropriate Index

To illustrate general rules for selection of the appropriate index, assume the following quarterly and yearly index numbers:

	Quarterly Indices				
Year	1st	2nd	3rd	4th	Annual Average
19X0	102.1	102.6	103.1	103.5	102.8
19X1	104.0	104.3	104.5	104.5	104.3
19X2	105.1	105.5	105.6	105.8	105.5
19X3	106.3	106.7	107.0	107.2	106.8
19X4	107.8	108.2	108.5	109.1	108.4

The general rules for selection of index numbers are as follows:

(a) All restatements are to be made in terms of the index of the quarter in which the balance sheet is dated. Thus, for a balance sheet dated December 31, 19X4, all restatements would be made on the basis of the index 109.1. A balance sheet dated September 30, 19X4 would require all restatements to be made by use of the index 108.5.

(b) Assets acquired in prior years should be restated by using the annual average index of the year of acquisition and the last quarter of the year, or fiscal year, of the latest balance sheet date. The same treatment should be applied to costs and liabilities incurred, when required to be restated. For example, a machine purchased for \$10,000 in 19X1 would be restated in units of general purchasing power at December 31, 19X4 as follows:

$$\$10{,}000 \times \frac{109.1}{104.3} = \$10{,}460$$

(c) Transactions occurring evenly throughout the year of restatement should be restated using the annual average index and the last quarter index for that year. For example, if inventory were acquired evenly throughout 19X4, it would be restated by using the annual average index of 19X4 and the index for the last quarter of that year. As an illustration, an inventory of \$15,000 at December 31, 19X4, acquired evenly during the year, would be restated as follows:

$$\$15{,}000 \times \frac{109.1}{108.4} = \$15{,}097$$

However, had all significant components of the inventory been acquired in, for example, the first quarter of 19X4, it would have been appropriate to use that quarter's index in lieu of the annual average index, as follows:

$$\$15{,}000 \times \frac{109.1}{107.8} = \$15{,}181$$

Rollover Formula

Where financial statements reported in units of general purchasing power are presented for the current and prior years, the general purchasing power amounts for the earlier periods should be converted to units of general purchasing power of the current period. This conversion can be accomplished by the following rollover formula applied to the units of general purchasing power amounts for the prior years.

$$\text{Amounts Stated in Units of General Purchasing Power of Prior Periods} \times \frac{\text{Index at End of Current Period}}{\text{Index at End of Prior Period}} = \text{Amounts Stated in Current Period Units of General Purchasing Power}$$

For example, assume the following net sales stated in units of general purchasing power for the years and at the indices indicated:

Year	Sales Stated in UGPP	Index at End of Year
19Y2	2,692,038	146.5
19Y3	3,020,167	155.7
19Y4	2,245,577	171.9

The sales in units of general puchasing power reported in comparative statements at December 31, 19Y4 should be computed as follows:

19Y2	\$2,692,038	x	$\frac{171.9}{146.5}$	= \$3,158,780
19Y3	3,020,167	x	$\frac{171.9}{155.7}$	= 3,334,404
19Y4	2,245,577	x	1.000	= 2,245,577

MONETARY AND NONMONETARY ITEMS

The key to accurate restatement in terms of units of general purchasing power lies in a proper classification of balance sheet items into monetary and nonmonetary items.

Monetary items are those accounts that are automatically stated in current values and therefore require no price-level adjustments. Nonmonetary items are those accounts that require price-level adjustments in order to be stated in units of general purchasing power. Generally, monetary items are those balance sheet accounts that represent cash and claims to cash, and those receivables and payables that are fixed in terms of number of dollars, regardless of changes in prices. All other balance sheet accounts are nonmonetary items.

Since the unit of general purchasing power used in restated financial statements is for the latest balance sheet date, monetary items for the current period are stated in identical amounts for both units of purchasing power statements and conventional statements.

Nonmonetary assets and liabilities are restated

in terms of current units of general purchasing power based on the number of dollars expended or received for them at the time they were acquired or incurred.

Monetary Items

The following balance sheet items are normally classified as monetary items:

Cash on Hand
Time and Demand Bank Deposits
Investment in Bonds
Accounts and Notes Receivable
Allowance for Doubtful Accounts and Notes Receivable
Cash Surrender Value of Life Insurance
Accounts and Notes Payable
Accrued Expenses
Cash Dividends Payable
Long-Term Debt
Unamortized Premium or Discount on Debt Securities
Preferred Stock

Nonmonetary Items

The following accounts are generally considered to be nonmonetary items:

Foreign Currency on Hand and Claims for Foreign Currency
Investments in Stocks
Inventories
Prepaid Expenses
Property, Plant, and Equipment
Accumulated Depreciation of Property, Plant, and Equipment
Deferred Income Tax Charges
Intangibles and Deferred Charges
Goodwill
Deferred Income
Obligations Under Warranties
Deferred Income Tax Credits
Preferred Stock
Common Stock
Paid-In Capital
Retained Earnings

Items Having a Dual Nature

The following items have characteristics of both classifications and can be either monetary or nonmonetary:

Bonds. Bonds, including convertible bonds, generally are of a monetary nature when they are intended to be held to maturity and redeemed at a fixed number of dollars. However, if bonds are intended to be sold or converted prior to maturity, they are nonmonetary items.

Inventories. Inventories produced under fixed contracts and accounted for at the contract price are monetary. All other inventory items are nonmonetary.

Preferred Stocks. Generally, preferred stock is a monetary item. However, preferred stock carried at less than its redemption value is nonmonetary and becomes monetary when it is restated in an amount equal to its liquidation or redemption value.

Investments in Equity Securities

Investments in long-term equity securities require special treatment, as follows:

Investments in Unconsolidated Subsidiaries and Other Investees. If the investment is carried at cost, it is nonmonetary. If it is accounted for by the equity method, the financial statements of the investee should be restated and the equity method should then be applied for restatement purposes.

Minority Interests. The minority interest in statements restated in units of general purchasing power should be based on the restated financial statements of the subsidiary.

EFFECTS OF RESTATEMENT

Income and expense items developed evenly throughout the current year (other than expenses charged to nonmonetary items) are restated using the index number for the last quarter of the year. When there is inflation during the year, this restatement generally results in reporting units of general purchasing power amounts that are greater than the dollar amounts shown in the conventional statements. Consequently, the excess of general purchasing power income over dollar amount income results in a general purchasing power loss, and the excess of general purchasing power expenses over dollar amount expenses results in a purchasing power gain.

Nonmonetary assets acquired during an inflation year are restated in units of general purchasing power as of the last quarter, and normally that will result in a purchasing power gain.

Monetary items held at the beginning of the year are assumed to be taken into operations during the year. Therefore, the net difference between the dollar amount of monetary items at the beginning of the year and these same amounts restated to units of general purchasing power at the end of the year will result in a purchasing power gain or loss. During an inflation year the units of general purchasing power amounts will exceed the dollar amounts at the end of the year, and reflect a purchasing power loss.

All of the above-described purchasing power gains and losses should be shown in one line on the income statement, and should be captioned "Net General Purchasing Power Gain (Loss)."

In an inflationary period restated expenses that are charged to nonmonetary items, such as depreciation and amortization, will exceed the same expenses reported in dollar amounts. This, of course, results in a purchasing power gain. However, these amounts are not included in the one-line classification "Net General Purchasing Gain (Loss)" described above because gains and losses charged to nonmonetary items are classified in the dollar amount income statement as separate items, and the amounts are restated in the general purchasing power statements under the same captions.

The effects of general price-level changes on financial statements can be determined only by comprehensive restatement of the components of the statements. Partial restatement is likely to produce misleading information; under ordinary circumstances it should never be attempted.

GENERAL PROCEDURES FOR RESTATEMENT

Statement of the Accounting Principles Board No. 3 outlines a step-by-step approach to preparing statements in units of general purchasing power. The steps are quoted verbatim below, and each step is illustrated and commented on in the model case of Converter Company that follows:

Step 1: Identify monetary and nonmonetary assets and liabilities.

Step 2: Analyze all nonmonetary items in the balance sheet of the current year (and prior year for the first year of restatement) to determine when the component money amounts originated.

Step 3: Analyze all revenue, expense, gain, and loss items in the income statement of the current year to determine when the amounts originated that ultimately resulted in the charges and credits in the statements of income and retained earnings.

Step 4: Restate the nonmonetary items.

Step 5: Restate the monetary items in the balance sheet at the beginning of the first year.

Step 6: Apply the "cost or market" rule after the restatement to the items to which it applies before restatement.

Step 7: Compute the general price-level gain or loss for the current year.

Step 8: "Roll forward" the restated statements of the prior year to units of current general purchasing power.

MODEL CASE OF FINANCIAL STATEMENTS RESTATED IN UNITS OF GENERAL PURCHASING POWER

Converter Company is a closely held corporation that manufactures concrete products for the home construction industry. In the years 19Y2, 19Y3, and 19Y4 the company experienced significant variations in sales, cost of sales, and net income. In response to inquiries from stockholders, management sought to determine what effect general price-level changes had on their financial statements for the last two years, and accordingly requested their accountants to prepare comparative statements reported in units of general purchasing power for the years 19Y3 and 19Y4.

To start the process, the accountants assembled the dollar value balance sheets and income statements of Converter Company for the years 19Y2, 19Y3, and 19Y4. These statements are reproduced in Exhibits A and B.

EXHIBIT A

CONVERTER COMPANY
BALANCE SHEETS—UNITS OF MONEY

	December 31		
ASSETS	19Y4	19Y3	19X2
Current			
Cash	232,887	568,115	678,919
Accounts Receivable—Trade	254,372	296,293	305,305
Refundable Income Taxes	106,618	32,228	
Inventory	263,502	116,196	150,615
Investments	552,740	502,013	447,717
Prepaid Expenses	23,764	38,564	27,585
Total Current Assets	1,433,883	1,553,409	1,610,141
Fixed, less accumulated depreciation	663,686	363,969	282,099
Other			
Patent, less accumulated amortization	303	347	390
	2,097,872	1,917,725	1,892,630
LIABILITIES AND STOCKHOLDERS' EQUITY			
Current			
Notes Payable	120,000	—	—
Accounts Payable—Trade	189,255	173,819	190,907
Accrued Expenses and Withheld Taxes	25,331	33,636	14,745
Income Taxes Payable	9,835	—	61,119
Current Portion of Long-Term Debt	12,500	—	—
Total Current Liabilities	356,921	207,455	266,771
Long-Term Debt	100,000	—	—
Stockholders' Equity			
Common Stock (13,000 shares—par $100)	1,300,000	1,300,000	1,300,000
Retained Earnings	340,951	410,270	325,859
Total Stockholders' Equity	1,640,951	1,710,270	1,625,859
	2,097,872	1,917,725	1,892,630

EXHIBIT B

CONVERTER COMPANY
STATEMENT OF INCOME AND RETAINED EARNINGS—UNITS OF MONEY

	For Year Ended December 31		
	19Y4	19Y3	19Y2
Net Sales	2,161,287	2,940,766	2,660,117
Cost of Goods Sold			
Inventory—beginning	116,196	150,615	133,217
Material Purchases	1,243,506	1,451,212	1,321,826
Direct Labor	244,013	314,640	233,170
Manufacturing Expense	479,396	479,315	425,619
	2,083,111	2,395,782	2,113,832
Less: Inventory—ending	263,501	116,196	150,615
Cost of Goods Sold	1,819,610	2,279,586	1,963,217
Gross Profit	341,677	661,180	696,900
Selling and Delivery Expense	279,704	365,762	341,733
General and Administrative Expense	203,548	181,617	131,168
Total Expenses	483,252	547,379	472,901
Income (Loss) Before Income Taxes	(141,575)	113,801	223,999
Provision for Income Taxes	(72,255)	29,390	105,614
Net Income (Loss)	(69,320)	84,411	118,385
Retained Earnings—beginning	410,270	325,859	207,474
Retained Earnings—end	340,950	410,270	325,859

IDENTIFICATION OF MONETARY AND NONMONETARY ITEMS

An inquiry into the nature of the balance sheet accounts revealed that the following were nonmonetary items:

Prepaid Expenses
Fixed Assets and Accumulated Depreciation
Patent Cost and Amortization Allowance

Investments consisted of demands for specific amounts of cash, and the long-term debt was fixed in the number of dollars payable. Therefore, both these accounts were classified as monetary items.

ANALYSIS OF NONMONETARY ITEMS

Schedules of Fixed Assets and Depreciation revealed that the buildings were actually leaseholds that had been acquired 24 and 14 years earlier, in 19W0 and 19X0, respectively. Equipment still in use had been acquired over the years from 19X5 to the current year. Unamortized prepaid expenses that had been purchased over the last five years were on the books, and unamortized patent expense was recorded on a patent granted ten years previously.

To facilitate restatement computations, index numbers were listed from the GNP Deflator and conversion factors computed as shown in Table 1.

	INDEX NUMBERS					CONVERSION FACTORS		
	Quarters					100 = 4th quarter	100 = 4th quarter	100 = 4th quarter
	1st	2nd	3rd	4th	Annual Average	19Y2	19Y3	19Y4
19W0	78.9	79.5	78.0	80.8	79.3	1.847	1.963	2.168
19X0	102.1	102.6	103.1	103.5	102.8	1.425	1.515	1.672
19X1	104.0	104.3	104.5	104.5	104.3	1.405	1.493	1.648
19X2	105.1	105.5	105.6	105.8	105.5	1.389	1.476	1.629
19X3	106.3	106.7	107.0	107.2	106.8	1.372	1.458	1.610
19X4	107.8	108.2	108.5	109.1	108.4	1.351	1.436	1.586
19X5	109.6	110.2	110.7	111.0	110.4	1.327	1.410	1.557
19X6	111.5	112.4	113.5	114.5	113.0	1.296	1.378	1.521
19X7	115.4	116.2	116.8	118.0	116.6	1.256	1.335	1.474
19X8	119.5	120.4	121.6	122.9	121.1	1.210	1.286	1.419
19X9	124.3	125.6	127.2	129.1	126.6	1.157	1.230	1.358
19Y0	130.9	132.9	134.4	135.8	133.5	1.097	1.166	1.288
19Y1	137.9	139.5	141.1	142.0	140.1	1.046	1.111	1.227
19Y2	142.7	144.6	145.3	146.5	144.8	1.012	1.075	1.187
19Y3	148.0	150.0	152.6	155.7	151.6		1.027	1.134
19Y4	158.9	163.6	167.3	171.9	165.4			1.039

TABLE 1

The conversion factors listed under the columnar heading for 19Y2, 19Y3, and 19Y4 were computed by dividing the *annual average* index number for each year shown in the extreme left column into the *fourth-quarter* index number of the respective years shown under the conversion columnar captions. For example, the conversion factor necessary to convert 19W0 costs to December 31, 19Y3 values was computed by dividing the *annual average* index of 19W0 (79.3) into the fourth-quarter index for the year 19Y3 (155.7), as follows:

$$155.7 \div 79.3 = 1.963$$

The conversion factor of 1.963 is found on a line with 19W0, under the conversion factor columnar heading "100 = 4th Quarter 19Y3." All of the other conversion factors were computed in the same manner.

ANALYSIS OF REVENUE AND EXPENSE ACCOUNTS

A review of income and expense accounts revealed that charges and credits to these accounts had occurred evenly throughout the year. Therefore, it was decided to restate the income and expense accounts, other than inventory adjustments, for each year by multiplying the dollar amount by the index for the last quarter of that year, and dividing the result by the annual average index of the same year.

All expenses charged to nonmonetary items (depreciation, amortization) were restated on the basis of the restatement shown in Schedules 1(c), 2(c), and 3, found in the following section of this chapter.

It was determined that the inventory components at the end of each year were acquired during that year in the following manner:

December 31, 19Y2—Acquired in the last quarter of 19Y2.
December 31, 19Y3—Acquired in the last quarter of 19Y3.
December 31, 19Y4—Acquired evenly throughout 19Y4.

RESTATEMENT OF NONMONETARY ITEMS

Since the first year of restatement was to be 19Y3, it was necessary to compute restated amounts as of December 31, 19Y2 in order to have a basis for beginning the restatement process. Therefore, analyses of prepaid expenses, fixed assets and depreciation, and patent costs were acquired from the accounting department, and restatement amounts were computed as described below.

Prepaid Expense

Schedule 1(a) is a reproduction of the prepaid expense schedule maintained by the accounting department to record costs of acquisition and amortization of such expenses.

Schedule 1(b) reflects restated amounts at December 31, 19Y2, 19Y3, and 19Y4 based on the dollar amounts shown on Schedule 1(a) at the respective dates. Restated amounts were computed by use of conversion factors shown in Table 1. For example, Protection Service acquired in 19Y1 had an unamortized cost of $5,547 at December 31, 19Y2. This value is restated in terms of units of general purchasing power at December 31, 19Y3 by use of the conversion factor 1.111, which converts 19Y1 dollar amounts to 19Y3 units of general purchasing power. This factor is shown on the conversion table in line with 19Y1 and in the 19Y3 conversion factor column. The unamortized dollar amount of this Protection Service at December 31, 19Y3 was $3,698. Again, the amount is restated to December 31, 19Y3 units of general purchasing power of $4,109 by use of the same conversion factor that converts 19Y1 dollar values to 19Y3 units of general purchasing power. At December 31, 19Y4 the unamortized dollar amount of this Protection Service was $1,849. In this case the dollar amount is to be restated in terms of units of general purchasing power at December 31, 19Y4, and therefore the restatement was computed as $2,269 by use of the conversion factor 1.227, which is the factor required to restate 19Y1 dollar amounts to December 31, 19Y4 units of general purchasing power. This factor is shown on Table 1. Schedule 1(b) was prepared to support the balance sheet presentation of prepaid expenses restated in units of general purchasing power for the three years indicated in the schedule.

Schedule 1(c) shows the computation of restated amortization of prepaid expenses for income statement presentation. The restated expense for each respective year is computed by adding restated purchases to the restated beginning balance, and then deducting the restated ending balance. The restated beginning and ending balances are shown on Schedule 1(a). The $18,000 acquisition in 19Y3 was made in January, 19Y3. Therefore, the conversion factor of 1.027 was computed by dividing the index for the last quarter of 19Y3 by the annual average index of 19Y3, thus: 155.7 ÷ 151.6 = 1.027. This conversion factor is listed on Table 1. The $1,943 and $10,500 acquisitions were made in December, 19Y3, so no restatement was necessary, and therefore the conversion factor is shown as 1.000. The computation for the year ended December 31, 19Y4 was made in the same manner as that for 19Y3, except that the beginning restated net book value was computed by rolling over the December 31, 19Y3 restated values to December 31, 19Y4 restated values by use of an appropriate conversion factor.

Schedule 1-a

CONVERTER COMPANY
PREPAID EXPENSES—(DOLLAR VALUES)

Date Paid		Amortization Period	Cost	Amortized at 12/31/Y2	Unamortized at 12/31/Y2	Amortization 19Y3	Unamortized at 12/31/Y3	Amortization 19Y4	Unamortized at 12/31/Y4
19Y0	Advertising	5 years	32,115	19,269	12,846	6,423	6,423	6,423	—
19Y1	Protection	5 years	9,245	3,698	5,547	1,849	3,698	1,849	1,849
19Y1	Insurance	3 years	18,000	12,000	6,000	2,000	4,000	2,000	2,000
6/Y2	Equipment Maintenance	1 year	6,384	3,192	3,192	3,192	—	—	—
			65,744	38,159	27,585				
1/Y3	Insurance	3 years	18,000			6,000	12,000	6,000	6,000
12/Y3	Equipment Maintenance	1 year	1,943			—	1,943	1,943	—
12/Y3	Protection	3 years	10,500			—	10,500	3,500	7,000
			96,187			19,464	38,564		
19Y4	Advertising	3 years	9,220					2,305	6,915
			105,407					24,020	23,764

Schedule 1-b

PREPAID EXPENSES
RESTATED IN UNITS OF GENERAL PURCHASING POWER

Date Paid		Unamortized at 12/31/Y2	Restatement Factor	Restated to Units of GPP at 12/31/Y3	Unamortized at 12/31/Y3	Restatement Factor	Restated to Units of GPP at 12/31/Y3	Unamortized at 12/31/Y4	Restatement Factor	Restated to Units of GPP at 12/31/Y4
19Y0	Advertising	12,846	1.166	14,978	6,423	1.166	7,489	—	—	—
19Y1	Protection	5,547	1.111	6,163	3,698	1.111	4,109	1,849	1.227	2,269
19Y2	Insurance	6,000	1.111	6,666	4,000	1.111	4,444	2,000	1.227	2,454
6/Y2	Equipment Maintenance	3,192	1.075	3,431	—	—	—	—	—	—
1/Y3	Insurance				12,000	1.027	12,324	6,000	1.134	6,804
12/Y3	Equipment Maintenance				1,943	—	1,943	—	—	—
12/Y3	Protection				10,500	—	10,500	7,000	1.134	7,938
19Y4	Advertising							6,915	1.039	7,185
		27,585		31,238	38,564		40,809	23,764		26,650

Schedule 1-c

CONVERTER COMPANY
PREPAID EXPENSES
COMPUTATION OF RESTATED AMORTIZATION FOR INCOME STATEMENT

Year Ended December 31, 19Y3		
Unamortized Value at December 31, 19Y2 restated to UGPP at December 31, 19Y3 (Schedule 1-b)		31,238
Additions in 19Y3 restated to UGPP at December 31, 19Y3		
18,000 x 1.027	18,486	
1,943 x 1.000	1,943	
10,500 x 1.000	10,500	30,929
		62,167
Less: Unamortized Value at December 31, 19Y3 restated to UGPP at December 31, 19Y3 (Schedule 1-b)		40,809
Amortization Expense for 19Y3 restated to UGPP at December 31, 19Y3		21,358
Year Ended December 31, 19Y4		
Unamortized value at December 31, 19Y3 restated in UGPP at December 31, 19Y3 rolled over to UGPP at December 31, 19Y4: 40,809 (Schedule 1-b) x 1.104		45,053
Additions in 19Y4 restated in UGPP at December 31, 19Y4		
9,220 x 1.039		9,580
		54,633
Less: Unamortized Value at December 31, 19Y4 restated to UGPP at December 31, 19Y4 (Schedule 1-b)		26,650
Amortization Expense for 19Y4 restated to UGPP at December 31, 19Y4		27,983

Fixed Assets and Depreciation

Schedule 2-a is a reproduction of the Schedule of Fixed Assets and Accumulated Depreciation in dollar amounts maintained by the accounting department.

Schedule 2-b reflects restated amounts for cost and net book value balances shown in Schedule 2-a. The restated cost and net book value was computed for each individual item, by use of the conversion factors listed in Table 1, in exactly the same manner that the unamortized values of prepaid expenses were restated, as described in the preceding paragraphs.

Schedule 2-c shows the computation of restated depreciation expense for income statement presentation, and it is computed in exactly the same manner as that for prepaid expenses shown in Schedule 1-c, and described above.

There are two important circumstances to note concerning this model case:

(a) Original dollar costs of the fixed assets have not been converted to units of general purchasing power in this study. If it is deemed necessary to show original cost in units of general purchasing power, such costs could be computed by using the same conversion factors for each year's acquisitions that were applied to the respective year's additions for converting net book value on Schedule 2-b. The accumulated depreciation then would be the difference between the restated cost computed as above and the restated net book value amounts shown on Schedule 2-b.

(b) The model case demonstrates the disposition of a group of *fully* depreciated assets. This disposition had no effect on cost, book value, or depreciation expense. However, had assets having a net book value been sold or abandoned, the gain or loss thereon would have been computed by restating the cost, accumulated depreciation, and net book value, using appropriate conversion factors. The restated net book value of the item disposed of then would have been deducted from the restated beginning net book value in Schedule 2c to arrive at the proper restated depreciation expense for the year.

Patent Cost and Amortization

Schedule 3 shows the restated amounts for patent costs and amortization for the years ended December 31, 19Y3 and 19Y4. The net book value was restated by appropriate conversion factors, and the restated amortization expense was computed by subtracting the ending restated value from the beginning restated value.

Schedule 2-a

CONVERTER COMPANY
FIXED ASSETS AND DEPRECIATION
(DOLLAR VALUES)

Year Acquired	Cost	Depreciation Allowance 12/31/Y2	Net Book Value 12/31/Y2	Depreciation 19Y3	Depreciation Allowance 12/31/Y3	Net Book Value 12/31/Y3	Depreciation 19Y4	Depreciation Allowance 12/31/Y4	Net Book Value 12/31/Y4
BUILDINGS									
19X0	150,000	69,000	81,000	3,000	72,000	78,000	3,000	75,000	75,000
19Y0	60,000	19,500	40,500	1,500	21,000	39,000	1,500	22,500	37,500
	210,000	88,500	121,500	4,500	93,000	117,000	4,500	97,500	112,500
EQUIPMENT									
19X5 (a)	377,265	301,812	75,453	37,727	339,539	37,726	37,726	377,265	
19X6	36,140	25,298	10,842	3,614	28,912	7,228	3,614	32,526	3,614
19X7	19,750	11,850	7,900	1,975	13,825	5,925	1,975	15,800	3,950
19X8	30,000	15,000	15,000	3,000	18,000	12,000	3,000	21,000	9,000
19X9	11,400	4,560	6,840	1,140	5,700	5,700	1,140	6,840	4,560
19Y0	15,000	4,500	10,500	1,500	6,000	9,000	1,500	7,500	7,500
19Y1	31,160	6,232	24,928	3,116	9,348	21,812	3,116	12,464	18,696
	520,715							473,395	47,320
19Y2	10,151	1,015	9,136	1,015	2,030	8,121	1,015	3,045	7,106
	530,866	370,267	160,599						
19Y3	154,952			15,495	15,495	139,457	15,496	30,991	123,961
	685,818			68,582	438,849	246,969			
19Y4	414,221						41,422	41,422	372,799
19Y4 (a)	(377,265)						–	(377,265)	–
	722,774						110,004	171,588	551,186
Total Net Book Value			282,099			363,969			663,686

Schedule 2-b

CONVERTER COMPANY
NET BOOK VALUE OF FIXED ASSETS
RESTATED IN UNITS OF GENERAL PURCHASING POWER

	December 31, 19Y2			December 31, 19Y3			December 31, 19Y4		
Year Acquired	Net Book Value	Restatement Factor	Restated to Units of GPP at 12/31/Y3	Net Book Value	Restatement Factor	Restated to Units of GPP at 12/31/Y3	Net Book Value	Restatement Factor	Restated to Units of GPP at 12/31/Y4
BUILDINGS									
19W0	81,000	1.963	159,003	78,000	1.963	153,114	75,000	2.168	162,600
19X0	40,500	1.515	61,357	39,000	1.515	59,085	37,500	1.672	62,700
	121,500		220,360	117,000		212,199	112,500		225,300
EQUIPMENT									
19X5	75,453	1.410	106,389	37,726	1.410	53,194	—	—	—
19X6	10,842	1.378	14,940	7,228	1.378	9,960	3,614	1.521	5,497
19X7	7,900	1.335	10,546	5,925	1.335	7,910	3,950	1.474	5,822
19X8	15,000	1.286	19,290	12,000	1.286	15,432	9,000	1.419	12,771
19X9	6,840	1.230	8,413	5,700	1.230	7,011	4,560	1.358	6,192
19Y0	10,500	1.166	12,243	9,000	1.166	10,494	7,500	1.288	9,660
19Y1	24,928	1.111	27,695	21,812	1.111	24,233	18,696	1.227	22,940
19Y2	9,136	1.075	9,821	8,121	1.075	8,730	7,106	1.187	8,435
19Y3	—	—	—	139,457	1.027	143,222	123,961	1.134	140,572
19Y4	—	—	—	—	—	—	372,799	1.039	387,338
	160,599		209,337	246,969		280,186	551,186		599,227
TOTALS	282,099		429,697	363,969		492,385	663,686		824,527

Schedule 2-c

CONVERTER COMPANY
COMPUTATION OF RESTATED DEPRECIATION EXPENSE FOR INCOME STATEMENTS

Year Ended December 31, 19Y3	
Buildings	
Net Book Value at December 31, 19Y2 restated to UGPP at December 31, 19Y3 (Schedule 2-a)	220,360
Less: Net Book Value at December 31, 19Y3 restated to UGPP at December 31, 19Y3 (Schedule 2-a)	212,199
Depreciation—Building—Restated to UGPP at December 31, 19Y3	8,161
Equipment	
Net Book Value at December 31, 19Y2 restated to UGPP at December 31, 19Y3 (Schedule 2-a)	209,337
Add: Purchases in 19Y3 restated to UGPP at December 31, 19Y3: 154,952 x 1.027	159,136
	368,473
Less: Net Book Value at December 31, 19Y3 restated to UGPP at December 31, 19Y3 (Schedule 2-a)	280,186
Depreciation—Equipment—Restated to UGPP at December 31, 19Y3	88,287
Year Ended December 31, 19Y4	
Buildings	
Net Book Value at December 31, 19Y3, restated to UGPP at December 31, 19Y3, rolled over to UGPP at December 31, 19Y4: 212,199 (Schedule 1-a) x 1.104	234,268
Less: Net Book Value at December 31, 19Y4 restated to UGPP at December 31, 19Y4 (Schedule 1-a)	225,300
Depreciation—Building—Restated to UGPP at December 31, 19Y4	8,968
Equipment	
Net Book Value at December 31, 19Y3, restated to UGPP at December 31, 19Y3, rolled over to UGPP at December 31, 19Y4: 280,186 (Schedule 1-a) x 1.104	309,325
Add: Purchases in 19Y4 restated to UGPP at December 31, 19Y4: 414,221 x 1.039	430,376
	739,701
Less: Net Book Value at December 31, 19Y4 restated to UGPP at December 31, 19Y4 (Schedule 1-a)	599,227
Depreciation—Equipment—Restated to UGPP at December 31, 19Y4	140,474

Schedule 3

CONVERTER COMPANY
PATENT COST AND AMORTIZATION SCHEDULE
AND
COMPUTATION OF RESTATED PATENT
EXPENSE FOR INCOME STATEMENTS

	Dollar	Net Book Value Restated to UGPP at: December 31, 19Y3		December 31, 19Y4	
	Cost and Amortization	Restatement Factor	Amount	Restatement Factor	Amount
Cost	748				
Amortization to December 31, 19Y2	358				
Net Book Value—December 31, 19Y2	390	1.410	550		
Amortization—19Y3	43				
Net Book Value—December 31, 19Y3	347	1.410	489	1.104	540
Amortization—19Y4	44				
Net Book Value—December 31, 19Y4	303			1.557	472
Restated Amortization			61		68

RESTATEMENT OF THE BALANCE SHEET AT THE BEGINNING OF THE FIRST YEAR

In Exhibit C the dollar amounts of the balance sheet items at the beginning of 19Y3 (December 31, 19Y2) are restated in units of general purchasing power for December 31, 19Y3. This restatement is necessary to establish beginning balances of units of general purchasing power on which to base the transactions in such units during 19Y3, the first year of restatement.

The following notes are referenced to the conversion factors used in the restatement:

(1) These amounts were restated by dividing the index for the last quarter of 19Y2 into the index for the last quarter of 19Y3, as follows:

$$\frac{155.7}{146.5} = 1.063$$

(2) Inventory was assumed to have been acquired in the last quarter of 19Y2, and therefore restatement was made on the basis shown in (1) above.

(3) It was not feasible to restate the components of retained earnings and capital stock. The restated stockholders' equity was computed as the difference between the restated assets and the restated liabilities.

Restatement of nonmonetary amounts was made in accordance with the schedules indicated on the statement.

LOWER OF COST OR MARKET

The components of the balance sheet were reviewed to determine their market values, and in this case it was revealed that the amounts restated in units of general purchasing power did not exceed current values.

BALANCE SHEET RESTATED AT END OF FIRST YEAR

The balance sheet in units of money at December 31, 19Y3 is restated in units of general purchasing power at that date on Exhibit D.

EXHIBIT C

CONVERTER COMPANY
BALANCE SHEET
19Y2 DOLLAR VALUES RESTATED IN 19Y3 UGPP

	Dollar Values at December 31, 19Y2	Restatement Factor	Dollar Values at December 31, 19Y2 Restated in UGPP of December 31, 19Y3
ASSETS			
Current			
Cash	678,919	(1) 1.063	721,691
Accounts Receivable	305,305	(1) 1.063	324,539
Inventory	150,615	(2) 1.063	160,104
Investments (market equals cost)	447,717	(1) 1.063	475,923
Prepaid Expenses	27,585	(Schedule 1-b)	31,238
	1,610,141		1,713,495
Fixed—less depreciation	282,099	(Schedule 2-b)	429,697
Patent—less amortization	390	(Schedule 3)	550
	1,892,630		2,143,742
LIABILITIES AND STOCKHOLDERS' EQUITY			
Current			
Accounts Payable	190,907	(1) 1.063	202,934
Withheld Taxes and Accrued Expenses	14,745	(1) 1.063	15,674
Income Taxes Payable	61,119	(1) 1.063	64,969
Total Current Liabilities	266,771		283,577
Stockholders' Equity			
Common Stock	1,300,000		
Retained Earnings	325,859		
Total Stockholders' Equity	1,625,859		(3) 1,860,165
	1,892,630		2,143,742

The monetary items are stated in identical amounts for both dollar values and units of general purchasing power. The nonmonetary items are restated in accordance with the schedules indicated in the statement. Stockholders' equity is restated in the amount developed in the restated income statement, Exhibit E.

The following note is referenced to the conversion factors in the statement:

(1) It was assumed that inventory was acquired in the last quarter of 19Y3, and therefore no restatement was necessary.

EXHIBIT D

CONVERTER COMPANY
BALANCE SHEET
19Y3 DOLLAR VALUES RESTATED IN 19Y3 UGPP

	Dollar Values at December 31, 19Y3	Restatement Factor	Dollar Values at December 31, 19Y3 Restated in UGPP of December 31, 19Y3
ASSETS			
Current			
Cash	568,115	–	568,115
Accounts Receivable	296,293	–	296,293
Refundable Income Taxes	32,228	–	32,228
Inventory	116,196	(1)	116,196
Investments (market equals cost)	502,013	–	502,013
Prepaid Expenses	38,564	(Schedule 1-b)	40,809
	1,553,409		1,555,654
Fixed—less depreciation	363,969	(Schedule 2-b)	492,385
Patent—less amortization	347	(Schedule 3)	489
	1,917,725		2,048,528
LIABILITIES AND STOCKHOLDERS' EQUITY			
Current			
Accounts Payable	173,819	–	173,819
Withheld Taxes and Accrued Expenses	33,636	–	33,636
Total Current Liabilities	207,455		207,455
Stockholders' Equity			
Common Stock	1,300,000		
Retained Earnings	410,270		
Total Stockholders' Equity	1,710,270		1,841,073
	1,917,725		2,048,528

INCOME STATEMENT FOR FIRST YEAR

Restatement of revenue and expense items and stockholders' equity is shown on Exhibit E. The following notes are referenced to the conversion factors used in restatement:

(1) These amounts were assumed to have been spread evenly throughout the year. The conversion factor was computed by dividing the index of the last quarter of 19Y3 by the annual average index of 19Y3, as follows:

$$155.7 \div 151.6 = 1.027$$

(2) Inventory at December 31, 19Y2 was assumed to have been acquired in the last quarter of 19Y2. The conversion factor was computed by dividing the index for the last quarter of 19Y2 into the index for the last quarter of 19Y3, as follows:

$$155.7 \div 146.5 = 1.063$$

(3) Inventory at December 31, 19Y3 was assumed to have been acquired in the last quarter of 19Y3. Therefore, no restatement was necessary, and thus the conversion factor is 1.000.

Expenses charged to nonmonetary assets were restated in accordance with the schedules indicated in the statements. Net General Purchasing Power (Loss) is shown in the amount developed in Exhibit F.

GENERAL PURCHASING POWER GAIN OR (LOSS)

Exhibit F develops the net general purchasing power (loss) disclosed in Exhibit E.

Exhibit F was prepared on a basis that clearly identified gains and losses from restatement and simultaneously proved the arithmetical accuracy of the units of general purchasing power financial statements.

The gain or loss on restatement of monetary items represents the difference between the dollar amount and the units of general purchasing power of the monetary items at the *beginning of the year.* Both sets of values shown in Exhibit F are taken from the beginning-of-year restatement shown on Exhibit C. Since, for example, cash in the amount of $721,691 at December 31, 19Y3 would be required to replace the purchasing power of $678,919 at December 31, 19Y2, a purchasing power loss of $42,772 was suffered on conversion.

Since gain or loss on the conversion of monetary items at the beginning of the year was picked up on Exhibit F, the gain or loss on restatement of all the monetary items flowing through the operating statement must also be computed. The net result of these computations is to show the *average* cost of holding monetary items during the year.

The excess of the units of purchasing power over the dollar amount of sales results in a purchasing power loss. In other words, sales would have to be increased by $79,401 in order for the value of the revenue to be equivalent to the $3,020,167 in units of general purchasing power representing $2,940,766 at December 31, 19Y3. Similarly, the excess of units of general purchasing power over the dollar amount of expenses during the year represents purchasing power gains. The dollar amounts and units of general purchasing power for sales and expenses shown on Exhibit F are taken directly from Exhibit E.

The acquisition of nonmonetary items reflects a purchasing power gain when it is restated on the balance sheet in units of general purchasing power at the index for the last quarter of the year. The amounts on Exhibit F showing restated amounts for prepaid expenses and equipment acquired during the year are taken from Schedules 1-c and 2-c, respectively.

The net loss from restatement amounting to $74,444 is carried to Exhibit E, which develops the stockholders' equity to be carried to Exhibit D. This indicates that the computational procedure employed to construct Exhibit F makes the statement self-balancing.

Exhibit G was prepared to prove the flow of dollar value monetary items through operations, and it corresponds to dollar values shown on Exhibit F.

EXHIBIT E

CONVERTER COMPANY
INCOME STATEMENT
FOR THE YEAR ENDED DECEMBER 31, 19Y3
19Y3 DOLLAR VALUES RESTATED IN 19Y3 UGPP

	Dollar Values	Restatement Factor	Restated in UGPP
Sales	2,940,766	(1) 1.027	3,020,167
Inventory—beginning	150,615	(2) 1.063	160,104
Material Purchases	1,451,212	(1) 1.027	1,490,395
Direct Labor	314,640	(1) 1.027	323,135
Manufacturing Expense	410,733	(1) 1.027	421,823
Depreciation	68,582	(Schedule 2-c)	88,287
	2,395,782		2,483,744
Less: Inventory—ending	116,196	(3) 1.000	116,196
Cost of Sales	2,279,586		2,367,548
Gross Profit	661,180		652,619
Selling and Delivery Expenses	365,762	(1) 1.027	375,638
General and Administrative Expenses	157,610	(1) 1.027	161,865
Amortization of Prepaid Expenses	19,464	(Schedule 1-c)	21,358
Amortization of Patent	43	(Schedule 3)	61
Depreciation	4,500	(Schedule 2-c)	8,161
	547,379		567,083
Operating Income	113,801		85,536
Net General Purchasing Power (Loss)	—	(Exhibit F)	(74,444)
Income before Income Taxes	113,801		11,092
Provision for Income Taxes	29,390	(1) 1.027	30,184
Net Income (Loss)	84,411		(19,092)
Stockholders' Equity—beginning	1,625,859		1,860,165
Stockholders' Equity—ending	1,710,270		1,841,073

EXHIBIT F

CONVERTER COMPANY
NET GENERAL PURCHASING POWER GAIN OR LOSS
FOR YEAR ENDED DECEMBER 31, 19Y3

	Dollar Values December 31, 19Y2	Restated to UGPP December 31, 19Y3	Gain or (Loss) on Restatement	
Gain or (Loss) from Restatement of Monetary Items				
Cash	678,919	721,691	(42,772)	
Accounts Receivable	305,305	324,539	(19,234)	
Investments	447,717	475,923	(28,206)	
Accounts Payable	(190,907)	(202,934)	12,027	
Withheld Taxes and Accrued Expenses	(14,745)	(15,674)	929	
Income Taxes Payable	(61,119)	(64,969)	3,850	
	1,165,170	1,238,576	(73,406)	
Net (Loss) from Restatement of Monetary Items				(73,406)

	Dollar Values for Year December 31, 19Y3	Restated to UGPP December 31, 19Y3	Gain or (Loss) on Restatement	
Gain or (Loss) from Restatement of Results of Operations				
Sales	2,940,766	3,020,167	(79,401)	
Net (Loss) from Restatement of Sales				(79,401)
Expenses (Other than Expenses Charged Against Nonmonetary Items)				
Material Purchases	1,451,212	1,490,395	39,183	
Direct Labor	314,640	323,135	8,495	
Manufacturing Expense	410,733	421,823	11,090	
Selling and Delivery Expenses	365,762	375,638	9,876	
General and Administrative Expenses	157,610	161,865	4,255	
Income Taxes	29,390	30,184	794	
	2,729 347	2,803,040	73,693	
Net Gain from Restatement of Expenses				73,693
Gain on Restatement of Nonmonetary Assets Purchased During Year				
Equipment	154,952	159,136	4,184	
Prepaid Expenses	30,443	30,929	486	
	185,395	190,065	4,670	
Net Gain from Restatement of Nonmonetary Assets Purchased				4,670
Net (Loss) from Restatement				(74,444)

EXHIBIT G

CONVERTER COMPANY
DEVELOPMENT OF CHANGES IN MONETARY ITEMS
FOR YEAR ENDED DECEMBER 31, 19Y3

Monetary Items at December 31, 19Y3		
Cash		568,115
Accounts Receivable		296,293
Refundable Income Taxes		32,228
Investments		502,013
Accounts Payable		(173,819)
Withheld Taxes and Accrued Expenses		(33,636)
Net Monetary Items at December 31, 19Y3		1,191,194
Changes in Monetary Items in 19Y3		
Monetary Items at December 31, 19Y2		1,165,170
Add: Sales		2,940,766
Less: Monetary Items Expended for Nonmonetary Items		4,105,936
Purchase of Equipment	154,952	
Purchase of Prepaid Expenses	30,443	185,395
		3,920,541
Less: Monetary Items Expended for Operating Costs		
Total Expenses		2,729,347
Net Monetary Items at December 31, 19Y3		1,191,194

ROLLOVER OF RESTATED AMOUNTS ON BALANCE SHEET

The restatement of dollar amounts in units of general purchasing power at December 31, 19Y4 on Exhibit H was made in the same manner as the restatement shown on Exhibit D for December 31, 19Y3, except that 19Y4 index numbers were used. The following note is cross referenced to the statement:

(1) Inventory was assumed to have been acquired evenly throughout the year, and the conversion factor was obtained by dividing the annual average index number for 19Y4 into the index number for the last quarter of that year, as follows:

$$171.9 \div 165.4 = 1.039$$

The units of general purchasing power representing assets, liabilities, and stockholders' equity at December 31, 19Y3 were rolled over to units of general purchasing power at December 31, 19Y4 by use of the rollover formula. This formula required that each balance sheet amount be multiplied by a conversion factor computed by dividing the index number of the last quarter of 19Y3 into the index number of the last quarter of 19Y4, as follows:

$$171.9 \div 155.7 = 1.104$$

EXHIBIT H

BALANCE SHEET CONVERTER COMPANY
19Y3 DOLLAR VALUES RESTATED IN 19Y3 UGPP AND IN 19Y4 UGPP
19Y4 DOLLAR VALUES RESTATED IN 19Y4 UGPP

	Dollar Values at December 31, 19Y3 Restated in UGPP of December 31, 19Y3	UGPP Values at December 31, 19Y3 Restated in UGPP of December 31, 19Y4	Dollar Values at December 31, 19Y4	Restatement Factor	Dollar Values at December 31, 19Y4 Restated in UGPP of December 31, 19Y4
ASSETS					
Current					
Cash	568,115	627,199	232,887	–	232,887
Accounts Receivable	296,293	327,107	254,372	–	254,372
Refundable Income Taxes	32,228	35,580	106,618	–	106,618
Inventory	116,196	128,280	263,502	(1) 1.039	273,779
Investments (cost equals market)	502,013	554,222	552,740		552,740
Prepaid Expenses	40,809	45,053	23,764	(Schedule 1-b)	26,650
	1,555,654	1,717,441	1,433,883		1,447,046
Fixed—less depreciation	492,385	543,593	663,686	(Schedule 2-b)	824,527
Patent—less amortization	489	540	303	(Schedule 3)	472
	2,048,528	2,261,574	2,097,872		2,272,045
LIABILITIES AND STOCKHOLDERS' EQUITY					
Current					
Notes Payable	–	–	120,000	–	120,000
Accounts Payable	173,819	191,896	189,255	–	189,255
Withheld Taxes and Accrued Expenses	33,636	37,134	25,331	–	25,331
Income Taxes Payable	–	–	9,835	–	9,835
Current Portion of Long-Term Debt	–	–	12,500	–	12,500
	207,455	229,030	356,921	–	356,921
Long-Term Debt	–	–	100,000	–	100,000
Stockholders' Equity					
Common Stock			1,300,000	–	
Retained Earnings			340,951		
Total Stockholders' Equity	1,841,073	2,032,544	1,640,951		1,815,124
	2,048,528	2,261,574	2,097,872		2,272,045

ROLLOVER OF RESTATED AMOUNTS ON INCOME STATEMENT

Restatement of the income and expenses for the year 19Y4 shown on Exhibit I was accomplished in the same manner as restatement of 19Y3 dollar amounts shown on Exhibit E. The following notes are cross referenced to the statement:

(1) The conversion factor is for amounts spread evenly throughout the year and was computed by dividing the index number of the last quarter of 19Y4 by the annual average index for 19Y4, as follows:

$$171.9 \div 165.4 = 1.039$$

(2) The beginning inventory was assumed to have been acquired in the last quarter of 19Y3. Therefore, the restatement factor was computed by dividing the index number of the last quarter of 19Y4 by the index number of the last quarter of 19Y3, as follows:

$$171.9 \div 155.7 = 1.104$$

Rollover of income and expense items was accomplished by using the same rollover conversion factor that was used for the rollover of asset and liability items on Exhibit H, which was computed to be 1.104.

NET GENERAL PURCHASING POWER LOSS FOR SECOND YEAR OF RESTATEMENT

Exhibits J and K were prepared to compute the net general purchasing power loss for the year ended December 31, 19Y4. They were prepared on the same basis as the computations shown on Exhibits F and G for 19Y3.

COMPARATIVE STATEMENTS IN UNITS OF MONEY AND UNITS OF GENERAL PURCHASING POWER

Balance sheets for December 31, 19Y3 and December 31, 19Y4, and related income statements for the two years then ended are shown on Exhibits L and M. Amounts are shown in units of money and are then restated for both years in units of general purchasing power at the latest balance sheet date, December 31, 19Y4.

EXHIBIT I

CONVERTER COMPANY
INCOME STATEMENT
19Y3 DOLLAR VALUES RESTATED IN 19Y3 UGPP AND IN 19Y4 UGPP
19Y4 DOLLAR VALUES RESTATED IN 19Y4 UGPP

	Dollar Values at December 31, 19Y3 Restated in UGPP of December 31, 19Y3	UGPP Values at December 31, 19Y3 Restated in UGPP of December 31, 19Y4	Dollar Values at December 31, 19Y4	Restatement Factor	Dollar Values at December 31, 19Y4 Restated in UGPP of December 31, 19Y4
Sales	3,020,167	3,334,264	2,161,287	(1) 1.039	2,245,577
Inventory—beginning	160,104	176,755	116,196	(2) 1.104	128,280
Material Purchases	1,490,395	1,645,396	1,243,506	(1) 1.039	1,292,003
Direct Labor	323,135	356,740	244,013	(1) 1.039	253,529
Manufacturing Expense	421,823	465,693	369,392	(1) 1.039	383,798
Depreciation	88,287	97,469	110,004	(Schedule 2-c)	140,474
	2,483,744	2,742,053	2,083,111		2,198,084
Less: Inventory—ending	116,196	128,280	263,502	(1) 1.039	273,779
Cost of Sales	2,367,548	2,613,773	1,819,609		1,924,305
Gross Profit	652,619	720,491	341,678		321,272
Selling and Delivery Expenses	375,638	414,704	279,704	(1) 1.039	290,612
General Expenses	161,865	178,699	174,984	(1) 1.039	181,808
Amortization of Prepaid Expense	21,358	23,579	24,020	(Schedule 1-c)	27,983
Amortization of Patent	61	67	44	(Schedule 3)	68
Depreciation	8,161	9,010	4,500	(Schedule 2-c)	8,968
	567,083	626,059	483,252		509,439
Operating Income (Loss)	85,536	94,432	(141,574)		(188,167)
Net General Purchasing Power (Loss)	(74,444)	(82,186)	—	Exhibit F	(104,326)
Income (Loss) Before Income Taxes	11,092	12,246	(141,594)		(292,493)
Provision for Income Taxes (Credit)	30,184	33,324	(72,255)	(1) 1.039	(75,073)
Net Income (Loss)	(19,092)	(21,078)	(69,319)		(217,420)
Stockholders' Equity—beginning	1,860,165	2,053,622	1,710,270		2,032,544
Stockholders' Equity—ending	1,841,073	2,032,544	1,640,951		1,815,124

EXHIBIT J

CONVERTER COMPANY
NET GENERAL PURCHASING POWER GAIN OR LOSS
FOR YEAR ENDED DECEMBER 31, 19Y4

Gain or (Loss) from Restatement of Monetary Items	Dollar Values December 31, 19Y3	Restated to UGPP December 31, 19Y4	Gain or (Loss) on Restatement	
Cash	568,115	627,199	(59,084)	
Accounts Receivable	296,293	327,107	(30,814)	
Refundable Income Taxes	32,228	35,580	(3,352)	
Investments	502,013	554,222	(52,209)	
Accounts Payable	(173,819)	(191,896)	18,077	
Withheld Taxes and Accrued Expenses	(33,636)	(37,134)	3,498	
	1,191,194	1,315,078	(123,884)	
Net (Loss) from Restatement of Monetary Items				(123,884)

Gain or (Loss) from Restatement of Results of Operations	Dollar Values for Year December 31, 19Y4	Restated To UGPP December 31, 19Y4	Gain or (Loss) on Restatement	
Sales	2,161,287	2,245,577	84,290)	
Net (Loss) from Restatement of Sales				(84,290)
Expenses (Other Than Expenses Charged Against Nonmonetary Items)				
Material Purchases	1,243,506	1,292,003	48,497	
Direct Labor	244,013	253,529	9,516	
Manufacturing Expenses	369,392	383,798	14,406	
Selling and Delivery Expenses	279,704	290,612	10,908	
General and Administrative Expenses	174,984	181,808	6,824	
Income Taxes	(72,255)	(75,073)	(2,818)	
	2,239,344	2,326,677	87,333	
Net Gain from Restatement of Expenses				87,333
Gain on Restatement of Nonmonetary Assets Purchased During Year				
Equipment	414,221	430,376	16,155	
Prepaid Expenses	9,220	9,580	360	
	423,441	439,956	16,515	
Net Gain from Restatement of Nonmonetary Assets Purchased				16,515
Net (Loss) from Restatement				(104,326)

EXHIBIT K

CONVERTER COMPANY
DEVELOPMENT OF CHANGES IN MONETARY ITEMS
FOR YEAR ENDED DECEMBER 31, 19Y4

Monetary Items at December 31, 19Y4		
Cash		232,887
Accounts Receivable		254,372
Refundable Income Taxes		106,618
Investments		552,740
Notes Payable		(120,000)
Accounts Payable		(189,255)
Withheld Taxes and Accrued Expenses		(25,331)
Income Taxes Payable		(9,835)
Current Portion of Long-Term Debt		(12,500)
Long-Term Debt		(100,000)
Net Monetary Items at December 31, 19Y4		689,696
Changes in Monetary Items in 19Y4		
Monetary items at December 31, 19Y3		1,191,194
Add: Sales		2,161,287
		3,352,481
Less: Monetary Items Expended for Nonmonetary Items		
Purchases of Equipment	414,221	
Purchases of Prepaid Expenses	9,220	423,441
		2,929,040
Less: Monetary Items Expended for Operating Costs		
Total Expenses		2,239,344
Net Monetary Items at December 31, 19Y4		689,696

EXHIBIT L

CONVERTER COMPANY
BALANCE SHEET

	Units of Money		Restated in Units of General Purchasing Power at December 31, 19Y4	
	December 31		December 31	
	19Y4	19Y3	19Y4	19Y3
ASSETS				
Current				
Cash	232,887	568,115	232,887	627,199
Accounts Receivable	254,372	296,293	254,372	327,107
Refundable Income Taxes	106,618	32,228	106,618	35,580
Inventory—at cost	263,502	116,196	273,779	128,280
Investments—cost market	552,740	502,013	552,740	554,222
Prepaid Expenses	23,764	38,564	26,650	45,053
	1,433,883	1,553,409	1,447,046	1,717,441
Fixed—less accumulated depreciation	663,686	363,969	824,527	543,593
Patent—less accumulated amortization	303	347	472	540
	2,097,872	1,917,725	2,272,045	2,261,574
LIABILITIES AND STOCKHOLDERS' EQUITY				
Current				
Notes Payable	120,000	—	120,000	—
Accounts Payable	189,255	173,819	189,255	191,896
Withheld Taxes and Accrued Expenses	25,331	33,636	25,331	37,134
Income Taxes Payable	9,835	—	9,835	—
Current Portion of Long-Term Debt	12,500	—	12,500	—
	356,921	207,455	356,921	229,030
Long-Term Debt	100,000	—	100,000	—
Stockholders' Equity				
Common Stock (13,000 shares—par $100)	1,300,000	1,300,000	—	—
Retained Earnings	340,951	410,270	—	—
Total Stockholders' Equity	1,640,951	1,710,270	1,815,124	2,032,544
	2,097,872	1,917,725	2,272,045	2,261,574

EXHIBIT M

CONVERTER COMPANY
STATEMENT OF INCOME AND STOCKHOLDERS' EQUITY

	Units of Money		Restated in Units of General Purchasing Power at December 31, 19Y4	
	December 31		December 31	
	19Y4	19Y3	19Y4	19Y3
Net Sales	2,161,287	2,940,766	2,245,577	3,334,264
Cost of Goods Sold				
Inventory—beginning	116,196	150,615	128,280	176,755
Material Purchases	1,243,506	1,451,212	1,292,003	1,645,396
Direct Labor	244,013	314,640	253,529	356,740
Manufacturing Expense	369,392	410,733	383,798	465,693
Depreciation	110,004	68,582	140,474	97,469
	2,083,111	2,395,782	2,198,084	2,742,053
Less: Inventory—ending	263,502	116,196	273,779	128,280
Cost of Goods Sold	1,819,609	2,279,586	1,924,305	2,613,773
Gross Profit	341,678	661,180	321,272	720,491
Selling and Delivery Expense	279,704	365,762	290,612	414,704
General and Administrative Expense	174,984	157,610	181,808	178,699
Amortization of Prepaid Expense	24,020	19,464	27,983	23,579
Amortization of Patent	44	43	68	67
Depreciation	4,500	4,500	8,968	9,010
	483,252	547,379	509,439	626,059
Operating Income (Loss)	(141,574)	113,801	(188,167)	94,432
Net General Purchasing Power (Loss)	—	—	(104,326)	(82,186)
Income (Loss) Before Income Taxes	(141,574)	113,801	(292,493)	12,246
Provision for Income Taxes (Credits)	(72,255)	29,390	(75,073)	33,324
Net Income (Loss)	(69,319)	84,411	(217,420)	(21,078)
Stockholders' Equity—beginning	1,710,270	1,625,859	2,032,544	2,053,622
Stockholders' Equity—ending	1,604,951	1,710,270	1,815,124	2,032,544
Earnings (loss) per Share	(5.33)	6.49	(16.72)	(1.62)

TRANSLATION OF FOREIGN CURRENCY

The financial statements of foreign branches, subsidiaries, and other investees should first be translated into United States dollars, and then restated for changes in the dollar's general purchasing power, in accordance with the principles set forth in this chapter. This procedure is necessary to ensure that units of general purchasing power are consistently based on the value of the United States dollar.

LOWER OF COST OR MARKET

Where nonmonetary assets are carried in conventional financial statements at the lower of cost or market, such accounts should be valued at the lower of restated cost or market in financial statements reported in units of general purchasing power.

INCOME TAX ALLOCATION

The income tax expense computed for statements reported in units of general purchasing power should be based on restated dollar amount income tax expense. The difference between pretax income in dollar amounts and such pretax income restated in units of general purchasing power is not a timing difference, and no interperiod income tax allocation should be made for such differences.

DEFERRED INCOME TAXES

Deferred income tax debits and credits that appear on conventional financial statements must be restated on financial statements reported in units of general purchasing power. An analysis should be made of the deferred income tax accounts. After the analyses have been prepared, the unamortized deferred income tax debits and credits should be restated in terms of units of general purchasing power by applying the conversion factor appropriate to the year in which the deferral occurred.

Illustration

In July 19Y1 Converter Company paid $75,000 for a machine having a useful life of five years, and decided to depreciate it on a straight-line basis for financial reporting and by the sum-of-the-digits method for tax purposes.

The depreciation expense computed for the books and for the tax returns, respectively, was as follows:

Year	Straight-Line Method	Sum-of-the-Digits Method	Timing Difference
19Y1	15,000	25,000	10,000
19Y2	15,000	20,000	5,000
19Y3	15,000	15,000	—
19Y4	15,000	10,000	(5,000)

Deferred tax credits on the books of the company at December 31, 19Y4 are summarized in the following schedule:

	Income		Income Tax Expense			Cumulative
Year	Accounting	Taxable	Paid	Pretax	Deferred	Net Deferred Tax Credits
19Y1	12,000	2,000	1,000	6,000	5,000	5,000
19Y2	14,000	9,000	4,500	7,000	2,500	7,500
19Y3	16,000	16,000	8,000	8,000	—	7,500
19Y4	17,000	22,000	11,000	8,500	(2,500)	5,000

Restatement in units of general purchasing power of December 31, 19Y4 would be computed by reversing the timing differences on a FIFO basis and then applying appropriate conversion factors, found in Table 1, to the net increment for each respective year, as follows:

Year		Deferred Tax Credit in Dollars	Conversion Factors	Deferred Tax Credit Restated in UGPP of December 31, 19Y4
19Y1	Deferred credit	5,000		
	Less: Reversal in 19Y4	2,500		
19Y1	Net deferred credit	2,500	1.227	3,068
19Y2	Deferred credit	2,500	1.187	2,968
19Y4	Net deferred tax credit	5,000		6,036

LIFO INVENTORY

Inventories are nonmonetary items and must be restated in units of general purchasing power. Where inventories are valued by the LIFO method, an analysis should be made in the manner demonstrated in chapter 3 of this volume, in order to determine the dollar amount of the base inventory and the dollar amount of layers added in subsequent years. When this has been done, restatement can be effected by applying an appropriate conversion factor to the base inventory, and to the subsequent net increments.

Illustration

Converter Company uses LIFO valuation of its inventory. The dollar amounts at December 31, 19Y4, and these amounts restated in units of general purchasing power at that date, are shown for the inventory base and subsequent layers in the following schedule. The conversion factors are found in Table 1, and it is assumed that inventory components were acquired evenly throughout the respective years.

	Dollar Amounts	Conversion Factors	Restated in UGPP of December 31, 19Y4
19Y0 Base	150,000	1.288	193,200
19Y1 Layer	50,000	1.227	61,350
19Y3 Layer	25,000	1.134	28,350
19Y4 Layer	30,000	1.039	31,170
Total LIFO Inventory at December 31, 19Y4	255,000		314,070

LEASES

Long-term leases that are capitalized and accounted for by the financing method are nonmonetary items and must be restated in units of general purchasing power. The property and the obligation are stated in the balance sheet at the discounted amount of future payments under the lease agreement. For accounting purposes, the asset is considered to be purchased and therefore the property, allowance for depreciation, and the depreciation expense are all restated in exactly the same manner as that for purchased assets demonstrated in the preceding schedules 2-a, 2-b, and 2-c. The lease obligation, and the imputed interest thereon, are monetary items. Therefore, the lease obligation is rolled over from year to year, and interest expense is restated on the assumption that it was incurred evenly throughout the year.

Lease payments on noncapitalized leases are treated as rent expense and such expense is restated on the income statement as having been incurred evenly throughout the year.

ASSETS WRITTEN DOWN TO MARKET

When inventory is written down from cost to market, it should be restated at the dollar cost restated in units of general purchasing power or market, whichever is lower. The write-down to market should be reflected in the value of the ending inventory and thus should be a part of cost of sales in both the conventional statements and in the statements reported in units of general purchasing power. The same principles apply to investments that have been written down to market, except that the expense of the write-down, both in terms of money on the conventional statements and in terms of units of general purchasing power on the restated statements, should go through the respective income statements as a separate item.

LIABILITIES WRITTEN DOWN TO ACTUAL OBLIGATION

Some liabilities are normally nonmonetary because, as in the case of warrants, they require providing nonmonetary goods or services whose prices may fluctuate, or, as in the case of estimated pension costs, the amounts payable under a contract are not fixed. Such liabilities must be restated in units of general purchasing power. However, at times it is determined by management that routine accrual of such liabilities has resulted in a book balance that is in excess of the cost of the actual obligation to perform. In such cases the liability is usually written down to the estimated dollar cost of the obligation. In these instances the reported liability should be identical on both the conventional and restated balance sheets, and the liability should be treated for restatement purposes as though it were a monetary item both at the beginning and at the end of the year.

GAINS AND LOSSES OF GENERAL PURCHASING POWER FROM MONETARY STOCKHOLDERS' EQUITY ITEMS

Gains and losses of general purchasing power that result from monetary stockholders' equity items should be charged or credited directly to *common* stockholders' equity in the general purchasing power financial statements. For example, assume that Converter Company had preferred stock with a fixed liquidation value of \$100,000 at December 31, 19Y3. In accordance with the procedures illustrated on Exhibit J of the model case, the monetary value of \$100,000 at December 31, 19Y3 would be rolled over to December 31, 19Y4 units of general purchasing power by use of a conversion factor of 1.104. The restated amount would be \$110,400, and would reflect a gain from restatement of \$10,400. This gain would not be used in the computation of net loss from restatement as shown on Exhibit J, but would be credited directly to restated stockholders' equity on Exhibit M, "Statement of Income and Stockholders' Equity."

INTERIM STATEMENTS

The exposure draft of the proposed Statement of Financial Accounting Standards on reporting in units of general purchasing power did not require general purchasing power information for interim periods. The practical problems that are involved in gathering and presenting the required data on an interim basis are so enormous that such disclosure normally would not be warranted.

STATEMENT OF CHANGES IN FINANCIAL POSITION

The FASB exposure draft did not require that conventional financial statements be accompanied by a statement of changes in financial position restated in units of general purchasing power. A statement of changes in financial position could readily be prepared under several methods, but since the balance sheet components for all years reported on are restated in units of general purchasing power as of the latest balance sheet date, such statement of changes in financial position would not only be of dubious interpretative value, but would, in fact, defy conceptual comprehension.

5

SYSTEMS OF DUAL ACCOUNTING:

Establishing Collateral Bad Debt Reserves for Financial Institutions

Dual accounting systems are used in a variety of ways to facilitate accounting operations in situations where it is necessary to accumulate more than one set of accounting data and also in circumstances where it is necessary to incorporate into a single system the accounting data derived from two or more accounting processes. Examples of such situations exist in certain industries, notably those that include banks, savings and loan associations, and insurance companies, where it is necessary to provide data for the separate, and often conflicting, purposes of accommodating the financial reporting format prescribed by statute; furnishing specific valuations required by the Internal Revenue Service; and preparing financial statements in accordance with generally accepted accounting principles. Other such situations exist where branch office accounting requires the integration of separate accounting processes; where company security requires that particular accounts be maintained in a "private ledger"; and where companies on the accrual method of accounting use the cash basis for income tax reporting.

The essential ingredient of a dual accounting system is a contra account, or reciprocal account, designed to represent and relate a series of accounts in a major system to a series of collateral accounts contained in a subsidiary system. To establish a dual accounting system for the purposes referred to above, it is necessary first to determine what accounts in the major system are involved in different reporting requirements. The total net value of such accounts should be set up as a contra account in a subsidiary system. For double-entry purposes, the subsidiary ledger contra account then should be expanded into, and offset by, the individual accounts that are necessary to provide the required reporting information. Subsequent entries made in the major system that affect accounts contained in the subsidiary system should be picked up in the contra account and distributed to appropriate accounts within the subsidiary system.

The purpose of this chapter is twofold. Its primary objective is to describe and illustrate dual accounting systems specifically designed to provide for a separation of regulatory and income tax reserves for banks and savings and loan associations. However, the descriptions and illustrations of these systems concurrently demonstrate sophisticated techniques that can be applied in any special situation where dual systems will facilitate the total accounting process.

SAVINGS AND LOAN ASSOCIATIONS

THE NATURE OF BAD DEBT RESERVES

Every federally chartered savings and loan association is required to maintain a Federal Insurance Reserve on its books. Conditions requiring additions to the reserve are specified in the rules and regulations of the federal supervisory agencies—the Federal Home Loan Bank Board and the Federal Savings and Loan Insurance Corporation. Reductions in the reserve may be made only to absorb losses on loans and real estate. State chartered associations may be state insured or federally insured. When they are insured by the federal agency, they are subject to the same rules and regulations as federally chartered associations. In addition, state associations are usually subject to the reserve requirements of state regulatory authorities.

The reserves required by the state and federal supervisory authorities are not loan valuation allowances and have not been created by charges against earnings. However, they do represent restrictions on retained income.

The federal tax laws allow a savings and loan association a special annual bad debt deduction limited to a percentage of income and subject to certain limitations based on aggregate loans and savings accounts at the end of the year. The use of income tax bad debt reserves is not restricted solely to absorbing losses, as in the case of regulatory reserves. However, if the amounts that qualify as deductions for federal income tax purposes are subsequently used for purposes other than to absorb losses, including distributions in liquidation, current taxable income will be generated in an amount equivalent to the reduction in the income tax bad debt reserves.

THE PROBLEM OF BAD DEBT RESERVES

Problems arise in accounting for bad debt reserves because the nature of the reserves required by the supervisory agencies is incompatible with that of the reserves permitted by the taxing authorities. In addition, the technical accounting requirements of both the supervisory and the taxing authorities, in some instances, are at variance with generally accepted accounting principles.

HISTORICAL BACKGROUND

Prior to 1952, savings and loan associations were not subject to any income tax law. In those halcyon days a vast majority of associations transferred only the minimum regulatory requirements to their bad debt reserves and retained the remainder of their annual earnings in undivided profits. This practice afforded maximum flexibility in management's discretionary use of association funds and, at the same time, produced a picture of relatively inflated retained earnings that was a significant attraction to prospective investors of savings funds.

The Revenue Act of 1951 made savings and loan associations subject to the income tax laws, and they were thenceforth taxed in the same manner as banks. There was one important difference, however. Banks, like all corporations, were permitted to take a *reasonable* bad debt deduction on their annual income tax returns, the reasonableness of which was subject to interpretation by the Secretary of the Treasury. Savings and loan associations, on the other hand, were presented with a statutory formula which, in effect, permitted them to take an annual bad debt deduction equivalent to their otherwise taxable income. The cumulative total of the reserve was limited to the difference between the sum of other net worth accounts and 12% of the aggregate withdrawable deposits at the end of the year. Practically every association took full advantage of the generous formula and immediately began transferring all taxable income, computed before the bad debt deduction, to the bad debt reserves.

The eleven years from 1952 through 1962 comprised a period of enormous expansion in the savings and loan industry. Continually increased earnings were transferred, in total, to bad debt reserves. While earnings were increasing, and bad debt reserves building up, the expanding savings accounts continued to render ineffective the restraint inherent in the 12% limitation. Retained earnings remained relatively level, but the resulting restriction on management's discretionary use of association funds was offset to some degree by the vast influx of cash into the industry.

During this eleven-year period, there was no distinction made on the books of savings and loan associations between regulatory bad debt reserves and income tax bad debt reserves. The Internal Revenue Service required that the bad debt deduction be transferred to bad debt reserves and, at the same time, the regulatory agencies required that amounts so transferred be locked up in the general reserves, and be used solely for the purpose of absorbing losses.

The Revenue Act of 1962 made drastic changes in the savings and loan bad debt formula. The new taxation formula was complicated, technically complex, and involved extensive additional recordkeeping. The major impact on the industry was effected by the provision that only a *percentage* of income could be taken as a bad debt deduction.[1] For the first time, *all* associations would pay direct income taxes.[2]

In order to accommodate the new bad debt formula, the 1962 Act required each savings and loan association to do the following, as of December 31, 1962:

(a) *Segregate its loan portfolio into the following two categories:*
   1. Qualifiying real property loans (in effect, loans secured by real estate); and,
   2. Nonqualifying loans (all other loans).

(b) *Determine the nature of its reserve accounts and reclassify them into two separate funds, as follows:*
   Fund 1. The net amount of reserves for which bad debt deductions had been taken in the years 1952-1962; and,
   Fund 2. The net amount of reserves, surplus, and undivided profits attributable to years before the association became taxable in 1952.

(c) *Realign its reserve accounts as of December 31, 1962 by establishing income tax reserve accounts and allocating funds thereto, as follows:*[3]

RESERVE I—Reserve for Losses on Nonqualifying Loans
An allocation to this reserve of a reasonable amount, based on experience, was required to be made from Fund 1.

RESERVE II—Reserve for Losses on Qualifying Loans
An amount equivalent to 3% of qualifying loans was required to be allocated to this reserve from Fund 1. (If the balance remaining in Fund 1 was insufficient to bring Reserve II up to 3% of qualifying loans, an allocation from Fund 2 was required for measurement purposes only. This allocation from Fund 2 could be drawn upon for appropriate purposes without tax effect.)

RESERVE III—Supplemental Reserve for Losses on Loans
Any balance remaining in Fund 1 after satisfaction of the requirements of Reserves I and II was required to be allocated to Reserve III.

RESERVE IV—Pre-1952 Reserves
The balance in Fund 2 was required to be allocated to Reserve IV.

RESERVE V—Tax-Paid Reserves
Tax-paid and tax-exempt portions of surplus, reserves, and undivided profits were required to be allocated to Reserve V.

After an association had completed all the operations referred to above, it was eminently equipped to maintain separate reserve accounts for both the Internal Revenue Service and for the regulatory authorities.

However, a peculiar situation developed in connection with maintaining separate income tax bad debt reserve accounts on the books of savings and loan associations. As early as September 1963, two months before even *proposed* regulations were is-

[1]The percentage was set at 60% by the Revenue Act of 1962. The Tax Reform Act of 1969 provided for a gradual reduction of 33-1/3% in the percentage over a ten-year period; to 40% in 1979.

[2]The Act did contain a "fill-up" method that permitted associations to build their reserves to 3% of qualifying loans without regard to taxable income. This provision was repealed by the Tax Reform Act of 1969.

[3]Special Tax Bulletin, T#1, dated October 24, 1962, issued by the United States Savings and Loan League, first used these Roman numeral designations. They have no official status, but afford a convenient method of identification in accounting for income tax reserves.

sued by the Internal Revenue Service, the Federal Home Loan Bank Board was busy issuing notices to insured institutions cautioning them not to lose or confuse the identity of the regulatory reserves on their books by rearranging or reclassifying them to conform to their understanding of the requirements under the Revenue Act of 1962. The confusion was compounded when the proposed regulations, issued on November 4, 1963, failed to contain the concept of permanent subsidiary ledgers. Consequently, when tax returns for 1963 were filed, most large professional tax consultants were under the impression that an amount equal to, or greater than, the bad debt deduction had to be credited to a locked-up supervisory reserve.

On May 5, 1964, final regulations were issued by the Internal Revenue Service, and Section 1.593-7(a) (2) (i) expanded on Section 1.593-8(a) (2) of the proposed regulations in an attempt to clarify the situation. In spite of the clear provision for permanent subsidiary ledger accounts contained in the final regulations, and in spite of the illustration of a reconciliation between regulatory and income tax bad debt reserves that appeared on page 23 of the United States Savings and Loan League Special Tax Bulletin of October 24, 1962, most large professional tax firms continued to advise their clients to lock up the total bad debt deduction in the supervisory reserve accounts, and continued to do so until Revenue Ruling 68-475, issued in 1968, made the following specific provision: "Permanent subsidiary ledger bad debt reserve accounts which are controlled to an undivided profits or surplus general ledger account will comply with the requirements of Section 1.593-7(a)(2)(i) of the regulations, provided proper records of the transactions are maintained." Meanwhile, millions of dollars had been unnecessarily credited to supervisory reserves and consequently locked up under the inflexible rules and regulations of the regulatory agencies.

PERMANENT SUBSIDIARY LEDGER ACCOUNTS FOR INCOME TAX RESERVES—CONTRA ACCOUNTS

A simple and efficent method of establishing and maintaining subsidiary ledger accounts for income tax reserves can be developed by using a contra account to represent the aggregate supervisory reserves carried on the books of the association. Use of a contra account will permit entries to be made in the income tax reserve accounts by use of standard, double-entry journal entries which, when posted to the contra account and to the income tax reserve accounts, will reflect the changes in the income tax reserves due to operations for the year.

In some cases it may be preferable to use two contra accounts. This situation occurs when the tax paid retained earnings (Reserve V) contains elements that are not in the supervisory reserves of the association. For example, initial service charges are taxable in the year received, but for supervisory purposes the income must be deferred over a period of time. In this case, the tax-paid portion of the general ledger account "Deferred Initial Service Charges" will not be in the supervisory reserve accounts in the general ledger, but it *will* be in the income tax reserves. To accommodate this kind of situation, a second contra account can be used to represent tax-paid income that is not carried in the net worth accounts in the general ledger.

SETTING UP SUBSIDIARY LEDGER ACCOUNTS

Subsidiary ledger accounts should be set up for each income tax reserve account. These ledger accounts should be columnarized to show the total of the account and the portion of each supervisory reserve included in the total.

"Subsidiary" columns in the subsidiary income tax reserves should be provided so that all entries made in the supervisory reserves can also be reflected in the income tax reserves. For example, if the association transfers $10,000 to its F.I.R. at the end of the year, but has an allowable bad debt deduction of $20,000, then $20,000 will be allocated to Reserve II in the income tax reserves; $10,000 will be added to the F.I.R. subsidiary balance and $10,000 to the Undivided Profits subsidiary balance, all within Reserve II.

ENTRIES TO THE SUBSIDIARY LEDGER ACCOUNTS

It is not feasible immediately to determine the eventual tax effect of every operation as it occurs during the year. Therefore, entries in the income tax reserves should be made only at year end. They should not be considered at all when making interim trial balances or in reports to management or the supervisory authorities, and they should not be changed at mid-year to reflect the results of operations for a six-month period. The purpose of the reserve accounts will be served by posting summarizing entries to them at the end of the taxable year. This procedure is, in effect, similar to the normal use of a Profit and Loss Account to summarize the results of operations for an accounting period. The year-end entries to the income tax reserves should summarize operations in the same manner as they are reported on the income tax return.

While it is not necessary to record entries in the income tax reserve accounts until year end, it is absolutely necessary that all entries be recorded and posted by the time the income tax return is filed. Bad debt deductions have been disallowed by the Internal Revenue Service because the entries to the income tax reserves had not been made within a reasonable time after the close of the year. Courts have ruled that a reasonable time would not extend beyond the effective due date of the tax return.

RELATING THE INCOME TAX RESERVES TO THE SUPERVISORY RESERVES

The total of the income tax reserves should, of course, equal the aggregate total of the supervisory reserves and the tax-paid deferred income accounts in the general ledger. Any transfers between supervisory reserves in the general ledger should be reflected as a transfer between balances within the respective income tax reserve accounts affected, so that the correct portion of the supervisory reserve will be reflected in each income tax reserve.

MODEL CASE IN ESTABLISHING AND MAINTAINING PERMANENT SUBSIDIARY LEDGER ACCOUNTS FOR SAVINGS AND LOAN ASSOCIATIONS

The following case study is presented as an illustration of the procedure for converting to, and maintaining, collateral bad debt reserve accounts.

The State Savings and Loan Association, a state-chartered, federally insured institution, followed a practice of recording the results of operations only in the general ledger supervisory reserve accounts. It accounted for its income tax bad debt reserve accounts by a process of analyzing the supervisory reserves at year end to determine the amounts that comprised the required income tax reserves. In 19X2 management decided to set up permanent subsidiary ledger accounts for income tax reserves. It was decided that the required reserves would be designated by Roman numerals as follows:

RESERVE I — Reserve for Losses on Nonqualifying Loans
RESERVE II — Reserve for Losses on Qualifying Loans
RESERVE III — Supplemental Reserve for Losses
RESERVE IV — Pre-1952 Reserves
RESERVE V — Tax-Paid Reserves

Management also decided to use two contra accounts to relate the income tax reserves to the general ledger accounts; one for supervisory reserve accounts and one for deferred income net of tax. The two accounts were designated:

Supervisory Reserve Control
Supervisory Deferred Income Control

The Association deferred the income from initial service charges over a ten-year period for financial accounting purposes, but recorded them as current income for tax purposes. The tax effect of the resulting timing difference was recorded in an account "Deferred Income Tax Debits." In accordance with Accounting Principles Board Opinion No. 23, no provision was made for deferred income tax on bad debt reserves that were accounted for as a part of the general reserves.

The "Deferred Income from Initial Service Charges" and the "Deferred Income Tax Debits" accounts were to be related to the "Supervisory Deferred Income Control," and the net worth reserves were to be related to the "Supervisory Reserve Control."

In order to establish permanent subsidiary ledger accounts for income tax reserves as of the beginning of the year, the general ledger accounts were analyzed as of December 31, 19X1, and the elements of income tax reserves contained therein were summarized as follows:

GENERAL LEDGER ACCOUNTS	INCOME TAX RESERVES					
	RESERVE I	RESERVE II	RESERVE III	RESERVE IV	RESERVE V	TOTAL
Deferred Income					149,298	149,298
F.I.R.	1,000	1,042,820	1,075,312	201,686	433,382	2,754,200
Legal Reserve		786,185				786,185
Undivided Profits		678,932		425,035	356,453	1,460,420
Deferred Tax Debits					(26,564)	(26,564)
Totals	1,000	2,507,937	1,075,312	626,721	912,569	5,123,539

The summary served as a basis for preparing the following journal entry to set up the income tax reserves as of December 31, 19X1:

Supervisory Reserve Control		5,000,805	
Supervisory Deferred Income Control		122,734	
Reserve I (F.I.R.)			1,000
Reserve II			
(F.I.R.	1,042,820)		
(Legal Reserve	786,185)		
(Undivided Profits	678,932)		2,507,937
Reserve III (F.I.R.)			1,075,312
Reserve IV			
(F.I.R.	201,686)		626,721
(Undivided Profits	425,035)		
Reserve V			
(Deferred Income	149,298)		
(F.I.R.	433,382)		
(Undivided Profits	356,453)		
(Deferred Tax Debits	(26,564))		912,569

To set up income tax reserves at December 31, 19X1 and relate them to appropriate general ledger accounts at that date.

At December 31, 19X2 the results of operations shown on the income statement were as follows:

Income before income taxes		539,366
Less—income taxes		
Current	152,233	
Deferred	(9,416)	142,817
Net Income		396,549

The following changes occurred during the year in general ledger accounts that affected income tax reserve accounts:

Net increase in deferred income		32,693
Net increase in deferred income tax debits		9,416
Transfers from Undivided Profits		
To Federal Insurance Reserve	200,000	
To Legal Reserve	19,134	219,134

The above information was summarized in the following schedule which shows the net changes in the general ledger accounts containing income tax reserve elements. These changes were the results of operations and reserve transfers.

GENERAL LEDGER ACCOUNTS

	Deferred Income	F.I.R.	Legal Reserve	Undivided Profits	Deferred Taxes	Total
Balance—12/31/X1	149,298	2,754,200	786,185	1,460,420	(26,564)	5,123,539
Net Income				396,549		396,549
Increase in Deferred Income	32,693					32,693
Increase in Deferred Taxes					(9,416)	(9,416)
Supervisory Reserve Transfers		200,000	19,134	(219,134)		—
Balance—12/31/X2	181,991	2,954,200	805,319	1,637,835	(35,980)	5,543,365

Entries for all the above changes had been made on the books of the Association as of December 31, 19X2, and the balances shown above were the actual balances in the respective general ledger accounts at that date.

Information shown on the income tax return was then analyzed to provide a basis for recording changes in the income tax reserves. That analysis produced the following reconciliation of pretax income to taxable income.

Net income per books			396,549
Federal income tax			
Current		152,233	
Deferred		(9,416)	142,817
Taxable income not on books			
Deferred initial service charges			32,693
Expenses recorded on books—not deducted on tax return			
Loss on loans		923	
F.S.L.I.C. premiums		5,485	6,408
			578,467
LESS			
Income on books—not on tax return			
F.S.L.I.C. interest	21,779		
F.H.L.B. dividend	5,533	27,312	
Deductions on return—not charged against income on books			
Bad Debt Deduction		220,462	247,774
Taxable income, per tax return			330,693

From the information provided by the income tax return, and with reference to the supervisory reserve transfers on the general ledger, the following series of journal entries were designed to reflect the tax effects of operations and reserve transfers during the year, and the resulting changes in the income tax reserves for that period.

Entry No.			Debit	Credit
1	Reserve II (Undivided Profits)		923	
	Reserve V (Undivided Profits)		5,485	
	Supervisory Reserve Control			6,408
	To record nonallowable deductions:			
	Loss on loans	923		
	F.S.L.I.C. premiums	5,485		
2	Supervisory Reserve Control		27,312	
	Reserve V (Undivided Profits)			27,312
	To record nontaxable income:			
	F.S.L.I.C. interest	21,779		
	F.H.L.B. dividends	5,533		
3	Supervisory Reserve Control		220,462	
	Reserve II (Undivided Profits)			220,462
	To record bad debt deduction.			
4	Supervisory Reserve Control		307,416	
	Supervisory Deferred Income Control		23,277	
	Reserve V			
	(Undivided Profits	307,416)		
	(Deferred Income	32,693)		
	(Deferred Income Tax	(9,416))		330,693
	To record taxable income for year.			

Entry No.			Debit	Credit
5	Reserve V (Undivided Profits)		152,233	
	Supervisory Reserve Control			152,233
	To record income tax expense for year.			
6	Reserve V (Undivided Profits)		219,134	
	Reserve V			
	(F.I.R.	200,000)		
	(Legal Reserve	19,134)		219,134
	To record transfers between supervisory reserves.			

Both the journal entry to set up the income tax reserves and the journal entries to record operations and transfers during the year were posted to the subsidiary income tax reserve ledger accounts. These ledger accounts are shown below.*

RESERVE I—RESERVE FOR LOSSES ON NONQUALIFYING LOANS

Date—Reference	Deferred Income	F.I.R.	Legal Reserve	Undivided Profits	Deferred Taxes	Balance (Dr.) Cr.
12/31/X1—Balance	—	1,000	—	—	—	1,000

RESERVE II—RESERVE FOR LOSSES ON QUALIFYING LOANS

Date—Reference	Deferred Income	F.I.R.	Legal Reserve	Undivided Profits	Deferred Taxes	Balance (Dr.) Cr.
12/31/X1—Balance	—	1,042,820	786,185	678,932	—	2,507,937
12/31/X2—JE #1				(923)		
12/31/X2—JE #3				220,462		
	—	1,042,820	786,185	898,471	—	2,727,476

RESERVE III—SUPPLEMENTAL RESERVE FOR LOSSES

Date—Reference	Deferred Income	F.I.R.	Legal Reserve	Undivided Profits	Deferred Taxes	Balance (Dr.) Cr.
12/31/X1—Balance	—	1,075,312	—	—	—	1,075,312

*For illustrative purposes, the journal entries prepared for the solution of this problem were deliberately designed to be somewhat elaborate. In actual practice, after the accountant has become familiar with the process, many shortcuts may be taken both in analyzing the relevant data and preparing the entries to be made in the income tax reserves.

RESERVE IV—PRE-1952 RESERVES

Date—Reference	Deferred Income	F.I.R.	Legal Reserve	Undivided Profits	Deferred Taxes	Balance (Dr.) Cr.
12/31/X1—Balance	—	201,686	—	425,035	—	626,721

RESERVE V—TAX-PAID RESERVES

Date—Reference	Deferred Income	F.I.R.	Legal Reserve	Undivided Profits	Deferred Taxes	Balance (Dr.) Cr.
12/31/X1—Balance	149,298	433,382	—	356,453	(26,564)	912,569
12/31/X2—JE #1				(5,485)		
—JE #2				27,312		
—JE #4	32,693			307,416	(9,416)	
—JE #5				(152,233)		
—JE #6		200,000	19,134	(219,134)		
12/31/X2—Balance	181,991	633,382	19,134	314,329	(35,980)	1,112,856

SUPERVISORY RESERVE CONTROL

Date—Reference	F.I.R.	Legal Reserve	Undivided Profits	Balance Dr. (Cr.)
12/31/X1—Balance	2,754,200	786,185	1,460,420	5,000,805
12/31/X2—JE #1			(6,408)	
—JE #2			27,312	
—JE #3			220,462	
—JE #4			307,416	
—JE #5			(152,233)	
—JE #6	200,000	19,134	(219,134)	
12/31/X2—Balance	2,954,200	805,319	1,637,835	5,397,354

SUPERVISORY DEFERRED INCOME CONTROL

Date—Reference	Deferred Income	Deferred Taxes	Dr. (Cr.)
12/31/X1—Balance	149,298	(26,564)	122,734
12/31/X2—JE #4	32,693	(9,416)	
12/31/X2—Balance	181,991	(35,980)	146,011

A trial balance taken on the income tax reserves and the subsidiary balances as of December 31, 19X2 is shown below

INCOME TAX RESERVES	SUBSIDIARY BALANCES					ACCOUNT BALANCE
	Deferred Income	F.I.R.	Legal Reserve	Undivided Profits	Deferred Taxes	
Reserve I		1,000				1,000
Reserve II		1,042,820	786,185	898,471		2,727,476
Reserve III		1,075,312				1,075,312
Reserve IV		201,686		425,035		626,721
Reserve V	181,991	633,382	19,134	314,329	(35,980)	1,112,856
Totals	181,991	2,954,200	805,319	1,637,835	(35,980)	5,543,365

The trial balance proved that the income tax reserves were in agreement with the general ledger accounts to which they related. The balances in the general ledger accounts at December 31, 19X2 were as follows:

Deferred Initial Service Charges	181,991
Federal Insurance Reserve	2,954,200
Legal Reserve	805,319
Undivided Profits	1,637,835
Deferred Income Tax Debits	(35,980)
	5,543,365

An inspection of the ledger cards for the Supervisory Reserve Control and the Supervisory Deferred Income Control revealed that the two contra accounts were in agreement with both the income tax reserve accounts and the related general ledger accounts.

The tax effects of every conceivable type of operation recorded on the general books of the association can be recorded in the income tax reserve accounts by the simple, direct, and accurate method described in this chapter. The procedures outlined herein may be performed manually or they can be adapted to either mechanical or electronic application.

BANKS

The problem of accounting for the bad debt reserves of banks is different from the accounting problem posed by savings and loan associations. Banks, unlike savings and loan associations, are not required to combine their bad debt reserves and net worth accounts, and then reclassify the aggregate thereof into five separate income tax reserves. On the contrary, banks generally have one single account for their reserve for losses on loans and this one account satisfies the accounting requirements of both the regulatory agencies and the taxing authorities. However, many banks have not always charged operations with the full amount of the periodic addition to their Reserve for Losses on Loans. Therefore, to present annual financial statements that are in conformity with generally accepted accounting principles, these banks must analyze their Reserve for Losses on Loans to segregate the following three elements:

(a) valuation portion, available for charging losses;
(b) contingency portion, not available for absorbing losses; and
(c) deferred tax portion.

Tax laws always have required corporations on the reserve method for bad debts to credit a loss reserve account for at least the amount taken as a tax deduction in any taxable year. However, in 1972 the Internal Revenue Service published Regulation 1.585-3(b) which permits banks to use permanent subsidiary ledger accounts to account for the income tax bad debt reserve. The remainder of this chapter illustrates a system for setting up and maintaining permanent subsidiary ledger accounts for income tax reserves for banks. This system will obviate the necessity for periodically analyzing the general ledger loan loss account, will comply with the technical accounting requirements of both the taxing and supervisory agencies, and will permit accurate statement presentation in accordance with generally accepted accounting principles.

THE NATURE OF BAD DEBT RESERVES

The diverse characteristics of loans made by banks make it difficult to project loan losses. Furthermore, the losses suffered by banks are of two different types: the recurring type that is common to all debt-creating activities, and the severe, unpredictable type that occurs at irregular and infrequent intervals.

The Internal Revenue Service recognizes the need for banks to provide reserves for both types of losses and its tax formula permits the accumulation of reserves for losses in amounts that are greater than that required to absorb only the recurring type. The maximum bad debt deduction permitted under the tax formula is credited to the loan loss reserve on the books of practically all banks, and such credits are normally in excess of supervisory requirements.

Banks are required to charge all loan losses to the Reserve for Losses on Loans. All recoveries on loans previously charged off are required to be added to the loss reserve. If, as a result of net recoveries during a taxable year, the reserve balance exceeds the permissible amount, no taxable income is generated, but the excess will affect future additions.

THE PROBLEM OF BAD DEBT RESERVES

The major problem connected with bad debt reserves of banks is one of accounting for them in accordance with generally accepted accounting principles. The accounting problem resolves largely into one of presentation on the financial statements. Since the Reserve for Losses on Loans is normally comprised of elements of valuation, contingency, and deferred tax, proper accounting for the reserve requires a separation of these three elements so that they can be accurately disclosed on the financial statements.

Another problem encountered in accounting for the Reserve for Losses on Loans is that the addition to the reserve permitted or required by the taxing and regulatory authorities may be greater or less than that which should be made under generally accepted accounting principles, which require that loan loss charges to operations be on a systematic and consistent basis.

HISTORICAL BACKGROUND

Most banks have always taken full advantage of the maximum bad debt deduction permitted by the Internal Revenue Service and have consistently credited their Reserve for Losses on Loans with the full amount of the deduction taken for tax purposes. The deductions permitted by the taxing authorities were, in almost every case, in excess of the regulatory requirements.

Prior to 1964, banks charged their provision for loan losses directly to undivided profits and disclosed their loan loss reserve on the balance sheet in a variety of ways. In some cases the loss reserve was deducted from loans as a valuation account; in other instances it was shown on the liability side as a reserve, either within or without the capital section.

Beginning in 1964, following new regulations by the Federal Reserve Board, the F.D.I.C., and the S.E.C., most banks adopted a method of presentation on the financial statements that reflected the loss provision as a nonoperating deduction on the income statement and the loss reserve as a valuation account on the balance sheet.

In 1969 revised regulations were issued following extensive discussions held by representatives of the banking industry, federal regulatory authorities, the S.E.C., and the A.I.C.P.A. The significant changes set forth in the revised regulations were the requirements that the provision for loan losses be included in the operating expenses of the bank, rather than shown as a nonoperating deduction, and that the reserve for loan losses be presented as a separate section on the credit side of the balance sheet, below total liabilities and above capital funds.

Meanwhile, in the same year, the Tax Reform Act of 1969 made substantial changes in the methods allowed to be used by banks in determining the deductible addition to bad debt reserves.

The Act added a new Code section to provide for losses on loans by banks. Banks were no longer allowed to build up their bad debt reserves to 2.4% of uninsured loans outstanding; instead, they were permitted to add to the reserve only the greater of a specified percentage of such loans or an amount computed on the basis of their experience, using a ratio of losses for the current year to the total losses over the current and preceding five years. The percentage method is to be phased out over an eighteen-year transitional period so that for taxable years beginning after December 31, 1987 banks will be required to use their own experience in determining the amount of their bad debt deductions.

The Tax Reform Act of 1969 still permits banks to take a bad debt deduction equivalent to that required by the regulatory authorities, since the revised federal regulations require an addition to the reserves based on a six-year experience average. However, the revised federal regulations permit banks to make a *greater* addition to the reserve when, in the opinion of management, such increased allocation is required for protection against expected future losses. This particular provision of the federal regulations provides for the possibility that the loan loss reserve of a particular bank may contain discordant elements that are incompatible with the requirements of both the taxing and the supervisory authorities and, at the same time, are at variance with generally accepted accounting principles.

As stated previously, in 1972 the Internal Revenue Service published the regulation that permits banks to account for their income tax bad debt reserves in permanent subsidiary ledger accounts. This provision of the law has the saving grace of allowing banks to install a system of accounting that provides easy resolution of all the accounting problems implicit in the complexities of bank loan loss reserves.

PERMANENT SUBSIDIARY LEDGER ACCOUNTS FOR INCOME TAX RESERVES

Establishing and maintaining subsidiary income tax reserves for banks is accomplished in the same manner as previously described for savings and loan associations. A contra account is used to represent the accounts carried in the general ledger; separate subsidiary accounts are set up for the elements contained in the reserve for losses on loans account; and entries are made only at the end of the taxable year by use of standard, double-entry journal entries.

MODEL CASE IN ESTABLISHING AND MAINTAINING PERMANENT SUBSIDIARY LEDGER ACCOUNTS FOR BANKS

This model case illustrates the procedure for setting up and maintaining permanent subsidiary ledger accounts for the income tax reserves of banks.

The State Bank, a state-chartered bank, insured by the Federal Deposit Insurance Corporation, followed a practice of taking a bad debt deduction on its tax return based on its loan loss experience, using a ratio of losses for the current year to the total losses over the current and preceding five years. In 19X2 management decided to set up permanent subsidiary ledger accounts so that income tax reserves could be separated from the general ledger accounts.

All of the annual additions to the reserve in past years were tax deductible, were in excess of supervisory requirements, and were charged to current operations. Therefore, at the end of the the prior year, December 31, 19X1, the Reserve for Losses on Loans account was "clean"; it contained no elements of contingency or deferred income tax.

Management decided that in 19X2 the bank should allocate to its Reserve for Losses on Loans a greater provision for bad debts than would be allowed as a tax deduction. Therefore, it decided to establish separate bad debt reserves in subsidiary ledger accounts as an accounting mechanism to handle the variance between financial accounting and tax accounting.

It was decided to set up the following income tax reserves:

Reserve for Losses on Loans—Tax Paid
Reserve for Losses on Loans—Tax Deferred
Surplus—Tax Paid
Undivided Profits—Tax Paid
Deferred Income Tax Debits

One contra account, Supervisory Reserve Control, was used to relate the income tax reserve accounts to the following general ledger accounts:

Deferred Income Tax Debits
Reserve for Losses on Loans
Surplus
Undivided Profits

At the beginning of the year, December 31, 19X1, the general ledger reflected balances in the following accounts in the amounts indicated:

Reserve for Losses on Loans	69,505
Surplus	587,500
Undivided Profits	132,948

The Reserve for Losses on Loans was "clean"; it had no contingency or deferred tax elements. The Surplus Account was required by the state supervisory agency, but for income tax purposes it was combined with Undivided Profits.

The following journal entry was prepared to set up the income tax reserves as of December 31, 19X1:

	Debit	Credit
Supervisory Reserve Control	789,953	
Reserve for Losses on Loans—Tax Paid		69,505
Surplus—Tax Paid		587,500
Undivided Profits—Tax Paid		132,948

To set up income tax reserves at December 31, 19X1 and relate them to appropriate general ledger accounts at that date.

At December 31, 19X2, the results of operations shown on the income statement were as follows:

Income, before bad debt expense		165,025
Bad debt expense (net increase in Reserve for Losses on Loans)		38,000
Income before income taxes		127,025
Less—income taxes		
Current	58,312	
Deferred	(8,640)	49,672
Net income		77,353

The following other changes occurred during the year in the general ledger accounts that affected income tax reserve accounts:

Stock dividend charged to Surplus	41,250
Transfer from Undivided Profits to Surplus	35,000

Estimated future tax benefits were set up in a Deferred Income Tax Debit account. These benefits are expected to derive when management's future allocations to the Reserve for Losses on Loans are less than those allowed as tax deductions.

The net change during the year in the general ledger accounts containing income tax components is shown in the following schedule:

	Reserve for Losses on Loans	Surplus	Undivided Profits	Deferred Income Tax	Total
Balance–12/31/X1	69,505	587,500	132,948		789,953
Net Income			77,353		77,353
Increase in Deferred Income Tax Debits				(8,640)	(8,640)
Increase in Reserve for Losses on Loans	38,000				38,000
Stock Dividend		(41,250)			(41,250)
Transfer between Net Worth Accounts		35,000	(35,000)		
Balance–12/31/X2	107,505	581,250	175,301	(8,640)	855,416

Entries for all the above changes had been made on the books of the bank as of December 31, 19X2, and the balances shown above were the actual balances in the respective general ledger accounts at that date.

The income tax return revealed the following reconciliation of pretax and taxable income:

Net income per books		77,353
Federal income tax–current	58,312	
–deferred	(8,640)	49,672
Expense on books–not on return		
Unallowable portion of bad debt deduction		18,000
		145,025
Less–Income on books–not on return		
Interest on state bonds (a permanent difference)		10,000
Taxable income		135,025

Based on the information provided by the tax return, and with reference to the stock dividend and transfers within the net worth accounts, the following series of journal entries were prepared to reflect the tax effects of operations and reserve transfers during the year, and the resulting changes in the income tax reserves.

Entry No.		Debit	Credit
1	Supervisory Reserve Control	10,000	
	Undivided Profits—Tax Paid		10,000
	To record nontaxable income—state bond interest.		
2	Supervisory Reserve Control	135,025	
	Undivided Profits—Tax Paid		135,025
	To record taxable income for year.		
3	Undivided Profits—Tax Paid	18,000	
	Supervisory Reserve Control		18,000
	To record unallowable portion of bad debt deduction.		
4	Undivided Profits—Tax Paid	49,672	
	Supervisory Reserve Control		49,672
	To record income tax expense—net.		
5	Supervisory Reserve Control	29,360	
	Deferred Income Tax Debits	8,640	
	Reserve for Losses on Loans—Tax Paid		20,000
	Reserve for Losses on Loans—Tax Deferred		18,000
	To record addition to Reserve for Losses on Loans, and related tax effect of timing difference.		
6	Surplus—Tax Paid	41,250	
	Supervisory Reserve Control		41,250
	To record stock dividend charged to Surplus.		
7	Undivided Profits—Tax Paid	35,000	
	Surplus—Tax Paid		35,000
	To record transfer between net worth accounts.		

The schedule below shows the detail of the subsidiary ledger accounts after all the journal entries had been posted.

	Reserve for Losses on Loans—Tax Paid	Reserve for Losses on Loans—Tax Deferred	Income Tax Debits	Surplus—Tax Paid	Undivided Profits—Tax Paid	Supervisory Reserve Control
Balance—1/1/X2	69,505			587,500	132,948	789,953
Journal Entry No.						
1					10,000	10,000
2					135,025	135,025
3					(18,000)	(18,000)
4					(49,672)	(49,672)
5	20,000	18,000	(8,640)			29,360
6				(41,250)		(41,250)
7				35,000	(35,000)	—
Balance—12/31/X2	89,505	18,000	(8,640)	581,250	175,301	855,416

The subsidiary balances relate to the balances in the following general ledger accounts at December 31, 19X2:

	Balance (Dr.) Cr.
Deferred Income Tax Debits	(8,640)
Reserve for Losses on Loans	107,505
Surplus	581,250
Undivided Profits	175,301
Total	855,416

The Reserve for Losses on Loans—Tax Paid has a credit balance in this case because the book allocation was greater than the allowable tax deduction. If the situation reverses and the tax deduction becomes greater than the book allocation, then the "tax deferred" portion of the reserve could have a debit balance, indicating that tax had not been paid on that portion, and deferred tax debits would develop into deferred income tax credits.

In this case there was no contingency element in the Reserve for Losses on Loans. Had there been, a separate subsidiary ledger account could have been set up in the income tax reserves for measurement purposes, even though it might be designated as a contingency for financial accounting purposes only and have no tax effect.

6

ACCOUNTING FOR BUSINESS COMBINATIONS:

Purchasing and Pooling of Interests Methods

In August 1970 the American Institute of Certified Public Accountants published Accounting Principles Board Opinion No. 16 for the purpose of providing guidance to accountants with respect to the accounting treatment of business combinations. In the Opinion the Board affirmed acceptance of both the purchase method and the pooling of interests method of accounting for business combinations, but it accepted neither to the exclusion of the other, and concluded that some business combinations should be accounted for by the purchase method and other combinations should be accounted for by the pooling of interests method. The Opinion states that the two methods are not alternatives in accounting for the same business combination; that a single method should be applied to an entire combination; and that circumstances surrounding the combination should dictate which method to apply.

The Opinion describes twelve distinctive conditions that require the pooling of interests method of accounting and states that a combination satisfying *all* of those conditions should be accounted for as a pooling of interests. Any business combination failing to satisfy any *one* of the specified pooling conditions should be treated as the acquisition of one company by another and accounted for by the purchase method. The Opinion also specifies the procedures to be followed in applying each accounting method.

This chapter provides explanations of the Opinion's provisions; illustrates both the purchase and the pooling of interests methods of accounting; and demonstrates accounting techniques that permit full compliance with the requirements of the Opinion.

METHODS OF ACCOUNTING FOR BUSINESS COMBINATIONS

The two acceptable methods of accounting for business combinations are: the purchase method, which is applied where the combination is treated as the acquisition of one company by another; and the pooling of interests method, which is used where the combination results in continuity of ownership by the stockholders of the constituent companies.

Purchase Method

In applying the purchase method, the principles normally applicable under historical-cost basis accounting are followed. The cost of the acquired company is equivalent to the fair value of the consideration exchanged for it, and such cost is allocated to the individual assets and liabilities acquired. Any excess of total cost over the costs assigned to individual assets and liabilities is recorded as goodwill and amortized over a period not exceeding forty years. The acquiring company picks up only that portion of income of the acquired company that was earned subsequent to the date of acquisition.

Pooling of Interests Method

Under the pooling of interests method, the assets, liabilities, and capital accounts of all the constituents are combined at their respective carrying values and no cost factors, or goodwill, are involved. The combined company reports its income combined with that of the constituent companies as though the pooling of interests had occurred on the first day of the fiscal year.

DEFINITION OF A BUSINESS COMBINATION

For purposes of APB Opinion No. 16, a business combination occurs when a corporation and one or more incorporated or unincorporated businesses are brought together into one accounting entity. The single entity carries on the activities of the previously separate, independent enterprises. The Opinion does not specifically discuss the combination of a corporation and one or more unincorporated businesses, or of two or more unincorporated businesses, but it states that its provisions should be used as a general guide.

CLASSIFICATION OF BUSINESS COMBINATIONS COVERED BY THE OPINION

The conclusions of the Opinion apply to the types of business combinations listed below. (Both incorporated and unincorporated enterprises are referred to as "companies" in this list.)

(a) Where a corporation and one or more incorporated or unincorporated businesses combine;
(b) Where one or more companies become subsidiary corporations;
(c) Where one company transfers its net assets to another; and,
(d) Where each company transfers its net assets to a newly formed corporation.

BUSINESS COMBINATIONS EXCLUDED FROM THE PROVISIONS OF THE OPINION

The following types of transactions are not considered to be business combinations to which the provisions of the Opinion are applicable:

(a) the acquisition of some or all of the stock held by minority stockholders of a subsidiary;
(b) a transfer by a corporation of its net assets to a newly formed substitute corporate entity chartered by the existing corporation; and,
(c) a transfer of net assets or exchange of shares between companies under common control, such as between a parent corporation and its subsidiaries, or between subsidiary corporations of the same parent.

MODEL CASE IN ACCOUNTING FOR A BUSINESS COMBINATION AS A POOLING OF INTERESTS

The following model case of Able Company, Baker Company, and Crystal Company has been prepared to illustrate the mechanics of accounting for an uncomplicated business combination as a pooling of interests. This model case is also used later in the chapter as the basis for illustrating certain pooling conditions and for demonstrating more complicated accounting techniques applicable to the pooling of interests method.

Able Company, Baker Company, and Crystal Company were unrelated, closely held corporations engaged in analogous enterprise. With respect to each of the three companies, earnings per share had been comparable for the several preceding years, fixed assets had been acquired over a corresponding time span, and the ratios of net book value of depreciable assets to replacement cost were estimated to be approximately equal.

At special meetings called in July, the Boards of Directors of the respective companies adopted identical resolutions to effect a pooling of interests of the three companies. Although the fiscal year of each company ended on December 31, the Boards directed that the pooling be consummated on September 30 of the current year.

The combination plan approved by the Boards provided that Able Company would issue its one-class voting stock for all of the voting common stock interests of the other two companies. Because of the comparability of earnings per share and replacement values of tangible assets, the number of shares to be issued to the combining companies was determined to be on the basis of the ratio of the net book value of a single share of stock of each respective combining company to the net book value of a single share of stock of the issuing company, applied to the number of shares outstanding at September 30.

All of the other conditions required to account for the combination as a pooling of interests were satisfied.

At September 30 adjusted general ledger trial balances of the constituent companies were as follows:

	Trial Balances			Combined	
	Able Company	Baker Company	Crystal Company	Combining Companies	All Constituents
	Dr. (Cr.)	Dr. (Cr.)	Dr. (Cr.)	Dr. (Cr.)	Dr. (Cr.)
Cash	22,000	18,750	17,500	36,250	58,250
Accounts Receivable	52,000	44,000	40,000	84,000	136,000
Inventories					
Finished Goods	66,000	56,000	49,500	105,500	171,500
Work in Process	27,500	23,250	22,500	45,750	73,250
Raw Materials	44,000	37,500	35,250	72,750	116,750
Land	75,000	64,000	56,250	120,250	195,250
Buildings	247,500	188,750	165,000	353,750	601,250
Depreciation Allowance	(25,000)	(18,750)	(15,000)	(33,750)	(58,750)
Machinery and Equipment	344,000	322,750	237,250	560,000	904,000
Depreciation Allowance	(11,000)	(40,250)	(29,750)	(70,000)	(81,000)
Notes Payable	(80,000)	(71,000)	(60,250)	(131,250)	(211,250)
Other Liabilities	(7,000)	(2,500)	(5,000)	(7,500)	(14,500)
Capital Stock	(610,000)	(400,000)	(375,000)	(775,000)	(1,385,000)
Retained Earnings	(87,500)	(166,500)	(91,500)	(258,000)	(345,500)
Sales	(920,500)	(787,750)	(693,750)	(1,481,500)	(2,402,000)
Raw Materials Purchases	272,250	230,000	204,250	434,250	706,500
Direct Labor	165,000	140,000	123,750	263,750	428,750
Manufacturing Expense	253,000	215,000	189,750	404,750	657,750
Selling Expense	66,000	56,000	49,500	105,500	171,500
Administrative Expense	93,500	79,500	70,250	149,750	243,250
Interest Costs	1,750	1,500	1,250	2,750	4,500
Inventory Adjustments	11,500	9,750	8,250	18,000	29,500
	-0-	-0-	-0-	-0-	-0-

Income tax expense, based on taxable income, was computed for each respective company. Since Baker Company and Crystal Company were to be dissolved, they were required to file a return as of September 30. Therefore, income tax expense was based on actual tax liability, and no attempt was made to follow accepted interim statement procedure, which requires that interim tax expense be based on an estimated effective *annual* rate.

The trial balances were adjusted to reflect income, tax liability, and expense, and the following financial statements were prepared as of September 30:

Balance Sheets—September 30

	Able Company	Baker Company	Crystal Company	Combined
Assets				
Current				
Cash	22,000	18,750	17,500	58,250
Accounts Receivable	52,000	44,000	40,000	136,000
Inventories	137,500	116,750	107,250	361,500
	211,500	179,500	164,750	555,750
Fixed—Net of Depreciation	630,500	516,500	413,750	1,560,750
	842,000	696,000	578,500	2,116,500
Liabilities and Stockholders Equity				
Current Liabilities				
Notes Payable	80,000	71,000	60,250	211,250
Other Current Liabilities	7,000	2,500	5,000	14,500
Income Taxes Payable	23,000	22,500	18,250	63,750
	110,000	96,000	83,500	289,500
Stockholder's Equity				
Capital Stock—Par $100				
Authorized, 50,000—Issued, 6,100 shares	610,000			
Authorized, 20,000—Issued, 4,000 shares		400,000		
Authorized, 20,000—Issued, 3,750 shares			375,000	1,385,000
Retained Earnings	122,000	200,000	120,000	442,000
Total Capital	732,000	600,000	495,000	1,827,000
	842,000	696,000	578,500	2,116,500

Statements of Income and Retained Earnings for Nine Months Ended September 30

	Able Company	Baker Company	Crystal Company	Combined
Sales	920,500	787,750	693,750	2,402,000
Cost of Sales	701,750	594,750	526,000	1,822,500
Gross Profit	218,750	193,000	167,750	579,500
Expenses				
Selling	66,000	56,000	49,500	171,500
Administrative	93,500	79,500	70,250	243,250
Interest	1,750	1,500	1,250	4,500
Total Expenses	161,250	137,000	121,000	419,250
Income Before Income Taxes	57,500	56,000	46,750	160,250
Provision for Income Taxes	23,000	22,500	18,250	63,750
Net Income	34,500	33,500	28,500	96,500
Retained Earnings—January 1	87,500	166,500	91,500	345,500
Retained Earnings—September 30	122,000	200,000	120,000	442,000
Earnings Per Share	5.65	8.38	7.60	

The net book value of one share of common stock was determined for each company by dividing the stockholders' equity by the number of shares outstanding, as follows:

Able Company	— $732,000 ÷ 6,100 shares	= $120
Baker Company	— $600,000 ÷ 4,000 shares	= $150
Crystal Company	— $495,000 ÷ 3,750 shares	= $132

The number of shares of stock of the issuing company (Able Company) that was issued in exchange for each share of stock of the combining companies was computed simply by dividing the book value of a share of the issuing company's stock into the book value of a share of stock of the respective combining companies, as follows:

Baker Company	— $150 ÷ $120	= 1.25
Crystal Company	— $132 ÷ $120	= 1.10

Thus, Baker Company stockholders received one and one-fourth share of Able Company stock in exchange for each share of Baker Company stock surrendered, and stockholders of Crystal Company received one and one-tenth share of Able Company stock for each of their shares in Crystal Company. The 6,100 shares of Able Company stock outstanding at September 30 were simply retained by Able Company shareholders; there was no change in their holdings.

Upon completion of the exchange, the holdings of Able Company stock were as follows:

Former Baker Company Stockholders:		
4,000 shares exchanged at 1.25 for 1	= 5,000 shares at $100 par =	$ 500,000
Former Crystal Company Stockholders:		
3,750 shares exchanged at 1.10 for 1	= 4,125 shares at $100 par =	412,500
Original Able Company Stockholders:		
6,100 shares retained by stockholders	= 6,100 shares at $100 par =	610,000
Total Able Company Shares outstanding after exchange.	15,225 shares at $100 par =	$1,522,500

The following entry was made by Able Company to transfer the combined accounts of Baker Company and Crystal Company to the books of Able Company:

	Debit	Credit
Cash	36,250	
Accounts Receivable	84,000	
Inventories	224,000	
Land	120,250	
Buildings	353,750	
Accumulated Depreciation		33,750
Machinery and Equipment	560,000	
Accumulated Depreciation		70,000
Notes Payable		131,250
Other Current Liabilities		7,500
Income Taxes Payable		40,750
Capital Stock		775,000
Retained Earnings		258,000
Sales		1,481,500

	Debit	Credit
Raw Material Purchases	434,250	
Direct Labor	263,750	
Manufacturing Expense	404,750	
Selling Expense	105,500	
Administrative Expense	149,750	
Interest Costs	2,750	
Inventory Adjustments	18,000	
Income Tax Expense	40,750	
	2,797,750	2,797,750

After the above entry was posted to the general ledger accounts of Able Company, the balance in the capital stock account was $1,385,000. This balance is $137,500 less than the par value of the 15,225 shares outstanding after the exchange was completed, and the difference developed because the number of shares received in exchange was based on *total* stockholders' equity and not on the capital stock account alone.

Therefore, the following entry was made to reduce the *combined* retained earnings and bring the combined capital stock account into agreement with the total par value of the outstanding stock:

	Debit	Credit
Retained Earnings	137,500	
Capital Stock		137,500

Since the ratio of exchange was based on the book value of net assets of the respective companies, and the shares received in exchange were to be valued at the issuing company's book value of $120 per share, the fairness of the exchange can be demonstrated as follows:

Combined Assets	2,116,500
Combined Liabilities	289,500
Total Stockholders' Equity	1,827,000

Total Stockholders' equity of $1,827,000 divided by 15,225 shares outstanding gives a book value of $120 for each share. The $120 per share value corresponds to the book value of Able Company's stock before the exchange and is the value on which the exchange was based.

It is important to realize that all the foregoing entries were made because Baker Company and Crystal Company were dissolved after the combination was consummated, and all of the accounts of the combining companies were integrated into the general ledger accounts of Able Company at September 30, and comprehended in its financial statements at December 31.

Had Baker Company and Crystal Company continued to operate as subsidiaries subsequent to the consummation of the combination, their accounts would have been consolidated with Able Company's accounts in consolidated financial statements at December 31. In such case, the following journal entry would have been made on Able Company's books, instead of the entries described above, and the $137,500 difference mentioned previously would have been adjusted in the consolidated financial statements:

	Debit	Credit
Investment in Subsidiaries	912,500	
Capital Stock		912,500

The subsidiary companies would not make any entries on their books at all, since the only effect of the combination on them would be the transfer of stock ownership from the former stockholders to Able Company.

The consolidated financial statements of Able Company and its subsidiaries would not normally be prepared until December 31, and at that time they would include the operations of the parent and both subsidiaries for the full fiscal year.

However, to complete this demonstration without complicating it further, the following condensed consolidating statements, prepared immediately after the combination was consummated, illustrate the effect of the combination on the financial position and results of operations of Able Company for the first nine months of the fiscal year.

Able Company and Subsidiaries
Consolidating Statement of Financial Position—September 30

	Able Company	Baker Company	Crystal Company	Eliminations Dr. (Cr.)	Consolidated
Assets					
Current and Fixed Assets	842,000	696,000	578,500		2,116,500
Investment in Subsidiaries	912,500			(912,500)	
	1,754,500	696,000	578,500		2,116,500
Liabilities and Stockholders' Equity					
Liabilities	110,000	96,000	83,500		289,500
Stockholders' Equity					
Capital Stock	1,522,500	400,000	375,000	775,000	1,522,500
Retained Earnings	122,000	200,000	120,000	137,500	304,500
Total Capital	1,644,500	600,000	495,000		1,827,000
	1,754,500	696,000	578,500		2,116,500

Able Company and Subsidiaries
Consolidating Statement of Income and Retained Earnings
for the Nine Months Ended September 30

	Able Company	Baker Company	Crystal Company	Consolidated
Sales	920,500	787,750	693,750	2,402,000
Cost of Sales	701,750	594,750	526,000	1,822,500
Gross Profit	218,750	193,000	167,750	579,500
Expenses	161,250	137,000	121,000	419,250

	Able Company	Baker Company	Crystal Company	Consolidated
Income Before Income Taxes	57,500	56,000	46,750	160,250
Provision for Income Taxes	23,000	22,500	18,250	63,750
Net Income	34,500	33,500	28,500	96,500
Retained Earnings—January 1	87,500	166,500	91,500	345,500
				442,000
Less—Par value of excess of number of shares issued over number of shares cancelled				137,500
Retained Earnings—September 30				304,500
Earnings Per Share				6,34

APPLYING THE POOLING OF INTERESTS METHOD

The preceding model case illustrates accounting for an uncomplicated business combination as a pooling of interests. This section of the chapter explains and demonstrates all the pooling of interests accounting procedures prescribed by the Opinion.

Assets and Liabilities Combined

The combined corporation records the assets and liabilities of the separate companies at the same values ascribed to them on the books of the combining companies. This operation is illustrated in the foregoing model case where Able Company makes an entry to pick up the assets and liabilities from Baker Company and Crystal Company.

Where separate companies have assets and liabilities that are accounted for on different bases, such accounts may be adjusted to a uniform basis of accounting after the combination is consummated, if the change otherwise would have been appropriate for the separate companies.

Stockholders' Equity Combined

The stockholders' equities of the separate companies are also combined, as illustrated in the foregoing model case.

Treasury Stock Distributed in Pooling of Interests. If a corporation distributes treasury stock in effecting a pooling of interests, the treasury stock should be accounted for as though retired. The shares then issued for the common stock of the combining company are accounted for the same as the issuance of previously unissued shares.

Illustration

Able Company is the issuing company in a combination plan to be accounted for as a pooling of interests, and will issue treasury stock to effect the combination.

At the date of consummation, the stockholders' equity of Able Company is as follows:

Stockholders' Equity	
Capital Stock—Par $10— Issued 10,000 Shares	100,000
Capital in Excess of Par	35,000
Retained Earnings	20,000
	155,000
Less—Cost of Treasury Stock— 1,000 shares	15,000
Total Stockholders' Equity	140,000

The entry that will be made by Able Company to eliminate the treasury stock is:

	Debit	Credit
Capital Stock	10,000	
Capital in Excess of Par	5,000	
Treasury Stock		15,000

Able Company will then effect the combination as though it were exchanging unissued shares at the ratio prescribed in the combination plan.

Par Value of Outstanding Shares of Combined Company Exceeds Par Value of Outstanding Shares of Separate Companies

After the issuing company has made the required stock exchanges, the total par value of the outstanding shares of the combined companies may exceed the total par value of outstanding shares of separate companies before combination occurred. In such cases the excess should be charged to combined contributed capital, if any, or to combined retained earnings. An illustration of this situation is contained in the foregoing model case of Able Company, Baker Company, and Crystal Company.

Accounting for Intercompany Investments in Common Stocks

Accounting for intercompany investments of combining companies in common stocks of other combining companies is accomplished as follows:

(a) voting common stock of the issuing company held by other combining companies is taken up by the issuing company as treasury stock on the same basis as it was recorded on the books of the respective combining companies; and

(b) voting common stock of the other combining companies held by both the issuing company and the other combining companies is simply eliminated in the entry made by the issuing company to record the combination.

Illustration

This illustration is an expansion of the foregoing model case of Able Company, Baker Company, and Crystal Company. Able Company is the issuing company and issued its shares to stockholders of Baker Company and Crystal Company on the basis of an exchange ratio of 1.25 for 1 and 1.10 for 1, respectively. However, in this present circumstance it is assumed that the combination was consummated after business hours on the last day of the fiscal year, and that the balance sheets of the three companies at that time are shown in the first three columns of the following schedule:

Balance Sheets—December 31

	Able Company	Baker Company	Crystal Company	Eliminations and Adjustments Dr. (Cr.)	Combined
Assets					
Current and Fixed Assets	822,500	679,000	563,000		2,064,500
Intercompany Investments					
100 shares Baker Company	12,000			(b) (12,000)	—
50 shares Crystal Company	7,500			(c) (7,500)	—
100 shares Able Company		11,000		(a) (11,000)	—
50 shares Crystal Company		6,000		(c) (6,000)	—
50 shares Able Company			7,500	(a) (7,500)	—
50 shares Baker Company			8,000	(b) (8,000)	—
	842,000	696,000	578,500		2,064,500
Liabilities and Stockholders' Equity					
Liabilities	110,000	96,000	83,500		289,500
Stockholders' Equity					
Capital Stock—Par $100					
6,100 shares outstanding	610,000				610,000
4,000 shares outstanding		400,000		(b) 15,000	385,000
3,750 shares outstanding			375,000	(c) 10,000	365,000
Total Capital Stock	610,000	400,000	375,000		1,360,000
Capital in Excess of Par	30,000	10,000	5,000	(b) 5,000 (c) 3,500	36,500
Retained Earnings	92,000	190,000	115,000		397,000
	732,000	600,000	495,000		1,793,500
Less—Cost of Treasury Stock				(a) 18,500	(18,500)
Total Stockholders' Equity	732,000	600,000	495,000		1,775,000
	842,000	696,000	578,500		2,064,500

In order to prepare an entry to record the combination, Able Company made the following adjustments and eliminations to the combined accounts of the three companies:

(a) to transfer Able Company stock held by other combining companies to treasury stock account;

(b) to eliminate Baker Company stock held by other combining companies, and reduce the capital in excess of par; and

(c) to eliminate Crystal Company stock held by other combining companies and reduce the capital in excess of par.

Able Company then issued its shares in exchange for shares held by stockholders of the other two companies at the exchange rate specified above. The following table summarizes the exchanges made, and shows the total number of shares and total par value of Able Company stock issued after the exchange was completed.

		Par Value
Baker Company		
3,850 shares exchanged at 1.25 for 1	= 4,812 at $100 par =	481,200
Crystal Company		
3,650 shares exchanged at 1.10 for 1	= 4,015 at $100 par =	401,500
Able Company		
6,100 shares held by stockholders and held in Treasury	= 6,100 at $100 par =	610,000
	14,927	1,492,700

After the exchange of shares was completed, Able Company made the following entry to record the combination:

	Baker Company	Crystal Company	Debit	Credit
Cost of Treasury Stock			18,500	
Current and Fixed Assets	679,000	563,000	1,242,000	
Liabilities	(96,000)	(83,500)		179,500
Capital Stock	(385,000)	(365,000)		750,000
Capital in Excess of Par	(5,000)	(1,500)		6,500
Retained Earnings	(190,000)	(115,000)		305,000
Investment in Baker Company				12,000
Investment in Crystal Company				7,500

After the above entry was posted to Able Company's books, the capital stock account was $1,360,000. The par value of the 14,927 shares outstanding ($1,492,700) exceeded the amount on the books by $132,700. In order to bring the capital stock account into agreement with the total par value of the outstanding shares, this $132,700 was charged first to combined capital in excess of par and then to combined retained earnings. Able Company therefore made the following entry after the combination was consummated:

	Debit	Credit
Capital in Excess of Par	36,500	
Retained Earnings	96,200	
Capital Stock		132,700

A trial balance of Able Company's general ledger after consummation of the combination was as follows:

	Debit	Credit
Current and Fixed Assets	2,064,500	
Cost of Treasury Stock	18,500	
Liabilities		289,500
Capital Stock		1,492,700
Retained Earnings		300,800
	2,083,000	2,083,000

Reporting Combined Operations

The pooling of interests method requires that results of operations for the period in which the combination occurs be reported as though the companies had been combined from the beginning of the period. This method of reporting operations for the period can be accomplished by integrating into the accounts of the issuing company the income and expense accounts of the companies that are to be dissolved; and preparing consolidated financial statements with those companies that are to continue as subsidiaries of the issuing company. Both methods are illustrated in the foregoing model case of Able Company, Baker Company and Crystal Company.

Any intercompany transactions that occurred before the combination that significantly affect results of operations should be eliminated.

Expenses Related to Combination

Costs incurred to effect a combination are expenses of the combined corporation and should be deducted in determining the net income of the combined corporation.

CONDITIONS FOR POOLING OF INTERESTS METHOD

Paragraphs 46 to 48 of the Opinion specify and explain twelve conditions that must be met by the combining companies to permit the combination to be accounted for as a pooling of interests. These conditions are classified by:

(1) attributes of the combining companies;
(2) manner of combining interests; and
(3) absence of planned transactions.

The twelve conditions are indicated below by their paragraph and subparagraph designations in the Opinion, and are quoted verbatim. Explanatory comments and illustrations of accounting techniques, where appropriate, are supplied for each condition listed.

Attributes of the Combining Companies

46-a. ***Each of the combining companies is autonomous and has not been a subsidiary or division of another corporation within two years before the plan of combination is initiated.***

Date of Initiation

The date of initiation is the earlier of:

(1) the date that the major terms of a plan, including the ratio of exchange of stock, are announced publicly or otherwise formally made known to the stockholders of any one of the combining companies; or,

(2) the date that stockholders of a combining company are notified in writing of an exchange offer.

New Company

A new company, incorporated within the preceding two years, meets this condition unless it is successor to a company, or part of a company, that is otherwise not autonomous for this condition.

Wholly Owned Subsidiaries

A wholly owned subsidiary may distribute voting common stock of its parent corporation to effect a combination under this condition, provided the *parent* meets all the required pooling conditions. For example, if a subsidiary owns 20% of its parent corporation's voting common stock, it could issue that stock to effect a combination, and the combination would be assumed to have been effected by the parent. A subsidiary is considered to be "wholly owned" for this condition if the parent owns substantially all its outstanding voting common stock. Usually the percentage not owned should be very small—legally required directors' shares, shares of a few dissenting stockholders, etc.—but in no case should the shares owned by the parent be less than 90% for the subsidiary to be considered wholly owned.

Ratio of Exchange

The actual exchange ratio need not be known at the time of initiation of a plan so long as the ratio of exchange is absolutely determinable by objective means in the future. A formula, including such factors as earnings, market prices of securities, etc., usually provides for such determination.

Options

Initiation of a plan may be based on stock options if they *require* unilateral performance by either party or bilateral performance by both parties. Options that grant only "first refusal" and the like cannot constitute initiation of a plan of combination.

Divestiture of Assets to Comply with Legal Requirements

Divestiture of assets to comply with an order of a legal authority constitutes an exception to the terms of this condition. Either a subsidiary divested under a legal order, or a new company that acquires assets disposed of under such order, are autonomous for this condition.

> **46-b.** ***Each of the combining companies is independent of the other combining companies.***

Limits to Intercompany Investments as a Condition of Independence

The Opinion specifies that this condition means that at the dates the plan of combination is initiated and consummated the combining companies hold as intercorporate investments no more than ten percent in total of the outstanding voting common stock of any combining company.

For example, if Able Company plans to issue its stock to combine with Baker Company and Crystal Company, and if Able Company and Baker Company each own eight percent of the outstanding voting common stock of Crystal Company, accounting for the combination as a pooling of interests will not be allowed because Able Company and Baker Company own over ten percent of the outstanding voting common stock of Crystal Company.

Date of Consummation

The consummation date means the date the assets are transferred to the issuing company.

Interim Intercompany Holdings

An official interpretation of the Opinion holds that if intercorporate investments in excess of ten percent are held at any time between the dates of initiation and consummation, even though the investments are disposed of at the date of consummation, the Opinion proscription is violated, and the combination must be accounted for as a purchase.

Intercompany Investments Held to Effect Combination

Voting common stock that is acquired after the date the plan of combination is initiated in exchange for the voting common stock issued to effect the combination is excluded from the ten percent limitation.

Investments of Ten Percent or Less

Intercorporate investments of ten percent or less are explained and illustrated in the comments under paragraph 47-b.

Manner of Combining Interests

> **47-a.** ***The combination is effected in a single transaction or is completed in accordance with a specific plan within one year after the plan is initiated.***

Altering Terms of Exchange of Stock

Altering the terms of exchange of stock constitutes initiation of a new plan of combination. However, if earlier exchanges of stock have been made under the plan, a new plan is not initiated if the earlier exchanges are adjusted to the new terms.

Consummation Delayed by Litigation or Governmental Authority

If consummation of a plan is delayed beyond one year because of delay caused by litigation or governmental authority, this condition of the Opinion is not violated.

Effect of Termination

This condition specifies that a combination must be effected within one year in accordance with a specific plan. If a plan is terminated after it has been initiated, subsequent negotiations would constitute a new plan.

47-b. ***A corporation offers and issues only common stock with rights identical to those of the majority of its outstanding voting common stock in exchange for substantially all of the voting common stock interest of another company at the date the plan of combination is consummated.***

Distributions of Cash and Other Consideration

Cash or other consideration may be distributed for fractional shares, shares held by dissenting stockholders, and other similar purposes, but a pro rata distribution of cash or other consideration will violate this condition.

Exchange of Substantially All of the Voting Common Stock

Substantially all of the voting common stock means 90 percent for this condition. The number of shares constituting the 90 percent excludes the following shares held by the issuing company and its subsidiaries:

(a) shares acquired before the date the plan is initiated;
(b) shares acquired after the date the plan is initiated other than by issuing its own voting common stock; and,
(c) shares outstanding after the date the combination is consummated.

Intercorporate Investments of Ten Percent or Less

An investment in the stock of the issuing corporation held by a combining company may violate this condition even though it is not more than ten percent of the issuing company's outstanding voting common stock. An investment in ten percent or less of the outstanding voting common stock of the issuing corporation affects the percentage of shares exchanged in the combination as follows:

(a) the number of shares of the issuing company held by the investor combining company is restated as an equivalent number of shares of common stock of the investor combining company based on the ratio of exchange of stock in the combination;
(b) the restated number of shares is deducted from the number of shares of the investor combining company exchanged for shares of the issuing company as a part of the plan of combination; and,
(c) the reduced number of shares is considered the number of shares exchanged, and is compared with 90 percent of the shares of the investor combining company to determine if the terms of this condition are met.

Illustration

A plan of combination was initiated that required Issuing Company to issue shares of its voting common stock to acquire all of the voting common stock of Combining Company at an exchange ratio of one issued share for two acquired shares.

At the date of consummation of the plan, the balance sheets of the two companies were as follows.

	Issuing Company	Combining Company
Assets		
Cash	100,000	46,000
Investment Account		
400 shares of Issuing Company		4,000
	100,000	50,000
Stockholders' Equity		
Common Stock—$10 Par		
5,000 shares issued	50,000	
3,000 shares issued		30,000
Retained Earnings	50,000	20,000
	100,000	50,000

Computation of Percentage of Stock to be Exchanged

(a) Shares of Issuing Company held by Combining Company restated as an equivalent number of shares of Combining Company based on the exchange ratio of 1 for 2.	400 x 2	800
(b) Number of Shares of Combining Company to be Exchanged:		
Total number of shares outstanding		3,000
Less: number of shares of Issuing Company held by Combining Company restated in (a) above		800
Remaining number of shares as potential combining consideration		2,200
(c) 90 percent of the total outstanding shares of Combining Company (90% x 3,000)		2,700

Since the number of shares to be exchanged by stockholders for Issuing Company stock is less than 90 percent of the total shares outstanding at the date the plan was consummated, the combination must be accounted for as a purchase.

Combination of More Than Two Companies

A combination of three or more companies is evaluated in the same manner as for two companies. The number of shares exchanged for stock of the issuing corporation includes only shares to be exchanged by stockholders other than the several combining companies themselves. Thus, intercompany investments in common stock are included in the number of shares of stock outstanding, but are excluded from the number of shares of stock exchanged to effect the combination. An illustration of this situation for two companies is shown in the preceding paragraph. The same computations would be made for each company in a three or more company combination.

New Corporation Formed to Effect Combination

A new corporation formed to issue its stock to effect the combination of two or more companies meets condition 47-b if it issues shares for at least 90 percent of the outstanding stock of the combining companies, and if the combining companies themselves would have met condition 47-b if any one of them had issued its stock to effect the combination.

Debt and Equity Securities of Combining Companies

An issuing company may liquidate any liabilities assumed in the combination in any way it chooses. It can pay cash, issue common stock or equity debt securities, or may exchange identical securities. However, the issuing company may exchange *only voting common stock* for outstanding equity and debt securities that had been issued by a combining company in exchange for common stock of that company during a period beginning two years preceding the date the plan of combination was initiated.

Transfer of Net Assets to Effect a Combination

A transfer of net assets of a combining company satisfies condition 47-b, provided all net assets of the company at the date of consummation are transferred in exchange for stock of the issuing corporation.

Warrants

The issue of warrants in lieu of common stock in exchange for voting common stock of the combining company in a combination violates condition 47-b.

Partial Exchange of Stock

In a business combination to be accounted for as a pooling of interests, each common shareholder of the combining companies must agree to exchange *all* of his voting common stock or refuse to exchange *any* of it.

> **47-c.** ***None of the combining companies changes the equity interest of the voting common stock in contemplation of effecting the combination either within two years before the plan of combination is initiated or between the dates the combination is initiated and consummated; changes in contemplation of effecting the combination may include distributions to stockholders and additional issuances, exchanges, and retirements of securities.***

This condition does not preclude a combining company's distribution of its regular normal dividends in common stock during the period between the dates of initiation and consummation of the plan of combination.

> **47-d.** ***Each of the combining companies reacquires shares of voting common stock only for purposes other than business combinations, and no company reacquires more than a normal number of shares between the dates the plan of combination is initiated and consummated.***

This condition does not prevent a combining company from acquiring treasury stock for distribution in accordance with stock option and compensation plans.

Acquisitions made by other combining companies of voting common stock of the issuing corporation after the date of initiation of the plan are essentially the same as if the issuing company had reacquired its own common stock, and therefore would violate the condition.

> **47-e.** ***The ratio of the interest of an individual common stockholder to those of other common stockholders in a combining company remains the same as a result of the exchange of stock to effect the combination.***

This condition means that each individual common stockholder who exchanges his stock receives a voting common stock interest exactly in proportion to his relative voting common stock interest before the combination was effected. Thus, no common stockholder is denied or surrenders his potential shares of a voting common stock interest in a combined corporation.

It is important to remember, however, that the shareholder in a combining company receives a voting common stock interest proportionate to his interest in the combining company that is being combined, as compared to other shareholders in the same company. Because of differences in exchange ratios, proportionate ownership in the continuing entity will not necessarily be the same as the proportionate interest he had in the company that was combined.

47-f. ***The voting rights to which the common stock ownership interests in the resulting combined corporation are entitled are exercisable by the stockholders; the stockholders are neither deprived of nor restricted in exercising those rights for a period.***

This condition is not met, for example, if shares of common stock issued to effect the combination are transferred to a voting trust.

However, the issuing company will not violate the condition if it issues shares in exchange for restricted shares received from a combining company.

47-g. ***The combination is resolved at the date the plan is consummated and no provisions of the plan relating to the issue of securities or other consideration are pending.***

This condition means that the combined corporation does not agree to the issuance of additional shares of a security or the transfer of cash or other consideration contingent on specified events or transactions in the future.

Absence of Planned Transactions

48-a. ***The combined corporation does not agree directly or indirectly to retire or reacquire all or part of the common stock issued to effect the combination.***

48-b. ***The combined corporation does not enter into other financial arrangements for the benefit of the former stockholders of a combining company, such as a guaranty of loans secured by stock issued in the combination, which in effect negates the exchange of equity securities.***

48-c. ***The combined corporation does not intend or plan to dispose of a significant part of the assets of the combining companies within two years after the combination other than disposals in the ordinary course of business of the formerly separate companies and to eliminate duplicate facilities or excess capacity.***

These three conditions are designed to prevent combinations from being accounted for as poolings of interest in situations where planned future transactions are inconsistent with the combining of entire existing interests of common stockholders.

Subsidiaries After Pooling

The Opinion does not require the dissolution of a combining company as a condition for applying the pooling of interests method of accounting for a business combination. One or more combining companies may be subsidiaries of the issuing corporation after the combination is consummated if the other considerations are met. The operation of a combining company as a subsidiary is illustrated in the foregoing model case of Able Company, Baker Company, and Crystal Company.

Disclosure in the Financial Statements of a Combined Company

Paragraph 64 of the Opinion contains seven subparagraphs that describe the information that should be included in notes to financial statements for the period in which a business combination occurs, and is accounted for by the pooling of interests method. The seven subparagraphs are quoted verbatim.

(a) Name and brief description of the companies combined, except a corporation whose name is carried forward to the combined corporation.

(b) Method of accounting for the combination—that is, by the pooling of interests method.

(c) Description and number of shares of stock issued in the business combination.

(d) Details of the results of operations of the previously separate companies for the period before the combination is consummated that are included in the current combined net income. The details should include revenue, extraordinary items, net income, other changes in stockholders' equity, and amount of and manner of accounting for intercompany transactions.

(e) Descriptions of the nature of adjustments of net assets of the combining companies to adopt the same accounting practices and of the effects of the changes on net income reported previously by the separate companies and now presented in comparative financial statements.

(f) Details of an increase or decrease in retained earnings from changing the fiscal year of a combining company. The details should include at least revenue, expenses, extraordinary items, net income, and other changes in stockholders' equity for the period excluded from the reported results of operations.

(g) Reconciliations of amounts of revenue and earnings previously reported by the corporation that issues the stock to effect the combination with the combined amounts currently presented in financial statements and summaries. A new corporation formed to effect a combination may instead disclose the earnings of the separate companies which comprise combined earnings for prior periods.

MODEL CASE IN ACCOUNTING FOR A BUSINESS COMBINATION AS A PURCHASE

The following model case of North Company, East Company, and West Company illustrates accounting for a business combination as a purchase.

North Company, East Company, and West Company were unrelated, closely held corporations engaged in regional operations. In July, North Company entered into separate agreements to purchase the stock of East Company and to purchase the net assets of West Company. North Company was identified as the acquirer in the combination plan with East Company and, of course, as the purchaser in the purchase plan with West Company.

The combination plan with East Company provided that stockholders of 80 percent of the outstanding stock of the acquired company would exchange their stock for shares of the acquiring company at the rate of two shares of East Company stock for one share of North Company stock. The plan further provided that East Company would survive as a corporate entity and be operated as a controlled subsidiary of North Company.

The purchase plan with West Company provided that the acquirer would purchase the assets and assume the liabilities of the acquired company for a total purchase price of $150,000, to be paid in cash by the acquiring company. The purchase plan also provided that West Company be dissolved and its outstanding shares cancelled. Operations subsequent to the combination would continue at the former site of West Company as branch operations of North Company.

The conditions required to account for a combination as a pooling of interest were not satisfied in either plan, and therefore the acquisitions by North Company of both East Company stock and West Company net assets were required to be accounted for as purchases.

Although the fiscal year of each company ended on December 31, each separate plan provided that the respective combination would be consummated on September 30.

Balance sheets of the separate companies at September 30 were as follows:

Balance Sheets—September 30

	North Company	East Company	West Company
Assets			
Current			
Cash	387,696	4,348	18,949
Receivables—less allowance for losses	44,262	27,702	23,553
Inventories	178,058	49,338	37,871
Prepaid Expenses	12,474	2,619	2,400
	622,490	84,007	82,773
Investments		10,041	2,933
Property, Plant and Equipment—net of accumulated depreciation	152,949	34,058	105,664
Other	9,410	1,538	2,453
	784,849	129,644	193,823
Liabilities and Stockholders' Equity			
Current			
Notes Payable and Current Portion of Long-Term Debt	52,106	10,369	897
Accounts Payable and Accrued Expenses	124,346	24,393	14,288
Income Taxes Payable	3,690	3,394	2,586
	180,142	38,156	17,771
Long-Term Debt	357,818	27,644	73,920
Total Liabilities	537,960	65,800	91,691
Stockholders' Equity			
Capital in Excess of Par	71,880		
Capital Stock—$10 Par			
Authorized, 50,000; Issued, 4,640	46,400		
Authorized, 20,000; Issued, 2,380		23,800	
Authorized, 20,000; Issued, 3,800			38,000
Retained Earnings	128,609	40,044	64,132
Total Stockholders' Equity	246,889	63,844	102,132
	784,849	129,644	193,823

A summary of earnings of the separate companies for the nine months ended September 30 is shown below:

	North Company	East Company	West Company
Income Before Income Taxes	55,390	16,684	18,651
Provision for Income Taxes	25,649	7,270	8,708
Net Income	29,741	9,414	9,943
Earnings Per Share	6.41	3.96	2.62

The plan of combination with East Company specified that the value of the stock of North Company would be placed at $100 per share. This value was somewhat in excess of fifteen times the earnings per share for the nine months ended September 30.

In accordance with the plan, 80 percent of the shares of East Company were surrendered and exchanged for shares of North Company at the rate of 1 for 2. The number of shares to be exchanged was computed as follows:

East Company—total number of shares	2,380
Percentage Exchanged—80%	x 80%
Number of East Company Shares Exchanged	1,904
Rate of Exchange—1 for 2	x .5
Number of Shares of North Company Issued in Exchange	952

An evaluation of the assets and liabilities of East Company revealed that inventories, prepaid expense, investments, property, and other assets were carried on the books at approximately fair value. The allowance for losses on accounts receivable was found to be adequate, and the difference between carrying values and present values of receivables, payables, and long-term debt were considered to be insignificant. Therefore, it was determined that there should be no change in the book values of the assets and liabilities of East Company.

The cost to North Company for its investment in East Company was determined to be $95,200, computed by multiplying the 952 shares issued at the fair market value of $100 per share.

The equity in underlying net assets in East Company received by North Company was determined to be as follows:

Net Assets of East Company	
Total Assets	129,644
Total Liabilities	65,800
Net Assets	63,844
Less—Minority Interest—$63,844 x 20%	12,769
Equity of North Company in Net Assets	51,075

The cost of the investment in East Company exceeded the equity in underlying net assets received by North Company as follows:

Cost of Investment (952 shares at $100 per share)	95,200
Equity in Net Assets Received (above)	51,075
Excess of Cost over Value of Underlying Net Assets	44,125

Management decided to record the excess of cost over the fair value of underlying net assets of the subsidiary and to amortize it by the straight-line method over a period of ten years.

The excess of value received over par value of North Company stock issued in exchange for East Company stock was computed as follows:

Value of Shares Issued in Exchange— 952 Shares at $100	95,200
Par Value of Stock Issued— 952 Shares at $10	9,520
Capital Received in Excess of Par Value	85,680

On September 30, North Company made the following entry to record the purchase of East Company stock:

	Debit	Credit
Investment in Subsidiary	51,075	
Excess of Cost over Equity in Subsidiary	44,125	
Capital in Excess of Par		85,680
Capital Stock		9,520

No entries were made on the books of the subsidiary to record the purchase since the only effect on East Company was the transfer of ownership of capital stock.

Accounting for the Purchase of West Company's Net Assets

An evaluation of the assets and liabilities of West Company revealed that all units, except property, plant and equipment, were carried at fair value. The fair value of the building was determined to be approximately $20,000 in excess of the book value. Management decided to record property, plant and equipment at a cost of $125,000 and depreciate the cost over the remaining useful lives of the respective components.

The excess of cost to North Company over the fair value of net assets received in exchange was computed as follows:

Cash Paid by North Company for Net Assets of West Company		150,000
Less: Book Value of Net Assets	102,132	
Add: Excess of Fair Value over Value of Building	19,336	121,468
Excess of Cost over Net Assets Received in Exchange		28,532

Management decided to record the excess cost of $28,532 as goodwill and amortize it by the straight-line method over a period of twenty years.

The following entry was made by North Company to record the acquisition of the net assets of West Company:

	Debit	Credit
Cash (West Company's bank account)	18,949	
Receivables	23,553	
Inventories	37,871	
Prepaid Expenses	2,400	
Investments	2,933	
Property, Plant and Equipment	125,000	

	Debit	Credit
Other Assets	2,453	
Goodwill	28,532	
Notes Payable and Current Portion of Long-Term Debt		897
Accounts Payable and Accrued Expenses		14,288
Income Taxes Payable		2,586
Long-Term Debt		73,920
Cash (North Company's bank account)		150,000
	241,691	241,691

The assets and liability accounts of West Company were integrated into the accounts of North Company by the above entry immediately upon consummation of the combination on September 30. The equity in East Company was represented on the books of North Company by the single account, "Investment in Subsidiary," and the separate asset and liability accounts of East Company would be integrated with those of North Company only on the consolidated financial statements prepared at the end of the year.

However, to complete this demonstration without complicating it further, the following schedule of entries on the books of North Company made to accommodate the combination at September 30, and the following consolidating balance sheets of North Company and East Company prepared immediately after the combination was consummated, illustrate the effect of the combination on the financial position of North Company at September 30.

NORTH COMPANY
SUMMARY OF ENTRIES MADE TO ACCOMMODATE COMBINATION
SEPTEMBER 30

	North Company Accounts (Unadjusted)	Adjustments For East Company Dr. (Cr.)	Adjustments For West Company Dr. (Cr.)	North Company Accounts (Adjusted)
Cash	387,696		18,949	
			(150,000)	256,645
Receivables—net	44,262		23,553	67,815
Inventories	178,058		37,871	215,929
Prepaid Expenses	12,474		2,400	14,874
Investment in Subsidiary		51,075		51,075
Excess of Cost over Equity in Subsidiary		44,125		44,125
Investments—other			2,933	2,933
Property, Plant and Equipment—net of depreciation	152,949		125,000	277,949
Other Assets	9,410		2,453	11,863
Goodwill			28,532	28,532
	784,849			971,740

	North Company Accounts (Unadjusted)	Adjustments For East Company Dr. (Cr.)	Adjustments For West Company Dr. (Cr.)	North Company Accounts (Adjusted)
Notes Payable and Current Portion of Long-Term Debt	52,106		(897)	53,003
Accounts Payable and Accrued Expenses	124,346		(14,288)	138,634
Income Taxes Payable	3,690		(2,586)	6,276
Long-Term Debt	357,818		(73,920)	431,738
Capital in Excess of Par	71,880	(85,680)		157,560
Capital Stock	46,400	(9,520)		55,920
Retained Earnings	128,609			128,609
	784,849	-0-	-0-	971,740

NORTH COMPANY AND SUBSIDIARY CONSOLIDATING BALANCE SHEET—SEPTEMBER 30

	North Company (Adjusted for Combination)	East Company	Eliminations Dr. (Cr.)	Consolidated
Cash	256,645	4,348		260,993
Receivables—net	67,815	27,702		95,517
Inventories	215,929	49,338		265,267
Prepaid Expense	14,874	2,619		17,493
Investment in Subsidiary	51,075		(1) (51,075)	—
Excess of Cost over Equity in Subsidiary	44,125		(2) (44,125)	—
Investments—other	2,933	10,041		12,974
Property, Plant and Equipment—net of accumulated depreciation	277,949	34,058		312,007
Other Assets	11,863	1,538		13,401
Goodwill	28,532		(2) 44,125	72,657
	971,740	129,644	(51,075)	1,050,309
Notes Payable and Current Portion of Long-Term Debt	53,003	10,369		63,372
Accounts Payable and Accrued Expenses	138,634	24,393		163,027
Income Taxes Payable	6,276	3,394		9,670
Long-Term Debt	431,738	27,644		459,382
Minority Interests			(1) (12,769)	12,769
Capital in Excess of Par	157,560			157,560
Capital Stock	55,920	23,800	(1) 23,800	55,920
Retained Earnings	128,609	40,044	(1) 40,044	128,609
	971,740	129,644	51,075	1,050,309

APPLICATION OF THE PURCHASE METHOD

The Opinion does not make any changes in accounting principles concerning purchases but, on the contrary, reaffirms the general principles outlined below.

Acquiring Assets

Assets acquired by exchanging cash or other assets, or by the assumption of liabilities, are recorded at cost. The "cost" is determined by an appropriate combination of the amount of cash disbursed, the fair value of assets exchanged, and the present value of liabilities incurred.

Assets acquired by issuing stock of the acquiring corporation are recorded at the fair value of the assets received. In cases where the fair value of the assets acquired is not readily determinable, cost may be determined by either the fair value of the stock given in exchange or the fair value of the property acquired.

Allocating Cost

The principles of recording assets at cost, or fair value, described in the preceding paragraph, apply equally to assets acquired singly and to those acquired in groups. However, costs applicable to a group of assets should be allocated to the individual assets that comprise the group. The difference between the sum of the costs assigned to identifiable assets, less liabilities assumed, should be assigned to intangible goodwill.

Acquiring Corporation

It is important that the acquiring corporation in a business combination be clearly identified. The acquiring company normally issues the stock and is the larger company. However, where common stockholders of a particular combining company either retain or receive the larger portion of the voting rights of the combined corporation, there is presumptive evidence that that particular combining company is the acquirer, regardless of which company is the issuing company.

Determining the Cost of an Acquired Company

The same accounting principles applicable to recording the acquisition of single assets, or groups of assets, apply to recording the cost of an acquired company.

Recording Assets Acquired and Liabilities Assumed

An acquiring corporation should allocate the cost of an acquired company to individual assets acquired and liabilities assumed. The Opinion lists nine general guides for assigning costs. In essence, costs should be allocated on the basis of fair value. Fair value involves consideration of all of the following: cash received or disbursed, net realizable value of securities, present value of receivables and payables, estimated cost of inventories, replacement costs of plant and equipment, and appraised value of land and of nonmarketable assets.

An acquiring company should not record as a separate asset the goodwill previously recorded by an acquired company.

Deferred income tax recorded by an acquired company should not be recorded as a separate item by the acquiring company.

Differences between the tax base of assets acquired and the cost assigned to the assets by the acquiring company at acquisition are not timing differences, and the acquiring corporation should not record deferred tax accounts for such differences.

Contingent Consideration

A business combination agreement may provide for the issuance of additional shares of a security or the transfer of cash or other consideration contingent on specified events or transactions in the future. Additional consideration may be contingent on maintaining or achieving specified earnings levels in future periods, or may be contingent on the market price of a specified security issued to effect the business combination.

The accounting treatment of contingent consideration should be in accordance with the following general rules:

(a) Issuance of additional securities based on earnings should result in additional cost of the acquired company, and normally should be added to goodwill;

(b) Issuance of additional securities based on security prices should not change the recorded cost of an acquired company, but should be recorded as an adjustment of the cost of the securities issued. Reducing the value of debt securities previously issued requires recording a discount on such securities. The discount should be amortized from the date the additional securities are issued;

(c) A contingent issuance of additional consideration should be disclosed in the financial statements, but should not be recorded as a liability at the date of acquisition unless the outcome of the contingency, and the amount involved, is determinable beyond a reasonable doubt;

(d) Interest and dividends paid on securities held in escrow as contingent consideration should be given the same accounting treatment as that given the related securities;

(e) A tax reduction due to the tax effects of imputed interest on contingently issuable stock reduces the fair value of consideration contingent on earnings, and increases the additional capital recorded for contingent consideration based on security prices;

(f) Compensation for services and use of property and participation in profit sharing provided for in a contingent agreement should be accounted for as an expense of the period in which it is paid.

Costs of Acquisition

The direct costs of acquisition of a company acquired in a combination accounted for as a purchase are a part of the cost of the company. Costs of registering and issuing securities are a reduction in the fair value of the securities. Indirect and general expenses are charged to operations in the appropriate periods.

Accounting After Acquisition

Accounting for assets and liabilities subsequent to a combination is based on the costs assigned the individual items at the time the combination is recorded. Depreciation and amortization are based on the assigned costs and charged to operations over the remaining life of the respective assets. Deferred interest income or expense developed in assigning present values to receivables or payables is amortized over appropriate periods.

No part of earned surplus of the acquired companies is carried forward to the acquiring corporation, and the acquiring corporation does not report the results of operations of the acquired companies that occurred prior to the date of acquisition.

Amortization of Goodwill

Goodwill recorded in a business combination should be amortized systematically over the periods estimated to be benefited. The period of amortization should not exceed forty years and, normally, the annual charge to operations should be computed by the straight-line method.

Excess of Acquired Net Assets Over Cost

Normally, this type of situation will not occur, since the general presumption in historical-cost based accounting is that net assets acquired should be recorded at not more than cost. However, if an excess over cost is determined, the excess should be allocated to reduce values assigned to noncurrent assets, except for long-term investments in marketable securities. If the allocation reduces the noncurrent assets to a zero value, the remainder of the excess should be classified as a deferred credit and amortized by the straight-line method over a period not to exceed forty years.

An illustration of a similar situation is provided in chapter 7, "Equity Method of Accounting for Investments," where there was an excess of acquired equity in net assets over cost.

Step-by-Step Acquisition of a Subsidiary

An unofficial interpretation of APB Opinion No. 17, "Intangible Assets," very clearly outlines the procedures for recording the step-by-step acquisition of a subsidiary. The interpretation states that when a company in a series of purchases on a step-by-step basis acquires either a subsidiary which is consolidated or an investment which is accounted for under the equity method, the company should identify the cost of each investment, the fair value of the underlying assets acquired, and the goodwill for each separate purchase. This process would then identify the goodwill associated with each step.

Paragraph 43 of Opinion No. 16 provides that the acquisition of some or all of the stock held by minority stockholders of a subsidiary should be accounted for by the purchase method rather than the pooling of interests method.

The following illustration demonstrates the accounting procedures applicable to period acquisitions of stock in a subsidiary.

Illustration

On January 1 Investor Corporation purchased 1,712 shares of the voting common stock of Investee Company from its shareholders. At that time Investee Company had 4,280 shares outstanding, and its common stockholder equity amounted to $114,919.

During the year Investor Corporation made the following purchases of voting common stock from stockholders of Investee Company:

March 31 — 428 shares for $27,820
June 30 — 428 shares for $29,960
December 31 — 642 shares for $48,150

The following schedule discloses the computations necessary to determine the net equity acquired, and the goodwill involved in each separate purchase. Lines 1 to 4 show the net assets, income, and shares outstanding of Investee Company at the respective purchase dates. Lines 5 to 19 show the transactions to be recorded on Investor Corporation's books at the various purchase dates. It is assumed in this illustration that the book value of the net assets of Investee Company are equivalent to their fair value.

Period Acquisition of a Subsidiary

	January 31	March 31	June 30	December 31
Investee Company				
1. Net Assets—beginning	—	114,919	142,903	166,653
2. Net Income	—	27,984	23,750	24,730
3. Net Assets—ending	114,919	142,903	166,653	191,383
4. Number of Shares Outstanding	4,280	4,280	4,280	4,280
Investor Corporation				
5. Number of Shares Owned—beginning	—	1,712	2,140	2,568
6. Number of Shares Purchased	1,712	428	428	642
7. Number of Shares Owned—ending	1,712	2,140	2,568	3,210

	January 31	March 31	June 30	December 31
8. Percentage of Stock Owned beginning	—	40%	50%	60%
9. Percentage of Stock Purchased (line 6 ÷ line 4)	40%	10%	10%	15%
10. Percentage of Stock Owned—ending (line 7 ÷ line 4)	40%	50%	60%	75%
11. Cost of Investment—beginning	—	100,000	127,820	157,780
12. Cost of Stock Purchased	100,000	27,820	29,960	48,150
13. Cost of Investment—ending	100,000	127,820	157,780	205,930
14. Equity in Net Assets—beginning	—	45,968	60,258	76,923
15. Equity in Net Assets—purchased (line 9 x line 3)	45,968	14,290	16,665	28,707
16. Equity in Net Assets—ending	45,968	60,258	76,923	105,630
17. Excess of Cost Over Equity—beginning	—	54,032	67,562	80,857
18. Excess of Cost Over Equity in Purchase (line 12—line 15)	54,032	13,530	13,295	19,443
19. Excess of Cost Over Equity—ending	54,032	67,562	80,857	100,300

The entries to be made by Investor Corporation at the dates the stock was purchased are as follows:

	January 31	March 31	June 30	December 31
Debit—Investment in Subsidiary	45,968	14,290	16,665	28,707
Debit—Excess of Cost Over Equity in Subsidiary	54,032	13,530	13,295	19,443
Credit—Cash	(100,000)	(27,820)	(29,960)	(48,150)

The foregoing schedule shows that at December 31 the total amount of net assets of Investee Company was $191,383. Investor Corporation owned 75% of the common stock of Investee Company, but its equity in net assets of the investee (Investment in Subsidiary) reflects a balance of only $105,630, which amount is $37,907 less than 75% of the net assets of the subsidiary. This difference represents Investor Corporation's equity in net income of the subsidiary for the full fiscal year computed on the percentage of ownership held at each step of the acquisition. Therefore Investor Corporation would make the following entry to record such income:

	Debit	Credit
Investment in Subsidiary	37,907	
Increase in Equity in Subsidiary		37,907

To record equity in net income of subsidiary at percentage of ownership at each stock purchase date:

Date of Purchase	Subsidiary Income Between Dates of Purchase	Percentage Owned	Equity in Income
March 31	27,984	40%	11,194
June 30	23,750	50%	11,875
December 31	24,730	60%	14,838
			37,907

Disclosure in Financial Statements of an Acquiring Company

Paragraphs 95 and 96 of the Opinion outline, in eight subparagraphs, the required disclosures in connection with a business combination accounted for by the purchase method. The subparagraphs are quoted below directly from the Opinion:

Notes to Financial Statements:

(a) Name and a brief description of the acquired company.

(b) Method of accounting for the combination—that is, by the purchase method.

(c) Period for which results of operations of the acquired company are included in the income statement of the acquiring corporation.

(d) Cost of the acquired company and, if applicable, the number of shares of stock issued or issuable and the amount assigned to the issued and issuable shares.

(e) Description of the plan for amortization of acquired goodwill, the amortization method, and period.

(f) Contingent payments, options, or commitments specified in the acquisition agreement and their proposed accounting treatment.

Supplemental Information on a Pro Forma Basis:

(a) Results of operations for the current period as though the companies had combined at the beginning of the period, unless the acquisition was at or near the beginning of the period.

(b) Results of operations for the immediately preceding period as though the companies had combined at the beginning of that period if comparative financial statements are presented.

7

EQUITY METHOD OF ACCOUNTING FOR INVESTMENTS:

Common Stock and Consolidated and Unconsolidated Subsidiaries

For many years prior to 1971 there was a growing concern among accountants with regard to the methods used in accounting for long-term investments in common stocks. Much of the accountants' solicitude was focused on situations where one company held a substantial interest in another, but lacked the "over 50%" control that would permit of consolidated financial statements. The general rule was that parent companies would account for investments in subsidiaries by the equity method, and all other investors would account for investments in common stocks by the cost method. This rule was not universally accepted and, consequently, there was no uniformity in accountants' methods of accounting for substantial, long-term investments in equity securities. Many accountants not only had misgivings about the lack of consistency in accounting methods for investments, but also were persuaded that the cost method, in any event, did not properly report the economic consequences of holding substantial, long-term investments in common stocks.

In March 1971, the American Institute of Certified Public Accountants published Accounting Principles Board Opinion No. 18, which was an attempt to clarify the applicability of the equity method of accounting to investments in common stocks of subsidiaries, corporate joint ventures, and investees in which the investor did not hold a controlling interest.

In essence, the Opinion specifies that investors should use the equity method of accounting for investments in common stock of unconsolidated subsidiaries, corporate joint ventures, and of investees in cases where the investor holds less than a controlling interest but, nevertheless, has the ability to exercise significant influence over operating and financial policies of the investee.

This chapter provides explanations and illustrations of the equity method of accounting in accordance with the provisions set forth in the Opinion.

METHODS OF ACCOUNTING FOR LONG-TERM INVESTMENTS IN COMMON STOCKS

There are two basic methods of accounting for investments in equity securities that are intended by the investor to be retained for an indefinite period—the cost method and the equity method. The market value method is also used by some investors in special circumstances, but it is not covered by the Opinion, and it is not commented on in this chapter.

The Cost Method

Under the cost method of accounting the investor records the investment at cost. Income is recognized by the investor only from dividends paid by the investee out of earnings accumulated since the date of acquisition of the related stock. Any dividends paid to the investor that are in excess of earnings from the date of acquisition of the related stock are considered to be return of capital, and are recorded as a reduction in the cost of the investment. A significant decrease in the value of the investment, which is other than temporary, requires an appropriate valuation allowance to be set up and charged to current operations.

The Equity Method

Under the equity method of accounting the investor initially records the investment at cost. The carrying amount of the investment is adjusted periodically to record the investor's interest in the earnings and losses of the investee after the date of acquisition. The investment account is also adjusted to reflect the investor's share of changes in the investee's captial accounts; consequently, dividends received from the investee reduce the carrying amount of the investment. The net income or loss pickup from the investee is included in net income by the investor. However, the pickup amount is adjusted to eliminate intercompany gains and losses. Any excess of the investor's cost over its equity in net assets of the investee is amortized over a period not exceeding forty years.

Under the equity method an investment in common stock is generally shown on the balance sheet of the investor as a single amount. Similarly, an investor's share of the net increase or decrease in net assets of an investee is ordinarily shown in the income statement as a single amount. Amortization of excess of cost over equity is shown as a separate item on the income statement.

CLASSIFICATION OF INVESTMENTS REQUIRED TO BE ACCOUNTED FOR BY THE EQUITY METHOD

The Opinion specifies that the following classes of investments in common stock are to be accounted for by the equity method:

(a) domestic and foreign subsidiaries in consolidated financial statements;
(b) subsidiaries in parent-company financial statements;
(c) joint ventures in both parent-company and consolidated financial statements;
(d) investments of less than controlling interest where the voting stock gives the investor the ability to exercise significant influence over operating and financial policies of the investee—in both parent-company and consolidated financial statements.

INVESTMENTS EXCLUDED FROM THE PROVISIONS OF THE OPINION

The provisions of APB Opinion No. 18 do not apply to investments in common stock held by:

(a) investment companies registered under the Investment Company Act of 1940;
(b) companies that would be included under the above Act (including small business investment companies) except that the number of stockholders is limited and the securities are not offered publicly; and
(c) nonbusiness entities, such as estates, trusts, and individuals.

CORPORATE JOINT VENTURES

The Opinion is applicable to investments in corporate joint ventures in the same manner and to the same extent that it is to investments in ordinary corporate investees.

VOTING STOCK INTEREST

An investor's *voting stock interest* should be based on current outstanding securities whose holders have voting privileges, and his *share of the earnings or losses* should be based on the shares of *common* stock held. Potential voting privileges that may become available, and securities designated as "common stock equivalents" under APB Opinion No. 15, should be disregarded.

INVESTMENTS NOT PROVIDING CONTROLLING INTEREST IN INVESTEES

Paragraph 17 of the Opinion states that the equity method of accounting should be followed by an investor whose investment in voting stock gives it the ability to exercise significant influence over operating and financial policies of an investee, even though the investor holds only 50% or less of the voting stock. The Opinion attempts to describe how such influence may be indicated. However, it recognizes that the determination of the ability of an investor to significantly influence an investee is a matter of judgment, and, in order to achieve a reasonable degree of uniformity in application, it concludes that an investment of 20%

or more of the voting stock of an investee shall lead to a presumption that the investor has the ability to exercise significant influence over an investee, and that an investment of less than 20% shall lead to a presumption that no such influence can be exercised by the investor. Therefore, an investment providing a 20% voting interest in an investee requires that the investment be accounted for by the equity method, and an investment that does not provide a 20% voting interest cannot be accounted for by that method. The investor carries the burden of demonstrating the presence, or absence, of his ability to exercise significant influence when the decision to use, or not to use, the equity method is based on any criteria other than the 20% limitation specified in the Opinion.

INVESTMENTS IN MARKETABLE EQUITY SECURITIES

The adjective "long-term" does not appear anywhere in the Opinion, but there is an implied presumption running throughout that the equity method is to be applied only to common stock interests that are to be retained for an indefinite period. The Financial Accounting Standards Board has published Statement No. 12, which deals with marketable equity securities. The provisions of APB Opinion No. 18 are beyond the scope of FASB Statement No. 12, and there is no conflict between the two pronouncements. In short, if an investment in equity securities is surrounded by the conditions that require it to be accounted for by the equity method, it falls under the provisions of APB Opinion No. 18. If the investment does not qualify for the equity method, it should be accounted for, and reported on, under the provisions of FASB No. 12.

COMPLETE CASE IN ACCOUNTING FOR AN INVESTMENT BY THE EQUITY METHOD

The following model case of Investor Corporation and Investee Company has been prepared to illustrate the mechanics of accounting for an investment by the equity method, in accordance with the principles outlined in a foregoing paragraph describing such method. The model also forms the basis for the problems posed and solved later in this chapter, which are designed to demonstrate the accounting procedures required by the Opinion.

On March 31, Investor Corporation purchased 1,712 shares of the voting common stock of Investee Company for a total cash price of $100,000. The stock purchased by the Investor Corporation represented 40% of the outstanding voting common stock of Investee Company. Since the other 60% of voting common stock of Investee Company was scattered among small groups of shareholders, the 40% held by Investor Corporation gave it the ability to exercise significant influence over operations and financial policies of Investee Company. Management of Investor Corporation decided to account for the investment in Investee Company by the equity method. The fiscal year of each company corresponded with the calendar year.

At March 31 the balance sheets of the two companies were as follows:

Balance Sheet—March 31

	Investor Corporation	Investee Company
Current Asset		
Cash	581,544	57,826
Receivables—less allowance for losses	66,393	49,864
Inventories	267,087	88,808
Prepaid Expenses	18,711	4,714
	933,735	201,212

	Investor Corporation	Investee Company
Investments		18,074
Property, Plant and Equipment—net of accumulated depreciation	229,424	61,304
Other	14,115	2,768
	1,177,274	283,358
Liabilities and Stockholders' Equity		
Current Liabilities		
Notes Payable	78,159	18,664
Accounts Payable	139,888	32,929
Accrued Expenses	46,630	10,978
Income Taxes Payable	5,535	6,109
	270,212	68,680
Long-Term Debt	536,727	49,759
Total Liabilities	806,939	118,439
Stockholders' Equity		
Preferred Stock—Par $100		
6% cumulative—nonparticipating		
Authorized, 20,000; issued, 1,078:	107,800	
Authorized, 10,000; issued, 500:		50,000
Common Stock—Par $10		
Authorized, 50,000; issued, 6,960:	69,600	
Authorized, 20,000; issued, 4,280:		42,800
Retained Earnings	192,935	72,119
Total Stockholders' Equity	370,335	164,919
	1,177,274	283,358

The results of operations of each company for the first three months of the fiscal year are comprehended in the above balance sheets and are summarized below:

Summary of Results of Operations—Three Months Ended March 31

	Investor Corporation	Investee Company
Income before income taxes	20,771	7,508
Provision for income taxes	9,618	3,271
Net Income	11,153	4,237

The book value of the assets and liabilities of Investee Company were determined to approximate their fair value. Investor Corporation made the following computations to allocate the cost of its investment:

Investee Company	
Total Assets	283,358
Total Liabilities	118,439
Net Assets	164,919
Less—Par Value of Preferred Stock	50,000
Equity of Common Stockholders in Investee Company	114,919
Percentage of Stock Held by Investor Corporation	40%
Equity in Underlying Net Assets Acquired by Investor Corporation (114,919 x 40%)	45,968
Total Cash Paid for Stock in Investee Company	100,000
Equity in Underlying Net Assets Acquired by Purchase (above)	45,968
Excess of Cost Over Underlying Equity in Net Assets	54,032

Therefore, Investor Corporation made the following entry to record the acquisition of Investee Company stock:

	Debit	Credit
Investment in Investee Company	45,968	
Excess of Cost Over Equity in Investee Company	54,032	
Cash		100,000

Management determined to amortize the excess cost by the straight-line method over a period of 20 years.

Investee Company made no entries to record the purchase of stock by Investor Corporation other than to record the transfer in its capital stock register.

Following nine months of operations, the financial position of Investee Company at December 31 is shown in the following condensed balance sheet:

Investee Company
Balance Sheet—December 31

Assets

Current Assets	222,159
Investments	23,925
Property, Plant and Equipment—net	71,338
Other	8,037
	325,459

Liabilities and Stockholders' Equity

Current Liabilities	95,829
Long-Term Debt	55,477
Total Liabilities	151,306

Liabilities and Stockholders' Equity

Stockholders' Equity	
Preferred Stock	50,000
Common Stock	42,800
Retained Earnings	81,353
Total Stockholders' Equity	174,153
	325,459

The above balance sheet comprehended the following operations of Investee Company during the *full fiscal year:*

Net income for the year	19,039
6% cash dividend on common stock, declared and paid in December;	2,568
6% dividend, payable in cash in January, declared on preferred stock in December.	3,000

The following entries were made by Investor Corporation at December 31 to record the effects of operations of Investee Company and to adjust the values of Investor Corporation's accounts reflecting the investment in common stock of Investee Company:

		Debit	Credit
Cash		1,027	
Investment in Investee Company			1,027
To record cash received for 40% of common stock dividend of $2,568 paid by Investee Company.			
Investment in Investee Company		4,720	
Increase in equity in Investee Company			4,720
To record the effects of operations of Investee Company for nine months ended December 31, as follows:			
Net income for year	19,039		
Less—net income to March 31	4,237		
	14,802		
Less—dividends declared on preferred stock	3,000		
Increase in net assets, disregarding common stock dividend from April 1 to December 31	11,802		
Percentage of equity of Investor Corporation	x 40%		
Increase in value of investment	4,720		

	Debit	Credit
Amortization of goodwill	2,026	
Excess of cost over equity in Investee Company		2,026

To amortize three-fourths of annual amortization of excess of cost over equity in Investee Company.

Following are condensed parent-company financial statements at December 31:

Investor Corporation
Condensed Balance Sheet—December 31

Assets	
Current	776,863
Investment in Investee Company—at equity	49,661
Excess of Cost Over Equity in Investee Company	52,006
Property, Plant and Equipment—net of accumulated depreciation	285,850
Other	20,316
	1,184,696
Liabilities and Stockholders' Equity	
Current Liabilities	346,823
Long-Term Debt	430,921
Total Liabilities	777,744
Stockholders' Equity	
Preferred Stock—$100 Par	107,800
Capital Stock—$10 Par	69,600
Retained Earnings	229,552
Total Stockholders' Equity	406,952
	1,184,696

Investor Corporation
Condensed Statement of Income and Retained Earnings
For Year Ended December 31

Net Sales	1,491,869
Cost of Sales	1,085,100
	406,769
Selling and Administrative Expenses	325,246
	81,523
Other Income	
Increase in Equity in Investee Company	4,720
Income Before Income Taxes	86,243
Provision for Income Taxes	38,473
Net Income	47,770
Retained Earnings—January 1	181,782
Retained Earnings—December 31	229,552

APPLYING THE EQUITY METHOD

Paragraph 19 of the Opinion sets forth fourteen procedures that when appropriate to the circumstance should be followed by an investor in applying the equity method of accounting to investments in common stock of unconsolidated subsidiaries, corporate joint ventures, and other investees where such investment qualifies for the equity method. These procedures are disclosed in subparagraphs with lettered designations from (a) to (n). The respective procedures are indicated below by their lettered designations, and are quoted verbatim from the Opinion. Explanatory comments and illustrations of accounting techniques are supplied for each indicated procedure.

(a) ***Intercompany profits and losses should be eliminated until realized by the investor or investee as if a subsidiary, corporate joint venture or investee company were consolidated.***

An interpretation of APB Opinion No. 18 provides that in cases where the investor does not have a majority voting interest in the investee it is appropriate for the investor to eliminate intercompany profits in relation to the investor's common stock interest in the investee. Since *all* intercompany transactions are normally eliminated in consolidation, this interpretation appears to violate the intent of Paragraph 19 of the Opinion, which states that the investor's net income and stockholders' equity should be identical in both consolidated and unconsolidated statements where the investment is accounted for by the equity method.

However, the method of accounting prescribed by the interpretation is generally accepted in accounting for investments that represent 50% or less of the voting stock of an investee, and that is the method used in the following illustrations of eliminating intercompany unrealized profit.

The percentage of intercompany profit to be eliminated is the same regardless of whether the sale is made by the investor to the investee ("downstream") or whether the sale is made by the investee to the investor ("upstream").

Illustration of Downstream Transactions

Investee Company has items in its inventory for which it paid $100,000 and on which Investor Corporation made a profit of 25%, or $25,000.

Investor Corporation would compute the effects of the intercompany transaction as follows:

Unrealized intercompany profit made by Investor Corporation on sales of items residual in Investee Company inventory	25,000
Investor Corporation percentage of participation in Investee Company's profits	x 40%
Amount of unrealized profit applicable to Investor Corporation's equity in Investee Company	10,000
Less—Tax benefit (estimated at 45%) derived from reduction in income	4,500
Net reduction of income in Investor Corporation	5,500

The financial statements of Investor Corporation could reflect the effects of the intercompany transactions in a variety of ways. One accepted method would be to present, on the balance sheet, the gross unrealized profit of $10,000 as deferred income and the tax benefit as a deferred tax debit. The $5,500 net reduction in income would be reported on the income statement as a separate item. The following entry would adjust the statements to eliminate the unrealized profit if the method described above were used:

	Debit	Credit
Deferred income tax	4,500	
Deduction for intercompany profit on inventory items	5,500	
Deferred income		10,000

This entry may be made for statement purposes only. However, if it is entered on the books, it should be reversed as of the first day of the succeeding accounting period.

Illustration of Upstream Transactions

Investor Corporation has items in its inventory for which it paid $100,000 and on which Investee Company made a profit of 25%, or $25,000.

Investor Corporation computes the effects of the intercompany transactions as follows:

Unrealized intercompany profit made by Investee Company on sales of items residual in Investor Corporation's inventory	25,000
Less—Tax effect (estimated at 45%)	11,250
Unrealized intercompany profit—net of income tax	13,750
Investor Corporation's percentage of participation in Investee Company's profits	x 40%
Net reduction in income of Investor Corporation	5,500

The reduction of income of Investor Corporation could be shown in its financial statements in several ways: the investment account and the corresponding income from investee could be reduced; the investor's inventory could be reduced and his cost of sales correspondingly increased; or, the reduction could be reported as separate items on both the balance sheet and in the income statement.

To avoid presenting values that disturb the ratio of sales to gross profit or upset the correspondence of the investment account with equity in the net assets of the investee, it is recommended that the reduction in income of Investor Corporation be presented as deferred income on its balance sheet and reported as a separate expense item in its income statement. The following entry would adjust the statements to eliminate the unrealized profit by this method:

	Debit	Credit
Deduction for intercompany profit on inventory	5,500	
Deferred income		5,500

This entry may be made for statement purposes only. However, if it is entered on the books, it should be reversed as of the first day of the succeeding accounting period.

(b) ***A difference between the cost of an investment and the amount of underlying equity in net assets of an investee should be accounted for as if the investee were a consolidated subsidiary.***

This subparagraph requires that the difference between the cost of the investment and the value of the related underlying net assets of the investee be accounted for by the investor as described below.

Excess of Cost Over Equity in Net Assets of Investee

For investments made prior to November 1, 1970, this excess need not be amortized unless it has a limited term of existence.

For investments made subsequent to October 31, 1970, the excess must be amortized on a straight-line basis for a period not to exceed forty years.

Illustration

The foregoing model case of Investor Corporation and Investee Company demonstrated a method for computing the excess of cost to the investor over equity acquired in underlying net assets of the investee. In the model the excess cost was determined to be $54,032, and management directed that the excess be amortized over a period of twenty years. However, it is important to note that in the model case the book value of the assets and liabilities of Investee Company were determined by management to be their "fair value," and therefore the allocation of cost of the investment was made to identifiable assets and liabilities on the basis of their book value, and the excess was set up in a single intangible asset account, "Excess of Cost Over Equity in Investee Company."

Had the "fair value" of the assets and liabilities been different from their book value, it would have been necessary to allocate the cost of the investment on the basis of fair value, and the remaining cost would then have been set up as intangible goodwill, or excess of cost over equity in net assets of the investee. Also, depreciable or amortizable assets would have had to be subsequently depreciated or amortized on the basis of their assigned values.

For example, assume that, in the model case referred to above, instead of fair value being equivalent to book value, a "fair value" of $90,000 was allocated to a building having a book value of $40,000, and a remaining useful life of forty years. In such case Investor Corporation's equity in the additional assigned value would be 40% of $50,000, or $20,000. This amount would be added to the investment in Investee Company account and deducted from excess of cost over equity in Investee Company. An adjustment of $500 would have to be made to the income pickup from Investee Company over the next forty years.

Therefore, the computation by Investor Corporation for allocation of the cost of its investment and the related entries for amortization and income pickup would be changed from that demonstrated in the model case to the following:

Total Cash paid for stock in Investee Company	100,000
Equity in book value of net assets of Investee Company (from the model case)	45,968
	54,032
Less—Portion of cost allocated to increase the basis of the building	20,000
Excess of cost over fair value of equity in net assets of Investee Company	34,032

The following entry would be made to record the acquisition of Investee Company stock:

	Debit	Credit
Investment in Investee Company	65,968	
Excess of cost over equity in Investee Company	34,032	
Cash		100,000

The entries described in the model case to record dividends and equity in income of Investee Company would remain the same. However, the entry to record amortizaiton of goodwill and the entries to record additional depreciation would be as follows:

	Debit	Credit
Amortization of goodwill	1,276	
Increase in equity in Investee Company	500	
Excess of cost over equity in Investee Company		1,276
Investment in Investee Company		500

In the determination of the fair value of the building, the tax effects of additional depreciation, etc., should be considered. However, differences between amounts assigned and tax bases are not timing differences, and no deferred taxes should be recorded for the depreciation that will be applied to the additional $20,000 cost assigned to the building.

If the investee sells the building at a subsequent date, the investor would have to adjust his pickup of net income from the investee so as to eliminate the assigned values on his books at the time of sale.

As an illustration, let us assume that in the case at hand Investee Company sold the building after ten years at a gain of $30,000. At that time the excess assigned value of the building in the investment in Investee Company account on Investor Corporation's books would be:

Original excess assigned value contained in investment in Investee Company account	20,000
Less—Total depreciation expense credited to investment in Investee Company account (10 years at $500 annually)	5,000
Remaining assigned cost in investment in Investee Company account at date of sale	15,000

To eliminate the assigned value residual in the investment account on Investor Corporation's books at the time of sale of the asset, Investor Corporation would have to reduce the net income pickup from Investee Company for the period in which the sale occurred by $15,000.

The examples illustrated above indicate that assigning values in excess of book values to identifiable assets of investees in which the investor holds a 50% or less interest is of dubious accounting integrity, economic validity, and legal foundation, and such assignment should be avoided unless failure to make proper assignment would result in serious defects in disclosure in financial statements.

Excess of Equity in Net Assets Over Cost

Normally, this type of situation will not occur, since the general presumption in historical-cost based accounting is that net assets acquired should be recorded at not more than cost. However, if an excess over cost is determined, the excess should be allocated to reduce values assigned to noncurrent assets, except for long-term investments in marketable securities. If the allocation reduces the noncurrent assets to zero values, the remainder of the excess should be classified as a deferred credit and amortized by the straight-line method over a period not to exceed forty years. No part of the excess of acquired net assets over cost should be added directly to stockholders' equity by the investor at the date of acquisition.

Illustration

In the model case of Investor Corporation and Investee Company, it was demonstrated that Investor Corporation paid $100,000 for an equity of $45,968 in the net assets of Investee Company, resulting in an excess of cost over equity of $54,032.

However, had the purchase price been $15,000, there would have been an excess of acquired net assets over cost of $30,968, of which $25,629 would have been allocated to the assigned values of noncurrent assets, reducing their values to zero, and the remaining $5,339 would have been classified as a deferred credit to be amortized over a period not exceeding forty years.

The computation of the above values is as follows:

Equity in net assets acquired by Investor Corporation (from the model case)			45,968
Cash purchase price			15,000
Excess of unassigned equity over cost			30,968
Less—Amount applied to equity in net assets of Investee Company to reduce their values to zero:			
	Book Value	Equity (40%)	
Fixed assets	61,304	24,522	
Other	2,768	1,107	
	64,072	25,629	25,629
Excess of equity over cost			5,339

In the situation outlined above, Investor Corporation would make the following entry to record the acquisition of Investee Company stock:

	Debit	Credit
Investment in Investee Company	20,339	
Excess of equity in Investee Company over cost		5,339
Cash		15,000

A summary of values assigned to Investor Corporation's equity in individual assets and liabilities of Investee Company is as follows:

	Investee Company Book Value	Investor Corporation Percentage	Investor Corporation Amount of Equity
Assets			
Current	201,212	40%	80,485
Long-Term Investments	18,074	40%	7,230
Fixed	61,304	—	—
Other	2,768	—	—
	283,358		87,715
Liabilities			
Current	68,680	40%	27,472
Long-Term	49,759	40%	19,904
Preferred Stock	50,000	40%	20,000
	168,439		67,376
Net Assets	114,919		20,339

(c) ***The investment(s) in common stock should be shown in the balance sheet of the investor as a single amount, and the investor's share of earnings or losses of an investee(s) should ordinarily be shown in the income statement as a single amount except for the extraordinary items as specified in (d) below.***

In essence, this subparagraph requires that the investor report a "one-line consolidation" with the investee, both on the balance sheet and in the income statement. It is immaterial how many accounts may be carried on the books of the investor to accommodate the investment, (e.g., dividends received from investee, increase in equity in investee, etc.), but the cost of the investment and the income therefrom should be consolidated into single lines on the balance sheet and income statement, respectively.

This requirement is demonstrated in the financial statements presented in the foregoing model case of Investor Corporation and Investee Company, as follows:

Balance Sheet	
Investment in Investee Company—at equity	49,661
Income Statement	
Increase in Equity in Investee Company	4,720

(d) ***The investor's share of extraordinary items and its share of prior-period adjustments reported in the financial statements of the investee in accordance with APB Opinion No. 9 should be classified in a similar manner unless they are immaterial in the income statement of the investor.***

This subparagraph requires that the investor's income statement report its equity in extraordinary items of the investee separately, and in the same manner that the investor would report its own extraordinary income. (APB Opinion No. 9 was superseded by APB Opinion No. 30 insofar as criteria for extraordinary items are concerned.)

With reference to the foregoing model case, had the income of Investee Company included an extraordinary credit of $5,000, realized subsequent to March 31, and assuming a tax rate of 45%, Investor Corporation would have reported the income pickup from Investee Company at December 31, as follows:

Operating Income	81,523
Other Income	
Increase in equity in Investee Company	3,620
Income before income taxes and extraordinary item	85,143
Provision for income taxes	38,473
Income before extraordinary credit	46,670
Extraordinary item (description)	1,100
Net income	47,770

> (e) ***A transaction of an investee of a capital nature that affects the investor's share of stockholders' equity of the investee should be accounted for as if the investee were a consolidated subsidiary.***

Acquiring treasury stock and sales of preferred or common stock are examples of capital transactions by an investee that affect the investor's share of stockholders' equity of the investee.

Schedules 1 and 2, based on the foregoing model case of Investor Corporation and Investee Company, reveal the effect on the investor of capital transactions by the investee. The effects demonstrated are as follows:

Sale of Common Stock by Investee:

(a) the *percentage* of investor's equity in net assets will decrease proportionate to the number of shares sold;

(b) the *amount* of the investor's equity in net assets of the investee,

(i) will increase if the stock is sold at a price in excess of book value,

(ii) will remain the same if stock is sold at a price equivalent to book value, and

(iii) will decrease if stock is sold at a price that is less than book value.

Reacquisition of Common Stock by Investee for Treasury: The second schedule reveals that reacquisition of common stock for the treasury has precisely the opposite effect from that shown above on the *percentage* and *amount* of equity held by the investor.

Schedule 1

Effect on Investment of Investor of Sales of Common Stock by Investee

		Sale of 200 Shares by Investee Company		
	Status of Investment at March 31	At Excess of Book Value $40.00 Per Share	At Book Value $26.85 Per Share	At Less Than Book Value $21.00 Per Share
Investee Company				
1. Assets	283,358	283,358	283,358	283,358
2. Cash received for shares		8,000	5,370	4,200
3. Liabilities and preferred stock	(168,439)	(168,439)	(168,439)	(168,439)
4. Net assets	114,919	122,919	120,289	119,119

	Status of Investment at March 31	Sale of 200 Shares by Investee Company: At Excess of Book Value $40.00 Per Share	At Book Value $26.85 Per Share	At Less Than Book Value $21.00 Per Share
5. Number of shares outstanding before sale	4,280	4,280	4,280	4,280
6. Number of shares sold	–	200	200	200
7. Number of shares outstanding after sale	4,280	4,480	4,480	4,480
8. Book value per share (line 4 ÷ line 7)	26.85	27.44	26.85	26.59
Investor Corporation				
9. Number of shares owned	1,712	1,712	1,712	1,712
10. Percentage of outstanding shares owned (line 9 ÷ line 7)	40.0000%	38.2143%	38.2143%	38.2143%
11. Total equity in net assets (line 10 x line 4)	45,968	46,973	45,968	45,520

Schedule 2

Effect on Investment of Investor of Reacquiring Common Stock for Treasury by Investee

	Status of Investment At March 31	200 Shares Reacquired by Investee Company: At Excess of Book Value $40.00 Per Share	At Book Value $26.85 Per Share	At Less Than Book Value $21.00 Per Share
Investee Company				
1. Assets	283,358	283,358	283,358	283,358
2. Cash paid for treasury stock		(8,000)	(5,370)	(4,200)
3. Liabilities and preferred stock	(168,439)	(168,439)	(168,439)	(168,439)
4. Net assets	114,919	106,919	109,549	110,719
5. Number of shares outstanding before purchase	4,280	4,280	4,280	4,280
6. Number of shares reacquired	–	(200)	(200)	(200)
7. Number of shares outstanding after acquiring	4,280	4,080	4,080	4,080
8. Book value per share (line 4 ÷ by line 7)	26.85	26.21	26.85	27.14

	Status of Investment At March 31	200 Shares Reacquired by Investee Company — At Excess of Book Value $40.00 Per Share	At Book Value $26.85 Per Share	At Less Than Book Value $21.00 Per Share
Investor Corporation				
9. Number of shares owned	1,712	1,712	1,712	1,712
10. Percentage of outstanding shares owned (line 9 ÷ line 7)	40.0000%	41.9608%	41.9608%	41.9608%
11. Total equity in net assets (line 10 x line 4)	45,968	44,864	45,968	46,459

Changes in the *amount* of the investor's equity in net assets of the investee should be recorded by the investor as a capital change. They should not go through the income statement, but be charged or credited directly to paid-in capital or to retained earnings.

Illustration

(a) Schedule 1 above reveals that if Investee Company sold 200 shares of its common stock at a price of $21.00 per share the percentage of common stock held by Investor Corporation would change from 40% to 38%, and the amount of equity would decrease from $45,968 to $45,520.

Investor Corporation would make the following entry to record the decrease in equity in Investee Company:

	Debit	Credit
Retained Earnings	448	
Investment in Investee Company		448

(b) Schedule 2 above indicates that if Investee Company reacquired 200 shares of its common stock for its treasury at $21.00 per share, the percentage of common stock held by Investor Corporation would change from 40% to 42%, and the amount of equity would increase from $45,968 to $46,459. In such case, Investor Corporation would make the following entry to record the increase in equity in Investee Company:

	Debit	Credit
Investment in Investee Company	491	
Retained earnings.		491

The problem of recording an appropriate change in excess of cost over equity, or goodwill, in instances described above is discussed in the comments under subparagraph (f), following.

(f) ***Sales of stock of an investee by an investor should be accounted for as gains or losses equal to the difference at the time of sale between selling price and carrying amount of the stock sold.***

The requirements of this subparagraph present no special accounting problems. There should be no attempt to identify the shares sold, since the carrying value of each share represents equivalent equity in the net assets of the investee.

However, a problem does arise in identifying the effect of such transactions on the integrity of any excess of cost over equity, or goodwill, recorded on the investor's books. The goodwill resulting from an excess of cost over the fair value of net assets underlying the investment in an investee is separate and apart from the adjusted cost of the shares of stock purchased. The shares represent equity in net assets; the goodwill represents an intangible expected benefit. If the valuation of the goodwill was proper to begin with, it is logical to conclude that the expected benefits to be derived therefrom will depend on the percentage of participation of the investor in the investee's net income.

In APB Opinion No. 18 there are no guidelines on the matter of disposal of goodwill attending an investment accounted for by the equity method. However, paragraph 32 of APB Opinion No. 17 reads as follows:

> *Ordinarily goodwill and similar intangible assets cannot be disposed of apart from the enterprise as a whole. However, a large segment or separable group of assets of an acquired company or the entire acquired company may be sold or otherwise liquidated, and all or a portion of the unamortized cost of the goodwill recognized in the acquisition should be included in the cost of the assets sold.*

The quoted paragraph indirectly relates goodwill to segments of equity in net assets acquired from an investee, and appears to sanction disposal of the portions of goodwill that are directly related to shares of investee stock sold by the investor.

It well might be, however, that the sale of small blocks of stock of an investee would have no significant effect on the total expected benefits to be derived from the goodwill recognized in the acquisition of the investee's stock. In such cases, of course, there would be no impairment of goodwill, and no entries would be made to reduce its cost on the books of the investor.

Therefore, it appears that the matter of disposing of a portion of goodwill concurrent with the sale of stock related to its acquisition is a matter of judgment to be made by management and concurred in by the independent accountant.

In the following illustrations of accounting for the sale of stock of an investee accounted for by the equity method, it is assumed that management feels that unamortized goodwill should be reduced proportionate to each share of stock sold.

Illustration

In the foregoing model case of Investor Corporation and Investee Company, the carrying value and excess of cost over equity at December 31 were as follows:

Carrying Value Per Share:

$49,661 ÷ 1,712 shares = $29.01 per share.

Excess of Cost Over Equity:

$52,006 ÷ 1,712 shares = $30.38 per share.

If on January 1, Investor Corporation sold 100 shares of Investee Company at $75.00 per share, the gain would be computed as follows:

Proceeds of sale of 100 shares at $75.00 per share		7,500
Carrying Value of Shares Sold		
"Investment" account— 100 shares at $29.01	2,901	
"Excess of Cost" account— 100 shares at $30.38	3,038	5,939
Gain on sale		1,561

The entry to record the transaction would be:

	Debit	Credit
Cash	7,500	
Investment in Investee Company		2,901
Excess of cost over equity in Investee Company		3,038
Gain on sale of stock in Investee Company		1,561

(g) ***If financial statements of an investee are not sufficiently timely for an investor to apply the equity method currently, the investor ordinarily should record its share of the earnings or losses of an investee from the most recent available financial statements. A lag in reporting should be consistent from period to period.***

The dispensation afforded in this paragraph is for purely practical purposes and has no basis in theory. In consolidation, as well as in accounting by the equity method, it is permissible for the parent, or investor, to report the financial position and results of operations of a subsidiary or an investee on a date as much as three months prior to the date of the consolidated, or investor's, financial statements.

In the model case of Investor Corporation and Investee Company, for example, had the date of the financial statements of Investee Company been as of September 30 instead of December 31, it would have been acceptable for Investor Corporation to make its pickup as of September 30 and report it in its December 31 financial statements.

(h) ***A loss in value of an investment which is other than a temporary decline should be recognized the same as a loss in value of other long-term assets. Evidence of a loss in value might include, but would not necessarily be limited to, absence of an ability to recover the carrying amount of the investment or inability of the investee to sustain an earnings capacity which would justify the carrying amount of the investment. A current fair value of an investment that is less than its carrying amount may indicate a loss in value of the investment. However, a decline in the quoted market price below the carrying amount or the existence of operating losses is not necessarily indicative of a loss in value that is other than temporary. All factors to be evaluated.***

This subparagraph is long, detailed, and self-explanatory. An example of accounting for a loss in value of an investment is illustrated below.

Illustration

In the foregoing model case of Investor Corporation and Investee Company, the carrying value of Investee Company stock on Investor Corporation's books at December 31 was:

Investment in Investee Company	49,661
Excess of cost over equity in Investee Company	52,006
	101,667

If management of Investor Corporation decided, on the basis of criteria outlined in this subparagraph, that a loss in value sufficient to reduce the carrying value of the investment to $40,000 had occurred, and that goodwill recognized in its acquisition would afford no further benefits, the following entry would be made to record the decline in value. The entries described in the model case to pick up income from the investee and to amortize excess of cost over equity would not be made.

	Debit	Credit
Loss on investment in Investee Company	60,000	
Allowance for loss on Investee Company		5,968
Excess of cost over equity in Investee Company		54,032

The financial statements would then report the following information:

Balance Sheet	
Investment in Investee Company—net of allowance for loss of $5,968	40,000
Income Statement	
Loss on investment in Investee Company	60,000

(i) ***An investor's share of losses of an investee may equal or exceed the carrying amount of an investment accounted for by the equity method plus advances made by the investor. The investor ordinarily should discontinue applying the equity method when the investment (and net advances) is reduced to zero, and should not provide for additional losses unless the investor has guaranteed obligations of the investee or is otherwise commited to provide further financial support for the investee. If the investee subsequently reports net income, the investor should resume applying the equity method only after its share of that net income equals the share of net losses not recognized during the period the equity method was suspended.***

This subparagraph is self-explanatory and there are no special accounting problems involved in complying with its requirements. There is a problem, however, in determining how much pickup should be made, if any, by the investor when the investee reports income in years subsequent to the year in which the equity method was discontinued by the investor. Following is an illustration of such pickup of income after the investor abandoned the equity method of accounting.

Illustration

This illustration is based on the foregoing model case in which Investor Corporation holds 40% of the common stock of Investee Company. For purposes of illustration, the following table has been prepared and it is assumed that Investee Company's net income or loss is shown on line 2 for the years indicated and that 40% of such income or loss is reflected on line 4. The effects on Investor Corporation of Investee Company's operatons for each year are shown on lines 5 to 11.

Effects of Discontinuing Equity Method of Accounting

	Balance End of 1st Year	Balances at End of 2nd Year	3rd Year	4th Year	5th Year
Investee Company					
1. Net assets—beginning	—	124,153	74,153	(847)	(25,847)
2. Earnings (losses)	—	(50,000)	(75,000)	(25,000)	50,000
	124,153	74,153	(847)	(25,847)	24,153
Investor Corporation					
4. 40% equity in Investee Company earnings (loss)	—	(20,000)	(30,000)	(10,000)	20,000
5. Investment—beginning	—	49,661	29,661	—	
6. Income (loss) of Investee Company	—	(20,000)	(29,661)	—	9,661
7. Investment—ending	49,661	29,661	—	—	9,661
8. Excess of cost over equity—beginning	—	52,006	49,406	—	—
9. Amortization (5%)	—	(2,600)	—	—	—
10. Disposal	—	—	(49,406)	—	—
11. Excess of cost over equity—ending	52,006	49,406	—	—	—

At the end of the second year Investor Corporation would take up its share of Investee Company's loss and amortize the goodwill intangible at 5%.

At the end of the third year, however, Investor Corporation would not pick up 40% of Investee Company's loss, but, instead, would pick up only such amount as would reduce the investment account to zero ($29,661), and thus discontinue accounting for the investment by the equity method. At the same time, it is assumed that management decided that no future benefits would accrue from the goodwill intangible represented by the unamortized excess of cost over equity in Investee Company, and therefore decided to dispose of the entire remaining balance.

At the end of the fourth year, Investor Corporation would not pick up any part of the loss sustained by Investee Company.

At the end of the fifth year, Investor Corporation would resume accounting for the investment by the equity method and would pick up $9,661 income, computed as follows:

Investor Corporation equity in income of Investee Company		20,000
Less: Prior year losses of Investee Company not picked up by Investee Corporation		
Third Year—(30,000 - 29,661)	339	
Fourth Year	10,000	10,339
		9,661

The entries made by Investor Corporation at the end of each respective year would be as follows:

	Debit	Credit
Second Year		
Decrease in equity in Investee Company	20,000	
Amortization of goodwill	2,600	
Investment in Investee Company		20,000
Excess of cost over equity in Investee Company		2,600
Third Year		
Decrease in equity in Investee Company	29,661	
Loss on disposal of goodwill	49,406	
Investment in Investee Company		29,661
Excess of cost over equity in Investee Company		49,406
Fourth Year		
None		
Fifth Year		
Investment in Investee Company	9,661	
Increase in equity in Investee Company		9,661

(j) (This subparagraph concerned deferred income taxes on undistributed earnings of subsidiaries and investees, and has been superseded by APB Opinion No. 23.)

In the model case in this chapter no deferred income taxes have been provided for undistributed earnings because it was assumed that such earnings would be permanently reinvested.

(k) ***When an investee has outstanding cumulative preferred stock, an investor should compute its share of earnings (losses) after deducting the investee's preferred dividends, whether or not such dividends are declared.***

An illustration of deducting preferred dividends from the investor's pickup from the investee was made in the foregoing model case of Investor Corporation and Investee Company in the entry made by Investor Corporation to pick up the income from Investee Company at December 31.

(l) ***An investment in voting stock of an investee company may fall below the level of ownership described in paragraph 17 from sale of a portion of an investment by the investor, sale of additional stock by an investee, or other transactions, and the investor may thereby lose the ability to influence policy, as described in that paragraph. An investor should discontinue accruing its share of the earnings or losses of the investee for an investment that no longer qualifies for the equity method. The earnings or losses that relate to the stock retained by the investor and that were previously accrued should remain as a part of the carrying amount of the investment. The investment account should not be adjusted retroactively under the conditions described in this subparagraph. However, dividends received by the investor in subsequent periods which exceed his share of earnings for such periods should be applied in reduction of the carrying amount of the investment.***

There are no problems involved in accounting for an investment when it ceases to qualify for the equity method. The equity method is simply discontinued in such cases. The problems arise, however, when subsequent dividends received from the investee exceed the investor's equity in the income of the investee for the year in which the dividend is received. Following is an illustration of such a situation.

Illustration

This illustration is again based on the foregoing model case in which Investor Corporation holds 40% of the stock of Investee Company. For purposes of illustration, the following table has been prepared based on assumptions that, at the beginning of the second year, Investor Corporation's equity in Investee Company was 40% of $124,153, or $49,661, and that on January 1 of the fourth year Investee Company sold 12,840 of its own shares to a third party at the book value of $38.94 per share, for which Investee Company received $500,000. The sale of the stock to a third party reduced the percentage of common stock held by Investor Corporation from 40% to 10%. It is also assumed that the income, effect on net assets of the proceeds from sale of stock, and dividends paid of Investee Company are shown on lines 2, 3, and 4 for the years indicated. Line 6 shows the percentage of common stock owned by Investor Corporation and lines 7 to 11 reflect the effect of Investee Company's operations on the investment held by Investor Corporation.

At the end of the second and third years, Investor Corporation took up its shares of Investee Company's income by the equity method.

At the end of the fourth year, Investor Corporation's common stock interest was reduced to 10%, and it discontinued the equity method. The dividend received that year was less than Investor Corporation's 10% equity in the income of Investee Company; therefore, the total dividend of $1,027 was picked up by Investor Corporation and credited to dividend income.

Accounting Effects When Investment Ceases to Qualify for Equity Method

	Balance at End of:				
	2nd Year	3rd Year	4th Year	5th Year	6th Year
Investee Company					
1. Net assets—beginning	124,153	142,903	166,653	691,383	686,113
2. Effects of proceeds from sale of stock	—	—	500,000	—	—
3. Earnings (losses)	25,000	30,000	35,000	5,000	(10,000)
4. Dividends paid	(6,250)	(6,250)	(10,270)	(10,270)	(10,270)
5. Net assets—ending	142,903	166,653	691,383	686,113	665,843
Investor Corporation					
6. Percentage of common stock of Investee Company held by Investor Corporation	40%	40%	10%	10%	10%
7. Investment—beginning	49,661	57,161	66,661	66,661	66,134
8. Dividends received	(2,500)	(2,500)	—	—	—
9. Income of Investee Company	10,000	12,000	—	—	—
10. Reduction for excess of dividends over equity in earnings for year	—	—	—	(527)	(1,027)
11. Investment—ending	57,161	66,661	66,661	66,134	65,107

In the fifth year, Investor Corporation's equity in Investee Company's income was $527 less than the dividend received. Therefore, $527 was credited to the investment account and the remaining $500 was credited to the dividend income account.

In the sixth year, Investee Company had a loss, and the total amount of the dividend received by Investor Corporation was therefore credited to its investment account.

The entries made by Investor Corporation at the end of each respective year were as follows:

	Debit	Credit
Second Year		
Investment in Investee Company	7,500	
Increase in equity in Investee Company		7,500
Third Year		
Investment in Investee Company	9,500	
Increase in equity in Investee Company		9,500
Fourth Year		
Cash	1,027	
Dividend income		1,027

	Debit	Credit
Fifth Year		
Cash	1,027	
Investment in Investee Company		527
Dividend income		500
Sixth Year		
Cash	1,027	
Investment in Investee Company		1,027

(m) ***An investment in common stock of an investee that was previously accounted for on other than the equity method may become qualified for use of the equity method by an increase in the level of ownership described in paragraph 17 (i.e., acquisition of additional voting stock by the investor, acquisition or retirement of voting stock by the investee, or other transactions). When an investment qualifies for use of the equity method, the investor should adopt the equity method of accounting. The investment, results of operations (current and prior periods presented), and retained earnings of the investor should be adjusted retroactively in a manner consistent with the accounting for a step-by-step acquisition of a subsidiary.***

This subparagraph requires an investor to start to use the equity method of accounting whenever an investment qualifies for such method, even though the investment was accounted for by the cost method in prior years. It also specifies that at the time of change to the equity method the cost of the investment be adjusted on the books of the investor as if the respective shares had been accounted for by the equity method, or the step-by-step acquisition of a subsidiary. An illustration of the step-by-step acquisition of a subsidiary is provided in chapter 6, "Accounting for Business Combinations," and following is an illustration of accounting for an investment prior and subsequent to the time it qualifies for the equity method.

Illustration

This illustration is based on the model case of Investor Corporation and Investee Company. It is assumed that Investor Corporation purchased 10% of the outstanding common stock of Investee Company on January 1 of the first year for $25,000, and 30% on January of the third year for $100,000. This stock was purchased from a stockholder and did not increase the outstanding stock of Investee Company. For purposes of illustration, the following table has been prepared to reflect the operations of Investee Company in lines 1 to 4, and the effect of such operations on Investor Corporation's investment. Lines 6 to 17 indicate such effect and also disclose the effect of the purchase of additional shares on January 1 of the third year.

At the end of the first and second years, Investor Corporation recorded dividends received as dividend income in accordance with the cost method of accounting for investments.

At the beginning of the third year, Investor Corporation recorded the purchase of the additional 30% of outstanding stock for $100,000. At that time it credited the investment account and debited excess of cost of equity in investee account for the difference between the total cash paid for the investment ($125,000) and the equity in the book value of Investee Company's net assets at the beginning of the third year (40% x $166,653 = $66,661). At the end of the third year, it was necessary for Investor Corporation to adjust the cost of the investment as if it had been accounted for by the equity method from the beginning of the first year.

Effects of Initiating Use of Equity Method of Accounting

	Balance at End of:			
	1st Year	2nd Year	3rd Year	4th Year
Investee Company				
1. Net assets—beginning	124,153	142,903	166,653	180,403
2. Income	25,000	30,000	20,000	20,000
3. Dividends paid	(6,250)	(6,250)	(6,250)	(6,250)
4. Net assets—ending	142,903	166,653	180,403	194,153
Investor Corporation				
5. Percentage of common stock of Investee Company held by Investor Corporation	10%	10%	40%	40%
6. Investment—beginning	25,000	25,000	25,000	72,161
7. Cash paid for additional shares	—	—	100,000	—
8. Excess of cost over equity	—	—	(58,339)	—
9. Dividends received	—	—	(2,500)	(2,500)
10. Equity in income of Investee Company	—	—	8,000	8,000
11. Investment—ending	25,000	25,000	72,161	77,661
12. Excess of cost over equity—beginning	—	—	—	57,077
13. Excess of cost—beginning of 3rd Year	—	—	58,339	—
14. Equity in income not recorded—Years 1 and 2	—	—	1,742	—
15. Amortization (5% x $60,081)	—	—	(3,004)	(3,004)
16. Excess of cost over equity—ending	—	—	57,077	54,073

The increase in equity of the 10% interest held during the first two years that was in excess of cash dividends received is an increase in excess of cost over equity received at the time the additional 30% interest was purchased. At the same time, the amount of amortization that would have been applied to the excess of cost over equity at the time the 10% interest was purchased is a decrease in excess of cost over equity at the time the additional 30% interest was purchased.

The following summary shows how the investment would have been accounted for under the equity method, how it was actually accounted for, and develops the net difference that had to be added to the excess cost at the end of the third year.

		1st Year	2nd Year	Total
Increase in Equity				
10% of increase in net assets		1,875	2,375	4,250
Less—Amortization of excess of cost over net book value		629	629	1,258
Income under equity method		1,246	1,746	2,992
Income reported—dividends received		625	625	1,250
Income not reported in prior years		621	1,121	1,742

		1st Year	2nd Year	Total
Amortization of Excess Cost				
Excess cost—beginning		—	11,956	—
Excess cost—1st Year				
Cost	25,000			
10% of net book value	12,415	12,585	—	12,585
Amortization (5%)		(629)	(629)	(1,258)
Excess cost—ending		11,956	11,327	11,327

The entries made by Investor Corporation to account for the investment in Investee Company follow:

	Debit	Credit
Beginning of First Year		
Investment in Investee Company	25,000	
Cash		25,000
End of First Year		
Cash	625	
Dividend income		625
End of Second Year		
Cash	625	
Dividend income		625
Beginning of Third Year		
Investment in Investee Company	41,661	
Excess of cost over equity in Investee Company	58,339	
Cash		100,000
End of Third Year		
(a) Investment in Investee Company	5,500	
Amortization of goodwill	3,004	
Increase in investment in Investee Company		5,500
Excess of cost over equity in Investee Company		3,004
(b) Excess of cost over equity in Investee Company	1,742	
Retained earnings (prior period adjustment)		1,742

(n) ***The carrying amount of an investment in common stock of an investee that qualifies for the equity method of accounting as described in subparagraph (m) may differ from the underlying equity in net assets of the investee. The difference should affect the determination of the amount of the investor's share of earnings or losses of an investee as if the investee were a consolidated subsidiary. However, if he investor is unable to relate the difference to specific accounts of the investee, the difference should be considered to be goodwill and amortized over a period not to exceed forty years, in accordance with APB Opinion No. 17.***

This subparagraph concerns the difference between the carrying value of an investment at the time it qualifies for the equity method and the underlying equity in net assets of the investee.

If the fair value of the assets and liabilities of the investee are equivalent to their book value, the cost of the investment should be allocated to the equity in assets and liabilities of the investee on the basis of book value, and any excess cost should be recorded as an intangible and amortized over a period of not less than forty years. This situation is illustrated in the comments following subparagraph (m) above, where the fair value of the assets and liabilities of Investee Company were assumed to coincide with their book values, and the excess of cost over equity was set up in an account "Excess of Cost Over Equity in Investee Company."

If the fair value of the assets and liabilities of the investee do not correspond to their book values, the allocation of cost to the equity in assets and liabilities of the investee should be made on the basis of each respective item, and any excess of cost over fair value should be recorded as an intangible and amortized over a period not to exceed forty years. If any depreciable or amortizable assets are allocated a cost different from their book values, the investment account must be adjusted annually to account for the difference in amortization or depreciation between the amount recorded in investee's books and the amount calculated on the basis of the cost assigned in the investor's books. This situation is illustrated in the comments under subparagraph (b) above, where it is assumed that a building has a fair value that is $20,000 in excess of its book value.

DISCLOSURE IN FINANCIAL STATEMENTS

The following disclosure in financial statements is generally applicable to material investments in common stocks:

(a) names of investees, and percentages of ownership;

(b) the accounting policies of the investor with respect to investments in common stocks;

(c) any difference between carrying amount of the investment and the amount of underlying equity in net assets of the investee, and the accounting treatment of such differences;

(d) market value of common stocks held, when available (except for investments in subsidiaries);

(e) summarized information as to assets, liabilities, and results of operations of unconsolidated subsidiaries and joint ventures (presented in notes, or in separate statements of the subsidiaries);

(f) material effects of possible conversions of convertible securities; possible exercise of outstanding options and warrants; or contingent issuance of stock of the investee.

8

PRACTICAL TECHNIQUES FOR STATISTICAL SAMPLING

Statistical methods were developed to permit analysts to reach conclusions in situations where the only available information about the population was that derived from their own statistical tests. Accordingly, statisticians were not content to be concerned only with the validity, compatibility, and integrity of the sample data, but delved into the science of mathematics to come up with abstruse mathematical principles that would permit of a high degree of reliability in their conclusions.

Generally, the auditor is neither a statistician nor a mathematician, and cannot be expected to be equipped to cope with the intellectual demands inherent in the solution of complex statistical problems. However, the purpose of statistical sampling in auditing differs significantly from its purpose in other fields because the sample is not the auditor's only source of information about the population. Consequently, the auditor need not be concerned with achieving the high level of reliability required in the solution of conventional statistical problems. At the same time, neither does he need to be versed in all the ramifications of statistical propositions and solutions.

The purpose of this chapter is to provide a methodological routine that will permit the auditor to set up statistical tests and evaluate their results without any reference to the mathematical concepts involved. To that end, step-by-step techniques are demonstrated, and are designed to allow the auditor to project the factors of his own sampling problems into the format provided and then arrive at a satisfactory conclusion by completing the steps outlined in the model.

PURPOSE OF STATISTICAL SAMPLING

The purpose of statistical sampling is to provide the auditor with an objective method of testing and to furnish him with a mathematically valid means of measuring the precision and reliability of the results. The objectivity inherent in the statistical process does not obviate the auditor's broad responsibility for subjective judgmental decisions. In the first place, all tests are not susceptible to statistical interpretation, and therefore the auditor must make a choice of testing methods. If he chooses the objective statistical process, he must still decide what degree of precision limits and confidence level will demonstrate that he has exercised due care in his examination. Even after the results are in, his original decisions are subject to his reconsideration because he may decide, for example, that a precision limit not quite achieved is, nevertheless, satisfactory; or, in another instance, he may decide that even though precision limits and confidence levels specified in his sampling plan are attained, nevertheless, the errors observed require further investigation of the circumstances that permit the deviation.

STATISTICAL SAMPLING PLANS

The following statistical techniques are described and illustrated in this chapter:

Sampling for Attributes

This sampling process reveals the frequency of occurrence of a particular error, (qualitative characteristic), in the sample and permits an estimate to be made of the percentage of elements in the total population[1] that contains similar errors.

Discovery Sampling

Discovery sampling gives the auditor assurance that if no errors (qualitative characteristics) are found in his sample, the percentage of elements in the population that contains similar errors does not exceed a specified limit.

Variables Sampling

This method of sampling permits the auditor to estimate the total value of the population by determining the value of the samples selected for examination.

Stratified Sampling

Stratified sampling is a variation of variables sampling that requires the auditor to take samples from various segments of the population and permits him to estimate the total value of the population by determining the value of the samples selected from each segment.

THE ESSENTIALS OF STATISTICAL SAMPLING

The essence and very nature of statistical sampling as a valid auditing tool consists of the following essentials:

1. Samples are selected at random from the total population.
2. The quantity of samples observed is sufficient to support a conclusion at specified precision limits and confidence levels.
3. Determination of the required sample size and evaluation of the results of observation of the samples arise from appropriate mathematical procedures based on the laws of probability.

The principles of random sampling are discussed in the next section of this chapter, and the problems illustrated in later sections demonstrate a methodology for computing the required sample size, and the evaluation of results of observation, in accordance with appropriate mathematical laws of probability.

PRINCIPLES OF RANDOM SAMPLING

The method of selecting samples for a statistical problem is just as important as the mathematical theorems applied to its solution. The principles of random selection are outlined in the paragraphs that follow.

RANDOM SELECTION OF SAMPLES

The tables in this book are based on the mathematical laws of probability and are valid only for sampling plans where the samples are drawn on a random, or "probability," basis. The dictionary definition of "random" comprehends the word "haphazard" and is misleading when noted in connection with random selection as defined for the purpose of statistical sampling. Haphazard, judgmental selection of samples completely invalidates the use of the tables contained in this volume.

Random sampling for statistical analysis purposes requires that each element in the population, or subpopulation, have an equal opportunity for inclusion in the sample.

There are two basic methods of drawing samples: random number sampling and systematic sampling; and these two methods can be applied either as unrestricted random sampling or as stratified random sampling.

RANDOM NUMBER SAMPLING

Random number sampling generally requires the use of a random number table. In such tables there is approximately an equal number of digits from 0 through 9, and the order in which the digits appear is completely random. The tables consist of a column at the extreme left (which is used solely for identifying lines in the table) and five-digit

[1]In statistical literature the total body of data to be observed is referred to variously as "population," "universe," "field." All three words are synonymous and are used interchangeably. In this volume "population" is most often used.

numbers listed in columns to the right of the identifying column. These columns are numbered from 1 to 14 in a line at the top of the page. However, the columnar divisions have no significance except as a visual aid.

The auditor should clearly outline in writing a plan of section that includes the following.

Correspondence

He should describe the method of identifying the random number selected with the sample to be observed. For example, if the auditor is examining invoices numbered from 1 to 400, the selected random numbers would correspond with the invoice numbers. If the population elements are not numbered, the auditor must number them in order to have the required correspondence between the random number selected and the related population element.

Starting Point

The auditor should describe the method of selecting his starting point in the tables and label it as, for example, page 6, line 10, column 14." The starting point must be a random selection. This can be accomplished by making a "blind stab" at the table and starting from there. A perhaps better way is to use some random number, like the serial number of a randomly selected dollar bill, and to segregate the numbers thereon to represent the page, the line, and the column in the table from which he will start his selection.

Route

The route should be described in advance and should indicate whether the numbers will be selected downward, upward, across, etc.

Numbers Used in Correspondence

The auditor should indicate what numbers in the columns will be used in correspondence to the number of the elements in the sample. For example, he might use the last three numbers in the column, or the first two, or the last two in the column and the first two in the adjacent column, etc.

The following case demonstrates the use of Table 16 of Appendix II in the selection of random numbers:

1. The problem is to select random numbers that will correspond with samples to be drawn from invoices numbered from 1 to 75.
2. The serial number of a randomly selected dollar bill indicates that the starting point will be on line 1467, column 4.
3. The route to be followed will be down the column to the bottom of the page, and continue with the first number at the top of the page in the column adjacent to the right.
4. The numbers to be used in correspondence are to be the last digit in the column and the first digit in the column adjacent to the right.

Reference to Table 16 reveals that the following numbers are selected, or were rejected as being of greater magnitude than the numbers on the invoices to be tested:

Lead Column	Adjacent Column	Rejected—Exceeds 75	Selected
93362	46063		24
53751	80925		18
71109	12758	91	
61101	13373		11
45421	08755		10
21812	47574		24
85260	15936		1
27845	89662		58
99113	60898		36
01385	03650		50
70068	44249	84	
79899	79340	97	
23068	10820	81	
77078	38993	83	
40119	10822	91	
41118	45281	84	
32776	90315		69

The ten invoices indicated above would comprise the sample to be used in this statistical test.

SYSTEMATIC SAMPLING

The process of systematic sampling requires the selection of samples at uniform intervals, using a random start. For example, if ten samples are required from one hundred invoices numbered from

1 to 100, and the random starting point is 4, the invoices selected would be numbers 14, 24, 34, 44, 54, 64, 74, 84, and 94.

Randomness is increased when several random starts are made, and the uniform interval increased in proportion to the number of starts.

RANDOM SYSTEMATIC SAMPLING

The technique of *random* systematic sampling requires the selection of samples at random intervals, which are based on the average interval derived by dividing the population by the number of samples to be drawn. Random numbers are drawn between 1 and 2 times the average interval, and the numbers drawn represent the intervals between the instant sample and the preceding sample. An example of random systematic sampling follows:

Problem

To select ten samples from one hundred invoices numbered from 1 to 100 by a random systematic method.

Average Interval

2 x 10 = 20

Starting Point

Selected by use of serial number on dollar bill, as previously described. Line 1451, Column 2 (Table 16).

Route

Downward in column to bottom of page, continuing with first number at top of page in column adjacent to the right.

Numbers Used in Correspondence

Last two digits in column.

Numbers Selected between 1 and 20 from Table 16

10, 12, 13, 2, 20, 3, 9, 17, 9, 17

Correspondence of Number Selected to Invoice to Be Examined

The numbers listed above indicate the interval between samples to be selected. The selection would be scheduled as follows:

Sample Element	Interval	Invoice to be Selected
1	–	10
2	12	22
3	13	35
4	2	37
5	20	57
6	3	60
7	9	69
8	17	86
9	9	95
10	17	–

The auditor would select the invoices having numbers indicated in the last column above. The interval between the last two invoices makes the last interval extend beyond the number of invoices in the population, (No. 112), therefore the auditor must add one more sample, selected at random from the total population by means of random procedures previously described.

UNRESTRICTED AND STRATIFIED RANDOM SAMPLING

Unrestricted random sampling means random sampling of the *total* population. Stratified random sampling refers to random sampling of segments of the population. The use of unrestricted random sampling is illustrated in all the problems in this chapter, except the problem on stratified sampling, which, of course, illustrates the process of stratification and the use of stratified random sampling.

BIAS IN SELECTING SAMPLES

The auditor must ascertain that no bias attends his selection of random samples. The danger of bias is inherent in systematic sampling. For example, if a payroll register listed the same number of employees each week, a systematic sample might select the same employee for each sample drawn. Also, if the operations of the company being audited are of a cyclical nature, systematic sampling would tend to select too many samples from the slow period and too few from periods of intense activity. The auditor must analyze each situation to determine that the samples are representative of the population.

SAMPLES DRAWN WITH REPLACEMENT AND WITHOUT REPLACEMENT

Samples drawn with replacement means that a sample drawn once is put back in the population and can be drawn again. Therefore, it is possible that the auditor might use the same sample twice in tabulating his observations.

Samples drawn without replacement means that once a sample is drawn it is removed from the population and cannot be drawn again.

The tables for the various sampling processes described in this volume are designed to accommodate replacement as follows:

Sampling for Attributes	– With or Without Replacement
Discovery Sampling	– Without Replacement
Variables Sampling	– With Replacement
Stratified Random Sampling	– Without Replacement

THE APPROACH TO SAMPLING

The approach to statistical sampling and evaluation of results taken by the author in this chapter is similar to the approach taken in the Individual Study Program prepared by the Professional Development Division of the American Institute of Certified Public Accountants in a series of books entitled "An Auditor's Approach to Statistical Sampling." Tables 1 through 15 in Appendix II are reproduced from that volume with permission granted by the Institute.

Table No. 16, "Random Numbers," is a single page taken from "Table of 105,000 Random Decimal Digits," Bureau of Transport Economics and Statistics, Interstate Commerce Commission. This booklet is now out of print. However, the reader may obtain free a booklet "Guidelines for the Presentation of the Results of Sample Studies," Statement No. 71-1 from the Interstate Commerce Commission, Bureau of Economics, Washington, DC, 20423, which contains similar random number tables.

SAMPLING FOR ATTRIBUTES

The objective of sampling for attributes is to determine, from a sample, the estimated frequency of occurrence of some qualitative characteristic in the population. For example, the population might be all the sales invoices prepared during an accounting period, and the qualitative characteristic whose frequency of occurrence is desired to be tested could be errors in the pricing of individual invoices. The frequency of occurrence can be approximated for any kind of qualitative characteristic, or attribute, that is determinable from a sample. The list shown here offers examples of particular characteristics of the elements of the indicated populations that can be tested by the technique of statistical sampling for attributes.

Population	Characteristic to be Sampled
Sales Invoices	Billing errors.
Sales Invoices	Balances under $10.00.
Accounts Receivable	Overdue accounts.
Accounts Receivable	Errors in account balances—(determined from confirmation requests).
Inventory	Slow-moving items.
Inventory	Errors in pricing.
Inventory	Errors in quantities.
Vendors' Invoices	Errors in amounts.
Cash Disbursements	Errors in distributing charges.
Voucher Register	Errors in distributing charges.
Checks	Lack of documentary support.

The list could go on. However, the experienced auditor will know, in any audit engagement, what populations and what characteristics of the elements therein he wants to test.

SAMPLING PLAN

Prior to starting his sampling procedures, the

auditor must set up a definite sampling plan in which he specifies the following:

1. Method of selecting random samples.
2. Definition of the population.
3. Definition of the occurrence to be observed.
4. Required confidence level.
5. Required upper precision level.

The method of selecting the random sample should be in accordance with the principles set forth earlier in this chapter.

PRECISION LIMITS AND CONFIDENCE LEVEL

The frequency of occurrence of any attribute in a population can be expressed as a percentage of the total population. The auditor must decide on how close it is necessary to estimate the actual, though unknown, rate of error. If, for example, he decides that he would be satisfied with an estimate within 2% of the actual frequency, the 2% becomes the "precision limits" of his sampling plan.

The auditor must then decide on how many chances out of 100 he is willing to risk that the percentage of occurrence found in the sample will actually be within the precision limits of 2% from the true frequency existing in the population. If, for example, he is willing to accept ten chances in a hundred that his estimate is incorrect, then the "confidence level" of his sampling plan is 90%.

REQUIRED SAMPLE SIZE

In frequency tests a sample should be drawn that is large enough to permit valid statistical evaluation of the results. This required sample size is a function of the actual percentage of frequencies in the population. Since the population frequency is unknown, it becomes necessary to *estimate* a frequency rate that can be used in the determination of the required sample size. If the auditor has had prior experience with the type of data he is examining, an estimated rate of occurrence could be based on that experience. However, if he has no idea of the possible frequency rate, he can select a preliminary sample of 50 elements in the population, determine the number of occurrences found in the sample, and calculate an estimated frequency rate from that data. For example, if two occurrences are found in a sample of 50, the estimated frequency rate would be 4%.

DETERMINING THE REQUIRED SAMPLE SIZE

After the auditor has estimated a frequency rate, he can go to prepared tables and determine the sample size required to statistically validate conclusions about the population that can be drawn from his full sample. The required sample size can be determined from the tables in Appendix II by the following steps:

1. Select the table for the confidence level that corresponds with the confidence level required in the sampling plan.
2. Find the line reflecting various precision percentages and select the column whose heading coincides with the precision limits specified in the sampling plan.
3. Follow this column downward until he finds the frequency rate either estimated by him, or computed from a preliminary sample.
4. Follow to the left the line intersected by the column at the frequency rate.
5. The required sample size is shown in the extreme left column, which is conveniently headed "Required Sample Size."

EVALUATION OF RESULTS

After the additional samples have been drawn, examined, and the number of observed occurrences tabulated, the results must be evaluated by reference to the tables designed for such evaluation and found in Appendix II. This evaluation may be accomplished by the following steps:

1. Select the table that corresponds to the confidence level specified in the sampling plan.
2. From the extreme left column select the line indicating the sample size of the full sample.
3. Follow to the right on this line until the figure for the *number* of occurrences found in the full sample appears.
4. At the intersection of the sample size line and the column having the number of actual occurrences, read the column heading found in the line for precision percentage at the top of the table. The percentage shown in the heading is the upper precision limit of the sample.

AUDITOR'S CONCLUSION

The auditor cannot extrapolate directly from the sample to the population because, from his sample alone, he cannot calculate the value of the functions lying beyond an interval from values of the functions observed within that interval. However, a process of inductive reasoning, based largely on laws of probability, will permit him to make inferences from the mathematical relationships to the population that are determined from observations of the sample. Therefore, at the conclusion of his sampling procedure, he can state that frequencies of an occurrence in a population do not exceed a given percentage at a particular level of confidence.

NONSAMPLING ERROR

Mistakes and errors made in examining the items in the sample are referred to by statisticians as "nonsampling error." The risk involved in nonsampling error is not subject to measurement simply because the errors are not detectible. However, the same risk would exist even though the total data in the population was examined. The auditor must recognize the possibility that results obtained from observation of samples may be inaccurate because of the presence of nonsampling error; and it should behoove him to make sure that his examination procedures are designed to reduce the possibility of nonsampling error to a minimum.

ILLUSTRATION OF SAMPLING FOR ATTRIBUTES

The following model case illustrates the application of sampling for attributes.

The Situation

A wholesale distributor of machinery parts and supplies publishes a catalog containing individual product prices and a schedule of graduated quantity discounts. Sales and accounts receivable are accounted for by an in-house computer. Quantities, prices, and discounts must be key-punched for each individual sales invoice; extensions are made by the computer. Adequate control is not maintained over key-punch operations. Sales invoices are designated for the current year by the letter G, and are numbered sequentially from 00001 to 10200.

The Problem

The problem at a year-end audit date was to test the frequency of errors in applying correct quantities, prices, and discounts to customers' invoices for the entire year. The quantities were to be checked to the shipping orders, and the prices and discounts were to be checked to the company's catalog.

Desired Confidence Level and Precision Limits

The auditor wished to be 90% confident that the frequency of errors in applying correct quantities and prices to sales invoices did not exceed 5%, respectively, and that the frequency of errors in assigning correct discounts did not exceed 10%.

SAMPLING PROCEDURE

1. The problem required three separate tests, all of which were made from the same sample. An error found in one test would have no effect on the other two tests. The factors of the problem, and the assurance required, are tabulated below.

	Quantities	Prices	Discounts
Population	10,200 Sales Invoices	10,200 Sales Invoices	10,200 Sales Invoices
Frequency to Be Tested	Incorrect Quantity on Invoice	Incorrect Price on Invoice	Incorrect Discount on Invoice
Required Confidence Level	90%	90%	90%
Acceptable Upper Precision Percentages	5%	5%	10%
Estimated Frequency of Occurrence	Unknown	Unknown	Unknown

2. In this case there was no basis on which to estimate a percentage of occurrence rate. Therefore, a random selection of 50 items was made as a preliminary sample, with the following results:

Test	Sample Size	Actual Number of Errors Found in Sample	Percentage of Occurrences in Sample
Quantities	50	1	2%
Prices	50	0	None
Discounts	50	2	4%

3. Based on the estimated percentage of occurrences revealed in the preliminary sample, reference to the table for determination of sample size at the 90% confidence level (Table 3) indicated the following required sample sizes:

Test	Acceptable Upper Precision Percentage Limit	Percentage of Occurrences in Sample	Required Sample Size
Quantities	5%	2%	160
Prices	5%	None	50
Discounts	10%	4%	70

4. Since the sample size of 160 required to evaluate the quantities test was in excess of the required sample size for the other two tests, it was decided to completely examine all 160 samples for all three tests simultaneously. Therefore, an additional 110 samples were selected at random, and the actual number of errors observed in the total of 160 samples was as follows:

Quantities	2
Prices	0
Discounts	3

5. Reference to the table for evaluation of results at the 90% confidence level (Table 8) revealed the following upper precision percentages indicated by the occurrences in the samples:

Test	Sample Size	Number of Occurrences in Sample	Upper Precision Percentages
Quantities	160	2	4%
Prices	160	0	2%
Discounts	160	3	5%

6. The complete series of tests and results are tabulated below:

	Quantities	Prices	Discounts
Required Confidence Level	90%	90%	90%
Acceptable Upper Precision Percentage Limits	5%	5%	10%
Preliminary Sample	50	50	50
Actual Number of Errors in Preliminary Sample	1	0	2
Percentage of Occurrences in Preliminary Sample	2%	None	4%
Required Sample Size	160	50	70
Actual Samples Tested	160	160	160
Number of Errors In Total Sample	2	0	3
Upper Precision Limit Indicated by Table 8	4%	2%	5%

7. The tests satisfied the auditor's requirements, and he could make the following statements:

a. Errors in recording quantities on customers' invoices do not exceed 4%, at a confidence level of 90%.

b. Errors in the prices recorded on customers' invoices do not exceed 2%, at a confidence level of 90%.

c. Errors in appying discounts to customers' invoices do not exceed 5%, at a confidence level of 90%.

DISCOVERY SAMPLING

Discovery sampling is a variation of sampling for attributes that provides assurance, at a prescribed confidence level, that if occurrences in the population exceed a specified frequency percentage, at least one occurrence will be found in the required sample. For example, if an auditor wishes to assure himself that there is a 99% chance that errors in cutting the amount on checks do not exceed .5%, this assurance is derived when he has examined the required sample and found no deviations. If *one* occurrence is found, the test indicates that occurrences exceed the desired frequency percentage and is a clue that further investigation may be necessary to determine the circumstances that permitted the deviation. Discovery sampling generally is used where a low percentage of deviations is expected by the auditor because of the effectiveness of internal control, or where a single occurrence in the population would indicate a critical situation. Examples of critical deviations include differences between the balance in a depositor's passbook and the balance in the financial institution's records; the difference in amount between that shown on a duplicate check and that paid by the depository; the difference between the certificate numbers shown on marketable securities examined and the certificate numbers recorded on the company's books; and many other situations that might indicate embezzlement, gross negligence, or defalcation of the records.

SAMPLING PLAN

The auditor should prepare a schedule describing his sampling plan, in which he sets forth the following:

1. Method of selecting random samples.
2. Definition of the population.
3. Definition of the occurrence to be observed.
4. Required confidence level.
5. Maximum tolerable frequency percentage.
6. Estimated size of population.

As in attribute sampling, the method of selecting the random sample should conform to the principles set forth earlier in this chapter. Unlike the procedure for sampling for attributes, the sampling plan of discovery sampling must include the approximate population size in order to calculate the required sample size.

DETERMINING THE REQUIRED SAMPLE SIZE

When the auditor has determined the maximum tolerable frequency percentage and the confidence level that will satisfy his sampling requirements, the required sample size can be determined by the following steps, using Tables 11, 12 and 13 in Appendix II:

1. Select the table that corresponds to the population size.
2. Select the column headed by the maximum tolerable occurrence rate, shown on the line indicating the true rate of population occurrence.
3. Follow this column downward until the desired confidence level appears.
4. Follow to the left the line on which the confidence level intersects the true rate of occurrence.
5. The required sample size is shown in the extreme left column headed "Sample Size."

EVALUATION OF RESULTS

The primary objective of discovery sampling is to give assurance that if particular characteristics of elements in the population exceed a specified frequency rate, at least *one* such characteristic would be observed in the required sample. If there are no occurrences found in the sample, then the auditor can conclude that the frequency rate does not exceed that specified in the sampling plan and his objective has been accomplished. If there are one or more occurrences, then the auditor must decide whether or not to investigate the circumstances that compelled the deviation.

COMBINED DISCOVERY AND ATTRIBUTE SAMPLING

The techniques of discovery sampling are generally employed to discover critical errors or deviations. However, the samples selected for the discovery sampling plan can also be used to evaluate noncritical errors in accordance with the principles of attribute sampling. For example, if a discovery sampling plan is designed to detect a critical error such as a difference between the amount shown on a depositor's passbook and the amount on the financial institution's records, the frequency of noncritical errors such as incorrect names, addresses, account numbers, failure to have dividends entered in passbooks, etc. could also be tabulated from an examination of the same sample used in the discovery sampling plan. The frequency of the noncritical errors could then be evaluated by reference to the tables for required sample size and evaluation of results applicable to attribute sampling procedure as discussed earlier in this chapter.

ILLUSTRATION OF DISCOVERY SAMPLING

The process of discovery sampling is demonstrated in the following illustrative problem.

The Situation

At a year-end audit date the subsidiary ledger trial balance of a savings and loan association indicated that the association had balances in 20,000 depositors' accounts. These savings accounts were accounted for by on-line operations with a computer service center. The service center provided daily subsidiary ledger trial balances and it could produce confirmation forms for individual savings accounts selected on a systematic basis for any number of random starts.

The Problem

The problem was to confirm that number of depositors' accounts sufficient to disclose at least one error if such occurrences in the total population were likely to exceed the acceptable precision percentage limit at the confidence level desired by the auditor.

Error Defined

An error in this case was defined as a constructive difference between the balance recorded on the computer for an individual depositor and the balance evidenced by that depositor's passbook.

Desired Confidence Level and Precision Limit

The auditor wished to be 99% confident that such errors did not exist in more than one-half of one percent of 20,000 savings accounts held by the association.

SAMPLING PROCEDURE

1. The problem was analyzed as follows:

Population Size	20,000
Desired Confidence Level	99%
Acceptable Precision Percentage Limit	.5%

The auditor consulted the discovery sampling table for populations over 10,000 (Table 11). He selected the column showing a true rate of occurrence of .5%. By proceeding downward in that column, he found that the first incidence of a confidence level of 99% appeared on a line that indicated a required sample size of 900. In order to have additional assurance, the auditor elected to use a sample size of 1,000.

2. The auditor had the computer service center prepare 1,000 confirmation requests that were systematically selected from ten random starts.

3. The replies to the confirmation requests disclosed various types of differences, such as incorrect addresses, misspelled names, failure of the depositor to have dividends recorded in his passbook, etc. There were no errors, as defined for this test.

4. Since no errors were discovered from his sample, the assurance requirements of the auditor were satisfied and he could state, with 99% confidence, that differences between individual account balances shown in the association's records and the related balances evidenced by the passbooks of the respective depositors were not likely to exist in more than one-half of one percent of the 20,000 savings accounts held by the association.

5. The auditor could also make statements concerning each occurrence interval on the line with a sample size of 1,000. For example, he could state that errors are not likely to exceed—

.3% at a confidence level of 95%
.2% at a confidence level of 86%
.1% at a confidence level of 63%

EVALUATION OF OTHER ATTRIBUTE FREQUENCIES OBSERVED IN THE SAMPLE

For purposes of illustration, it is assumed that the auditor wished to evaluate the frequency of occurrence in the sample of the following noncritical errors: names, addresses, and account numbers. He wished to be 95% confident that the frequency rate for each of the three errors did not exceed 5%. From past experience he estimated that the expected frequency of all three did not exceed 3%. From Table 2 he determined that an estimated frequency rate of 3% at a confidence level of 95% with an upper acceptable precision limit of 5% required a sample of 460. Since the 1,000 samples required for his discovery sampling plan exceeded the sample size required for the attribute plan, he determined to examine all 1,000 samples for the noncritical errors defined in the attribute plan and to evaluate the individual results.

Examination of the 1,000 samples revealed the following noncritical errors.

Attribute	Number of Occurrences
1. Incorrect name.	8
2. Incorrect address.	20
3. Incorrect account number.	2

Reference to the table for evaluation of results at the 95% confidence level (Table 7) revealed the upper precision percentages shown in the schedule below:

Test	Sample Size	Number of Occurrences in Sample	Upper Precision Percentages
Names	1,000	8	2%
Addresses	1,000	20	3%
Account Numbers	1,000	2	1%

The tests satisfied the auditor's requirements and he could make the following statement:

> At a confidence level of 95%, errors in the savings and loan association's records concerning names, addresses, and account numbers did not exceed 2%, 3%, and 1%, respectively.

VARIABLES SAMPLING

The statistical method used to estimate dollar values is known as "variables sampling." Variables sampling permits the auditor to project dollar-value estimates by determining the average value of a small number of samples from the population. For example, if an auditor randomly selects 50 samples from an inventory of 2,000 items and finds that the total value of the 50 items is $2,800, he can divide 50 into $2,800 to arrive at an average sample value of $56. He then can estimate the total value of the inventory to be $112,000 by multiplying the average sample value of $56 by the 2,000 items in the inventory.

STANDARD DEVIATION

The measure used in variables estimation is the arithmetic mean of the sample elements. However, the range of values of the elements in the population creates a degree of variability that must be measured before estimating the total value from the arithmetic mean. Statisticians have developed a measurement called the "standard deviation," which provides a factor in the formula to allow for different degrees of variability.

There are two frequently used methods of computing the standard deviation, as follows.

Range Method

The standard deviation can be estimated by selecting a random sample of 50 elements from the population and separating them into groups of six or seven elements each. The range, or differences between the highest and lowest values, is obtained for each group and then averaged for all groups.

The resulting average range is then divided by an appropriate d_2 factor to obtain the estimated standard deviation.

Sum-of-the-Squares Method

The other widely used method, and the one that will be used and illustrated in this volume, is sometimes known as the sum-of-the-squares method. To use this method for estimating the standard deviation, the auditor selects 30 random samples from the population; determines the value of the sample mean; determines the square of the deviation from the mean for each sample element; obtains the sum of the squared deviations; divides this sum by the number of elements in the population, minus 1; and takes the square root of the dividend. The result is the estimated standard deviation.

A shortcut method permits computation of the sum of the squares of the sample values rather than the sum of squares of the deviation from the sample mean. In this instance, the square of the arithmetic mean is multiplied by the number of elements in the sample, and the result is subtracted from the sum of the squares of the sample values. The value obtained from the above operation is then divided by the number of elements in the population, minus 1, and the square root of the resulting dividend is the estimated standard deviation.

The shortcut method is fully demonstrated in Charts II and III of the illustrative problem for variables sampling that follows.

PRECISION LIMITS AND CONFIDENCE LEVEL

The degree of precision desired by the auditor must be determined in advance, since it is a factor in determining the required sample size. The prescribed precision limits must be stated in dollars; that is, plus or minus so many dollars.

The confidence level is a function of the precision limits in evaluating results of the statistical test. It is also a factor in computing the required sample size. Therefore, it must be determined in advance by the auditor and stated as a percentage. If, for example, the auditor wants to be assured that 90 times out of 100 the true value of the population would be contained within his prescribed precision limits, his desired confidence level would be 90%.

REQUIRED SAMPLE SIZE

The method of determining the required sample size suggested in this volume requires the solution of a formula in which the required sample size is the square of a fraction in which the precision limit is the denominator and the standard deviation of the population, the confidence coefficient, and the number of elements in the population are factors of the numerator. The methodology of solving the equation is fully demonstrated in Chart IV in the illustrative problem.

STANDARD ERROR OF THE MEAN

Statisticians have devised a formula for measuring the deviation of the sampling mean from the true population mean. This value is known as the "standard error of the mean" and is derived by dividing the standard deviation of the sample by the square root of the number of elements in the sample.

U VALUES (CONFIDENCE COEFFICIENT)

The standard deviation is the only variable in the formula for the normal distribution curve. Therefore, statisticians are able to determine the proportion of the area under the curve and thus the percentage of observations contained within any given distance measured from the arithmetic mean. The U values in Table 14 of Appendix II are based on the distance from the arithmetic mean in terms of the standard error of the mean, and the percentage of observations (samples) contained in the area under the curve. Thus, it can be seen from the table that in 65% of cases the difference between the sample mean and the true population mean will not exceed .93 times the standard error of the mean. The use of Table 14 in the evaluation of results is demonstrated in Charts VIII and IX of the illustrative problem.

CONVERSION OF U VALUES TO CONFIDENCE PERCENTAGES

The values in Table 15 of Appendix II have been prepared to permit the easy conversion of U values to confidence percentages. For example, line 9 in Chart VIII shows that the result of dividing the maximum allowable deviation between sample and population means by the standard error of the mean is 1.35. Table 15 shows that the conversion of this value (U value) to a confidence percentage indicates a confidence level of 82%.

EVALUATION OF RESULTS

The confidence level is a function of the precision limits in the mathematical evaluation of the results of variables sampling. Therefore, determination of the confidence level is computed at a given precision limit, and, conversely, precision is computed at a given confidence level. The method of evaluation prescribed in this volume is described below, and fully demonstrated in the illustrative problem that follows.

Confidence Level

The confidence level is determined by dividing the number of elements in the total population into the desired precision limits and then dividing the result by the standard error of the mean. The result of this computation is referred to the conversion table for U values (Table 15) to determine the confidence level for the specified precision limits.

Precision Limits

The confidence coefficient that corresponds to the desired confidence level is found from the tables (Table 14). This value is multiplied by the standard error of the mean and the result is then multiplied by the total number of elements in the population to arrive at the dollar value of the precision limits at the specified confidence level.

ILLUSTRATION OF VARIABLES SAMPLING

The technique of variables sampling tests is demonstrated in the following problem.

The Situation

A wholesale distributor of machinery parts and supplies maintains a perpetual inventory record. At a year-end audit date, after all adjustments had been made for physical count variations, the final inventory listing carried 8,000 lots at a total cost of $4,800,000.

The company also bills the customer for freight charges and credits him with discount on the respective sales invoices. At audit date 20,000 customers' invoices had been prepared during the year; all of the invoices reflected discounts; and 6,000 invoices included a billing for freight charges. An additional copy of each invoice having freight charges was filed numerically in a separate file. The general ledger balances for sales discounts and freight charges collected at year-end were $450,000 and $210,000, respectively.

The Problem

The auditor wishes to test the required number of inventory lots necessary to enable him to project the value of the items tested to an approximation of the total value of the inventory. He also wishes to test sufficient sales invoices to permit him to project the estimated total sales discounts allowed and the total freight charges collected from customers. The test of inventory requires verification by physical count of the lots selected; the freight test requires verification of the sample items by examination of the related freight bills; and the test of discounts requires verification of the test items by reference to a graduated discount schedule.

Desired Confidence Level and Precision Limits

The auditor wishes to be 80% confident that the projected inventory value is within $240,000 of its actual value; 90% confident that the projected values for freight charges and discounts allowed are within $10,500 and $22,500 of their respective actual values.

SAMPLING PROCEDURE

The auditor's requirements as to confidence levels and precision limits, and the other known factors of the sampling problem, should be stated in a reference chart, as shown in Chart I.

CHART I—SAMPLING REFERENCE MEMORANDA				
		Inventory Test	Freight Test	Discount Test
1.	Total value—per books	4,800,000	210,000	450,000
2.	Number of elements in population	8,000	6,000	20,000
3.	Preliminary sample size	30	30	30
4.	Required confidence level	80%	90%	90%
5.	Acceptable precision limit	240,000	10,500	22,500

SUM OF SAMPLE ELEMENTS AND SUM OF SQUARES OF SAMPLE ELEMENTS—PRELIMINARY SAMPLE

When 30 samples have been drawn for each test in accordance with the principles of random sampling, the total value of the samples, and the total value of the squares of the samples, should be determined so that these values will be available for computing the standard deviation. Chart II demonstrates the method of computing these values for the inventory test. Values for the freight and discount tests should be computed in like manner. For the purposes of this problem, it is assumed that the values for the freight and discount tests were computed, and the results of the computations are summarized at the foot of Chart II.

STANDARD DEVIATION—PRELIMINARY SAMPLE

The standard deviation is determined by the following computations:

1. Divide the sum of the sample elements by the number of elements in the sample to arrive at the sample arithmetic mean.
2. Square the arithmetic mean.
3. Multiply the square of the arithmetic mean by the number of elements in the sample.
4. Subtract the values developed in Step 3 above from the sum of the sample squares.
5. Divide the value found in Step 4 above by the number of sample elements, minus one.
6. The standard deviation is the square root of the value found in Step 5 above.

Chart III demonstrates the computation of the standard deviation for the problem at hand.

REQUIRED SAMPLE SIZE

The required sample size is computed by the steps shown beneath Chart III on page 183.

CHART II—COMPUTATION OF THE SUM OF SAMPLE ELEMENTS AND THE SUM OF THE SQUARES OF SAMPLE ELEMENTS

1. Detailed Illustration of Computation of Values of Sample Elements for Inventory Test.

Product Number	Sample Value	Square of Sample Value
98-169	917	840,889
36-765	48	2,304
72-938	729	531,441
17-885	125	15,625
01-116	304	92,416
48-541	325	105,625
48-94	914	835,396
63-821	296	87,616
08-584	330	108,900
58-151	255	65,025
11-728	744	553,536
13-766	975	950,625
62-38	59	3,481
27-982	706	498,436
33-121	159	25,281
99-527	430	184,900
72-151	427	182,329
21-228	1,256	1,577,536
29-277	717	514,089
41-146	149	22,201
24-964	562	315,844
56-320	946	894,916
84-529	232	53,824
01-228	743	552,049
36-088	1,669	2,785,561
81-292	1,502	2,256,004
56-135	810	656,100
69-786	588	345,744
44-879	359	128,881
61-285	1,203	1,447,209
Totals	(a) **18,479**	(b) **16,633,783**

2. Summary of Sample Values of Respective Tests—Computed in the Same Manner as That Used for the Inventory Test.

	Inventory Test	Freight Test	Discount Test
(a) Sum of Values of Sample Elements	18,479	1,050	690
(b) Sum of Sample Squares	16,633,783	53,454	23,294

CHART III—COMPUTATION OF STANDARD DEVIATION

		Inventory Test	Freight Test	Discount Test
1.	Sum of sample elements—(line 2(a), Chart II)	18,479	1,050	690
2.	Sum of sample squares—(line 2Ab), Chart II)	16,633,783	53,454	23,294
3.	Number of elements in sample—(line 3, Chart I)	30	30	30
4.	Sample arithmetic mean—(line 1 – line 3)	616	35	23
5.	Square of sample arithmetic mean—(line 4 x line 4)	379,456	1,225	529
6.	(line 3 x line 5)	11,383,680	36,750	15,870
7.	(line 2 – line 6)	5,250,103	16,704	7,424
8.	(line 7 – [line 3 – 1])	181,038.03	576	256
9.	Standard deviation—(square root of line 8)	425.5	24	16

1. Multiply the confidence coefficient by the standard deviation.
2. Multiply the number of elements in the population by the value developed in Step 1 above.
3. Divide the value found in Step 2 above by the dollar value of the acceptable precision limits.
4. The required sample size is determined by squaring the value found in Step 3.

Chart IV illustrates the procedure for computing the required sample size for this problem.

COMBINED SAMPLE VALUES

The sum of the sample elements and the sum of the squares of the sample elements of the additional samples must be computed in the manner illustrated in Chart II and combined with the corresponding values of the preliminary sample. For purposes of this problem, it is assumed that these computations were made, and the results are displayed in Charts V and VI.

STANDARD DEVIATION—COMBINED SAMPLE

The standard deviation of the combined sample must be computed in the same manner as that demonstrated in Chart III. This computation is shown in Chart VII.

CHART IV—COMPUTATION OF REQUIRED SAMPLE SIZE

		Inventory Test	Freight Test	Discount Test
1.	Number of elements in population—(line 2, Chart I)	8,000	6,000	20,000
2.	Required confidence level—(line 4, Chart I)	80%	90%	90%
3.	Confidence coefficient—(Table 14)	1.28	1.64	1.64
4.	Standard deviation—(line 9, Chart III)	425.5	24	16
5.	Acceptable precision limits—(line 5, Chart I)	240,000	10,500	22,500
6.	line 3 x line 4	544.6	39.4	26.2
7.	line 6 x line 1	4,356,800	236,400	524,000
8.	line 7 — line 5	18.15	22.5	23.3
9.	Required sample size—square of line 8 (line 8 x line 8)	330	506	543
10.	Assurance sample—(line 9 x 110%)	363	557	598
11.	Number of elements in preliminary sample—(line 3, Chart I)	30	30	30
12.	Required additional sample elements—(line 10 — line 11)	333	527	568

CHART V—EVALUATION OF ADDITIONAL SAMPLE VALUES

		Inventory Test	Freight Test	Discount Test
1.	Number of additional samples drawn—(line 12, Chart IV)	333	527	568
2.	Sum of additional sample elements	199,821	18,660	12,836
3.	Sum of the squares of additional sample elements	179,838,917	991,540	463,550

CHART VI—COMBINED PRELIMINARY AND ADDITIONAL SAMPLE VALUES

		Inventory Test	Freight Test	Discount Test
1.	Sample Elements			
	(a) Preliminary sample—(line 3, Chart I)	30	30	30
	(b) Additional samples drawn—(line 1, Chart V)	333	527	568
	(c) Combined total required sample—(line 10, Chart IV)	363	557	598
2.	Sum of Sample Elements			
	(a) Preliminary sample—(line 2(a), Chart II)	18,479	1,050	690
	(b) Additional samples—(line 2, Chart V)	199,821	18,660	12,836
	(c) Combined total	218,300	19,710	13,526
3.	Sum of Squares of Sample Elements			
	(a) Preliminary sample—(line 2(b), Chart II)	16,633,783	53,454	23,294
	(b) Additional samples—(line 3, Chart V)	179,838,917	991,540	463,550
	(c) Combined total	196,472,700	1,044,994	486,844

CHART VII—COMPUTATION OF STANDARD DEVIATION FROM COMBINED SAMPLE

		Inventory Test	Freight Test	Discount Test
1.	Sum of sample elements—(line 2(c), Chart VI)	218,300	19,710	13,526
2.	Sum of sample squares—(line 3(c), Chart VI)	196,472,700	1,044,994	486,844
3.	Number of elements in sample—(line 1(c), Chart VI)	363	557	598
4.	Sample arithmetic mean—(line 1 — line 3)	601.4	35.4	22.6
5.	Square of sample arithmetic mean—(line 4 x line 4)	361,682	1,254	511
6.	(line 3 x line 5)	131,290,566	698,478	305,578
7.	(line 2 — line 6)	65,182,134	346,516	181,266
8.	(line 7 — [line 3, minus one])	180,061.1	623.2	303.6
9.	Standard deviation—(square root of line 8)	424.3	25	17.4

EVALUATION OF RESULTS—CONFIDENCE LEVEL

The following steps will determine the confidence level obtained in the sampling process:

1. Determine the standard error of the arithmetic mean by dividing the standard deviation by the square root of the number of elements in the sample.
2. Determine the maximum allowable difference between the sample mean and the population mean by dividing the dollar amount of the acceptable precision limits by the number of elements in the population.
3. Divide this maximum allowable difference by the standard error of the mean to arrive at a U factor.
4. Refer to Table 15 to convert the U factor into the confidence level that applies to the computed precision percentage.

   Determination of the confidence level for this problem is illustrated in the Chart VIII.

CHART VIII—EVALUATION OF RESULTS—CONFIDENCE LEVEL

		Inventory Test	Freight Test	Discount Test
1.	Acceptable precision limits—(line 5, Chart I)	240,000	10,500	22,500
2.	Total elements in population—(line 2, Chart I)	8,000	6,000	10,000
3.	Standard deviation—(line 9, Chart VII)	424.3	25	17.4
4.	Number of elements in sample—(line 3, Chart VII)	363	557	598
5.	Square root of number of sample elements—(square root of line 4)	19.05	23.60	24.46
6.	Standard error of the mean—(line 3 – line 5)	22.27	1.06	71
7.	Confidence coefficient—(line 3, Chart IV)	1.28	1.64	1.64
8.	Maximum allowable difference between sample mean and population mean—(line 1 – line 2)	30	1.75	1.125
9.	Maximum allowable deviation between sample and population means divided by standard error of the mean—(line 8 – line 6)	1.35	1.65	1.58
10.	Confidence level at the acceptable precision limits stated on line 1 (from Table 15 for values shown on line 9, above)	82%	90%	88%

EVALUATION OF RESULTS—PRECISION LIMITS

The precision limits at the required confidence level are determined by the following steps:

1. Determine the maximum amount at the required confidence level by which the sample mean will differ from the population mean by multiplying the confidence coefficient by the standard error of the mean.
2. Determine the maximum error at the stated confidence level by multiplying the total elements in the population by the factor developed in Step 2, above. This will be the precision limits at the confidence level required by the auditor.

Chart IX illustrates the above computations for the problem at hand.

CHART IX—EVALUATION OF RESULTS—PRECISION LIMITS

		Inventory Test	Freight Test	Discount Test
1.	Total population—(line 2, Chart I)	8,000	6,000	20,000
2.	Desired confidence level—(line 4, Chart I)	80%	90%	90%
3.	Confidence coefficient—(line 3, Chart IV)	1.28	1.64	1.64
4.	Standard error of the mean—(line 6, Chart VIII)	22.27	1.06	.71
5.	Maximum amounts at stated confidence levels by which the sample mean will differ from the population mean—(line 3 x line 4)	28.51	1.74	1.16
6.	Precision limits at confidence levels stated on line 2 Maximum error, at the stated confidence levels, in estimate of total population—(line 1 x line 5)	228,080	10,440	23,200

EVALUATION OF RESULTS—PROJECTION OF SAMPLE MEAN

The estimated dollar value of the population and the upper and lower precision limits of estimated dollar value can be computed as follows:

1. Multiply the number of elements in the population by the sample arithmetic mean to arrive at the estimated value of the population.
2. Add and subtract the estimated dollar value of the maximum error found in the preceding evaluation of precision limits to determine the upper and lower limits, respectively, of the estimated dollar value of the population at the computed confidence level.

Chart X demonstrates the projection of the dollar value of the population and the projection of the upper and lower limits of the estimated dollar value of the population.

CHART X—EVALUATION OF RESULTS—PROJECTION OF SAMPLE MEAN

		Inventory Test	Freight Test	Discount Test
1.	Number of elements in population—(line 2, Chart I)	8,000	6,000	20,000
2.	Sample arithmetic mean—(line 4, Chart VII)	601.4	35.4	22.6
3.	Value of population projected by sample mean—(line 1 x line 2)	4,811.200	212,400	452,000
4.	Computed precision limits at desired confidence levels—(line 6, Chart IX)	228,080	10,440	23,200
5.	Computed confidence levels at desired precision limits—(line 10, Chart VIII)	82%	90%	88%
6.	Upper limit of estimated total dollar value—(line 3 + line 4)	5,039,280	222,840	475,200
7.	Lower limit of estimated total dollar value—(line 3 – line 4)	4,583,120	201,960	428,800

AUDITOR'S REPORT

Upon completion of Chart X, the auditor can report as follows:

1. The estimate of the total value of the inventory is $4,811,200, plus or minus $228,080 at a confidence level of 82%.
2. The estimated total of freight bills charged to customers is $212,400, plus or minus $10,440 at a confidence level of 90%.
3. The estimated total of discounts allowed customers is $452,000, plus or minus $23,200 at a confidence level of 88%.

Since the statements on the value of the inventory and the total freight charged to customers meet the auditor's requirements, no further sampling in these two tests is necessary. The statement on total discounts, however, reflects an excess of $700 in the required precision limits and a deficiency of 2% in the required confidence level. If desired, the auditor could make further sampling tests either to substantiate the computed confidence level and precision limits, or to determine the precision limits at a higher confidence level. It appears that the reasonable course to take in this situation would be to accept the small deficiency and change the original requirements to correspond with the results of the test.

STRATIFIED SAMPLING

There are many bodies of data that cannot be subjected to unrestricted random sampling for variables because the degree of variability in the population is so great that a satisfactory required sample size cannot be determined. For example, the inventory of a distributor of power tools, miscellaneous machinery, and parts and supplies might contain items ranging in unit price from fifteen cents to twenty-five hundred dollars. In such a situation the extensive range of values of elements in the inventory precludes making a reliable estimate of its true value by a method of unrestricted random sampling. If, however, the inventory were segregated into components of tools, machinery, parts, and supplies, random samples could be drawn from each category and a reliable estimate made of the total population based on evaluation of the results of sampling each inventory classification separately.

The method of segregating the data in the population into groups and making observations from random samples drawn from each category is called "stratified sampling." Stratified random sampling is an extension of the previously described method of sampling for variables. The same principles apply and the only difference in technique is that segments of the population are sampled separately and a final valuation is made by considering the results of each separate sampling process.

The value of stratified sampling is that it can be applied to any population, regardless of its degree of variability, if the population can be segregated into homogeneous components.

ILLUSTRATION OF STRATIFIED RANDOM SAMPLING

The processes of stratified random sampling are demonstrated in the following problem.

The Situation

This problem is based on the preceding problem illustrating variables sampling wherein a wholesale distributor of machinery parts and supplies follows the practice of billing customers for freight charges. At audit date the records showed that $210,000 had been billed to customers for freight charges on a total of 6,000 sales invoices. An additional copy of each sales invoice having freight charges thereon was filed numerically in two separate files—one file for local freight and one for regional freight. The total freight was not classified in the general ledger into local and regional charges, but the number of invoices on which freight had been billed was found from the files to be 4,000 for local freight and 2,000 for regional freight.

The Problem

The auditor wishes to stratify the total freight charges billed to customers into two strata—local and regional—and test the required number of samples to enable him to project the value of the items tested to an approximation of the total amount billed. The test will require examination of the related freight bills.

Desired Confidence Level and Precision Limits

The auditor wishes to be 95% confident that the projected total freight charges billed customers is within $10,500 of the actual total.

SAMPLING PROCEDURE

The auditor's requirements as to confidence level and precision limits, and other known factors of the sampling problem, should be stated in a sampling reference chart.

Chart XI contains the sampling reference memoranda necessary to the solution of the remaining phases of this sampling problem. For purposes of this problem it is assumed, at this point, that a preliminary sample of 30 items has been randomly selected from each of the files for local and regional freight, respectively. It is further assumed that the sum of the values of the sample elements and the sum of the sample squares has been computed for each stratum in a manner similar to that demonstrated in Chart II of the preceding problem, and that the standard deviation of the preliminary sample of each stratum has been computed by the same method as that illustrated in Chart III in the problem on variables sampling.

	CHART XI–SAMPLING REFERENCE MEMORANDA	
1.	Total value, per books	210,000
2.	Total number of elements in population	6,000
3.	Desired confidence level	95%
4.	Confidence coefficient (Table 14)	1.96
5.	Square of confidence coefficient (line 4 x line 4)	3.84
6.	Acceptable precision limits	10,500
7.	Square of acceptable precision limits (line 6 x line 6)	110,250,000
8.	Elements in the population	
	(a) Stratum I —Local Freight Charges	4,000
	(b) Stratum II—Regional Freight Charges	2,000
9.	Preliminary sample size	
	(a) Stratum I	30
	(b) Stratum II	30
10.	Sum of values of sample elements	
	(a) Stratum I	480
	(b) Stratum II	2,280
11.	Arithmetic mean of sample elements	
	(a) Stratum I—(line 10(a) ÷ line 9(a))	16
	(b) Stratum II—(line 10 (b) ÷ line 9(b))	76
12.	Sum of sample squares	
	(a) Stratum I	8,188
	(b) Stratum II	173,280
13.	Standard deviation—computed on preliminary sample	
	(a) Stratum I	5
	(b) Stratum II	25
14.	Square of standard deviation	
	(a) Stratum I—(line 13(a) x line 13(a))	25
	(b) Stratum II–(line 13(b) x line 13(b))	625

ALLOCATION OF STRATA SAMPLE SIZES

An acceptable method of allocating strata sample sizes can be accomplished by the following steps:

1. Multiply the number of elements in the population of each stratum by the standard deviation of each, to arrive at a separate result for each respective stratum.
2. Allocate the strata sample size for each stratum based on the ratio of the separate results arrived at in Step 1 for each stratum, divided by the sum of the two separate results.

This computation is illustrated in Chart XII.

CHART XII—ALLOCATION OF STRATA SAMPLE SIZES

		STRATUM I Local Freight	STRATUM II Regional Freight
1.	Number of elements in population—(line 8, Chart XI)	4,000	2,000
2.	Standard deviation computed on preliminary sample—(line 13, Chart XI)	5	25
3.	Population elements multiplied by standard deviation—(line 1 x line 2)	(a) 20,000	(b) 50,000
4.	Allocation of sample size Stratum I— (line 3(a) divided by sum of line 3(a) and 3(b)) Stratum II— (line 3(b) divided by sum of line 3(a) and 3(b))	.29	71

COMPUTATION OF REQUIRED POPULATION SAMPLE SIZE

The computation of the required sample size for the total population involves the solution of a complex algebraic formula. This formula has been developed by statisticians; it is acceptable for auditing purposes and is applicable to any problem in stratified random sampling. The steps in the solution of the formula are illustrated in Chart XIII.

CHART XIII—COMPUTATION OF REQUIRED SAMPLE SIZE

		STRATUM I	STRATUM II
1.	Number of elements in population—(line 8, Chart XI)	4,000	2,000
2.	Square of standard deviation—(line 14, Chart XI)	25	625
3.	Line 1 x line 2	100,000	1,250,000
4.	Line 1 x line 3	(a) 400,000,000	(b) 2,500,000,000
5.	Sample allocation factors—(line 4, Chart XII)	(a) .29	(b) .71
6.	Line 3 x line 5	(a) 29,000	(b) 887,500
7.	Line 5(b) ÷ line 5(a)		2.45
8.	Line 4(a) x line 7		980,000,000
9.	Line 4(b) + line 8		3,480,000,000
10.	Line 6(a) x line 7		71,050
11.	Line 6(b) + line 10		958,550
12.	Square of acceptable precision limits—(line 7, Chart XI)		110,250,000
13.	Line 12 x line 5(b)		78,277,500
14.	Square of confidence coefficient—(line 5, Chart XI)		3.84
15.	Line 9 x line 14		13,363,200,000
16.	Line 11 x line 14		3,680,832
17.	Line 13 + line 16		81,958,332
18.	Required sample size—(line 15 : line 17)		163

STRATUM SAMPLE SIZES

The required stratum sample sizes are based on the allocation ratios developed in Chart XII applied to the required sample size computed in Chart XIII. Chart XIV shows the required computations.

CHART XIV—STRATUM SAMPLE SIZES

		STRATUM I	STRATUM II
1.	Sample size allocation ratio—(line 4, Chart XII)	.29	.71
2.	Required strata sample sizes (a) Stratum I —(line 1 x line 18, Chart XIII) (b) Stratum II—(line 1 x line 18, Chart XIII)	47.27	115.73
3.	Assurance sample Stratum I —(line 2(a) x 110%)) Stratum II—(line 2(b) x 110%))	52	127
4.	Number of elements in preliminary sample—(line 9, Chart XI)	30	30
5.	Number of elements in additional sample—(line 3 – line 4)	22	97

COMBINED SAMPLE VALUES

The sum of the additional sample elements and the sum of the squares of the additional sample elements must be computed for each stratum by the method illustrated in Chart II of the preceding problem, and the results combined with the corresponding values of the preliminary sample. For the purpose of this problem, it is assumed that these computations were made and the results are shown in Charts XV and XVI.

CHART XV—SUMMARY OF ADDITIONAL SAMPLE VALUES

		STRATUM I	STRATUM II
1.	Number of additional samples drawn—(line 5, Chart XIV)	22	97
2.	Sum of additional sample elements	330	7,250
3.	Sum of squares of additional sample elements	5,583	552,813

CHART XVI—COMBINED PRELIMINARY AND ADDITIONAL SAMPLE VALUES

		STRATUM I	STRATUM II
1.	Sample elements		
	(a) Preliminary sample—(line 9, Chart XI)	30	30
	(b) Additional samples drawn—(line 5, Chart XIV)	22	97
	(c) Combined total	52	127
2.	Sum of sample elements		
	(a) Preliminary sample—(line 10, Chart XI	480	2,280
	(b) Additional sample—(line 2, Chart XV)	330	7,250
	(c) Combined total	810	9,530
3.	Sum of squares of sample values		
	(a) Preliminary sample—(line 12, Chart XI)	8,188	173,280
	(b) Additional sample—(line 3, Chart XV)	5,583	552,813
	(c) Combined total	13,771	726,093
4.	Sample mean—(line 2(c) ÷ line 1(c))	15.6	75
5.	Standard deviation—computed from combined sample	3	9.65
6.	Square of standard deviation—combined sample (line 5 x line 5)	9	93

EVALUATION OF RESULTS—PRECISION LIMITS

Evaluating the results of the test for precision limits involves the solution of an algebraic formula that has been developed by statisticians. The solution of the formula is achieved by the steps set forth in Chart XVII.

CHART XVII–EVALUATION OF RESULTS–PRECISION LIMITS	STRATUM I	STRATUM II
1. Number of elements in population–(line 8, Chart XI)	4,000	2,000
2. Number of elements in combined sample–(line 1, Chart XVI)	52	127
3. Line 1 ÷ line 2	3,948	1,873
4. Square of standard deviation–combined sample–(line 6, Chart XVI)	9	93
5. Line 1 x line 4	36,000	186,000
6. Line 5 x line 3	142,128,000	348,378,000
7. Line 6 ÷ line 2	2,733,231	2,743,134
8. Sum of amounts on line 7		5,476,365
9. Square root of line 8		2,340.09
10. Confidence coefficient Chart XI)		1.96
11. Precision limits–(line 9 x line 10)		4,586

EVALUATION OF RESULTS—PROJECTION OF SAMPLE MEAN

The computation of the estimated dollar value of the total population and the upper and lower limits of estimated dollar value are shown in detail on Chart XVIII.

CHART XVIII–EVALUATION OF RESULTS–PROJECTION OF SAMPLE MEAN

		STRATUM I	STRATUM II
1.	Number of elements in population–(line 8, Chart XI)	4,000	2,000
2.	Sample arithmetic mean–(line 4, Chart XVI)	15.6	75
3.	Value of population projected by sample mean–(line 1 x line 2)	62,400	150,000
4.	Value of total population projected by sample mean–(sum of amounts on line 3)		212,400
5.	Computed precision limits–(line 11, Chart XVII)		4,586
6.	Upper limit of estimated total dollar value–(line 4 + line 5)		216,986
7.	Lower limit of estinated total dollar value–(line 4 – line 5)		207,814
8.	Confidence level–(line 3, Chart XI)		95%

AUDITOR'S REPORT

After completing Chart XVIII, the auditor can report as follows:

The estimate of the total value of freight charges billed to customers is $212,400, plus or minus $4,586, at a confidence level of 95%.

Since the statement satisfies the auditor's requirements, no further sampling is necessary.

9

DESIGN AND APPLICATION OF FLOWCHARTS AND DECISION TABLES

FLOWCHARTS

Flowcharting is a technique that can be used by an accountant to achieve total comprehension of an information processing system. A flowchart is a diagram that shows the processing operations and the sequence in which they are performed. Symbols are used to represent input into and output from the system; and to picture the processing operations and delineate the flow of information within the system. The graphic presentation contained in a flowchart permits a visual comprehension that is superior to the auditory conception attained from a narrative description.

The evolution of the art of flowcharting occurred concurrent with the evolving application of electronic computers to problems of business and industry. In the early stages of their development flowcharts were designed exclusively for electronic computer systems. But it was not long before accountants became aware of the value of flowcharts as an accounting tool that could be applied to any system—manual, mechanical, or electronic. Accountants found the flowchart to be a useful and rapid method for committing to paperwork the different steps used in a given procedure. From the flowchart accountants could visualize the interrelationships of various procedures and could relate specific audit steps to weaknesses in internal control. Flowcharts were found to provide the most efficient method to alter existing procedures or plan new systems. Consequently, the use of flowcharting for manual systems has become widespread in the accounting profession. It therefore should behoove all accountants to develop a working knowledge of flowcharts, and this chapter is intended to aid in that endeavor.

In this chapter the author proposes first to disclose a simple flowchart, designed to picture the initial segment of a program, so that the reader will have a conceptual understanding of a flowchart before he attempts to master the art of preparing one. Having demonstrated, and thus assured the reader, that flowcharts are easy to prepare and when logically prepared are simple to read, the author then will follow with a description of standardized symbols, an exposition of basic rules, and illustrations of advanced techniques.

ILLUSTRATION OF A SIMPLE FLOWCHART

It is important for the reader to bear in mind that all logically prepared flowcharts are easy to read. At first glance an intricate flowchart may appear to be a mass of confusion, but a step-by-step approach to reading even the most complicated chart renders it elementary.

For example, the initial operations in a highly involved accounting process might begin with the following steps:

Mail Clerk
- (a) Opens the mail and distributes customers' checks to Secretary.

Secretary
- (a) Prepares a typed listing of checks,
- (b) runs an adding machine tape on checks,

(c) runs an adding machine tape on listing,
(d) if the amounts on the tapes do not agree, the Secretary rechecks the amounts, and makes the appropriate corrections,
(e) files the original listing and the related tape,
(f) prepares a bank deposit ticket from checks,
(g) sends the tape on the checks, the deposit ticket, and duplicate listing to the accounting department for processing.

A flowchart of the secretary's operations could be prepared in the manner shown in the following Program Flowchart.

The steps in processing the information are easy to follow. The flow of documents, and the sequence of operations, are indicated by flowlines. The flowlines normally proceed from left to right and from top to bottom. Arrowheads are used to denote flow in the opposite direction. Most of the symbols used in the chart are labeled and therefore the meaning of each is perfectly obvious to the reader.

A knowledge of only these rudiments of flowcharting generally will enable one to comprehend and interpret any well-prepared flowchart. However, facility in reading and skill in preparing flowcharts requires a knowledge of standardized symbols and the basic rules of the art.

STANDARDIZED SYMBOLS

In the first stage of the development of flowcharts, symbols were highly individualistic. However, individuals in a company began coordinating their work in flowcharting and later these company groups began exchanging flowcharts within the related industry. The industrial user groups then began an interchange among themselves and with governmental agencies. The standardization of flowchart symbols proceeded slowly until the initiative was grasped by the American National Standards Institute whose Committee on Computers and Information Processing in 1966 produced a standard for flowchart symbols and their usage. The symbols of the ANSI are the same as those of the International Organization for Standardization, and are universally recognized. The ANSI is dedicated to reviewing its standards every five years and promulgating new standards if it appears necessary to do so.

The functions of an information-processing system are input/output (I/O), processing, flow direction, and annotation. Basic symbols are established for each function and can always be used to represent that function. In addition to the basic symbols, however, specialized input/output and processing symbols have been developed to give additional information. Specialized input/output symbols not only represent the I/O function, but also can picture the medium on which the information is recorded or stored. The specialized processing symbols represent the processing function and also identify the specific type of operation to be performed on the information. If no specialized symbol exists for a function, the basic symbol is used.

The symbols shown on page 202 are applied extensively to flowcharts designed in connection with electronic computers. These symbols have been made conventional by sanction of the ANSI. Each of the symbols is either a cutout or a combination of shapes provided by cutouts in the flowcharting template recommended by International Business Machines for use in computerized flowcharting of their computer programs and systems. The reader should obtain a template from IBM.

The IBM template also contains the following three symbols that have not been adopted officially by the ANSI.

Keying Transmittal Tape Offpage Connector

All of these symbols are essential to flowcharting computer operations. An accountant involved in the layout of systems and programs for electronic processing must, of course, be familiar with all of them. However, accountants generally are only indirectly concerned with flowcharts for computers. Almost always the actual preparation of flowcharts for computer operations are prepared by technicians who are adept in organizing computer processes and the flow of input and output information within the computer processing operation. The accountant may act as an advisor in determining what information is needed from the computer, and he may be vitally interested in the features of internal control incor-

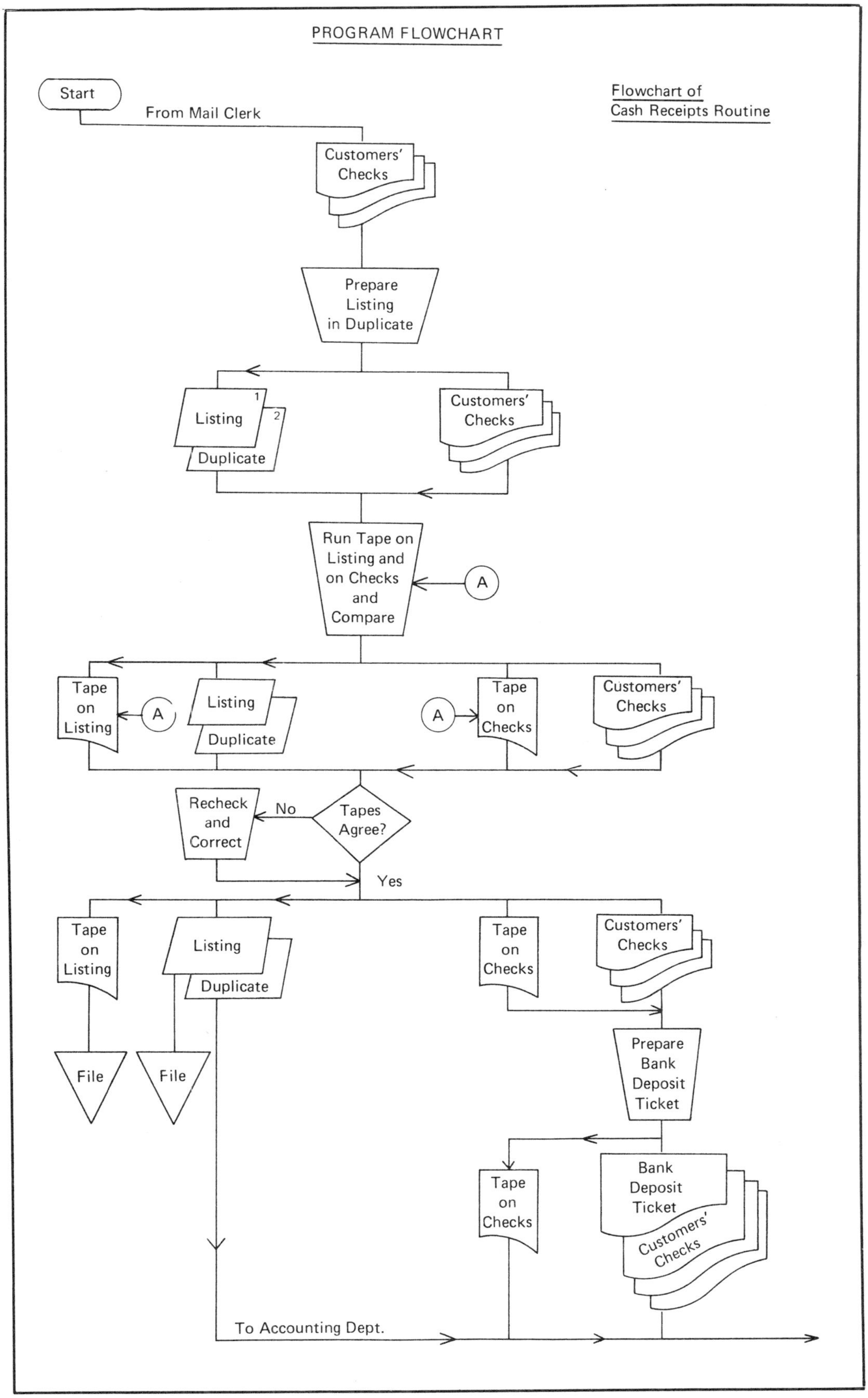
PROGRAM FLOWCHART
Flowchart of
Cash Receipts Routine
Start
From Mail Clerk
Customers' Checks
Prepare Listing in Duplicate
Listing
1
2
Duplicate
Customers' Checks
Run Tape on Listing and on Checks and Compare
A
Tape on Listing
A
Listing
Duplicate
A
Tape on Checks
Customers' Checks
Recheck and Correct
No
Tapes Agree?
Yes
Tape on Listing
Listing
Duplicate
Tape on Checks
Customers' Checks
File
File
Prepare Bank Deposit Ticket
Tape on Checks
Bank Deposit Ticket
Customers' Checks
To Accounting Dept.

BASIC SYMBOLS

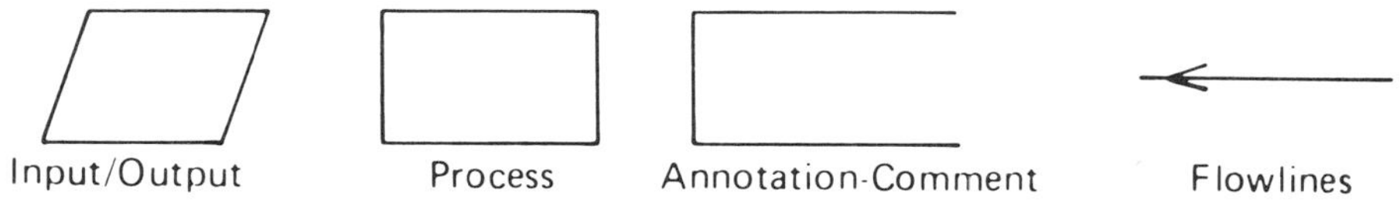

SPECIALIZED INPUT/OUTPUT SYMBOLS

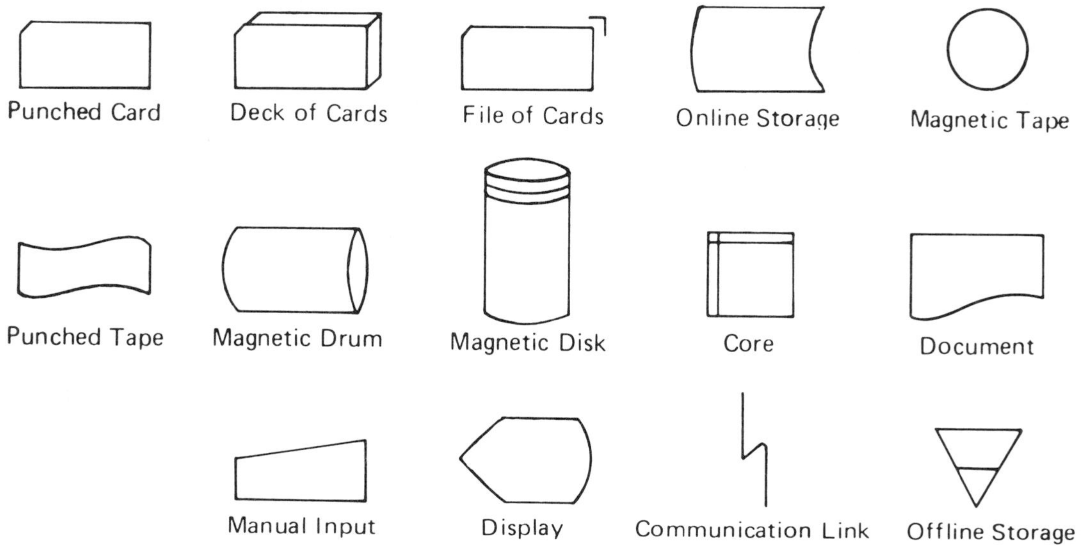

SPECIALIZED PROCESS SYMBOLS

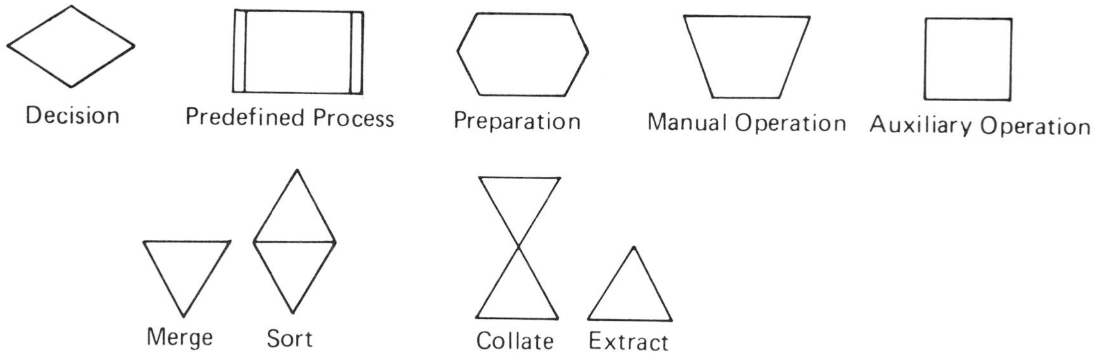

ADDITIONAL SYMBOLS

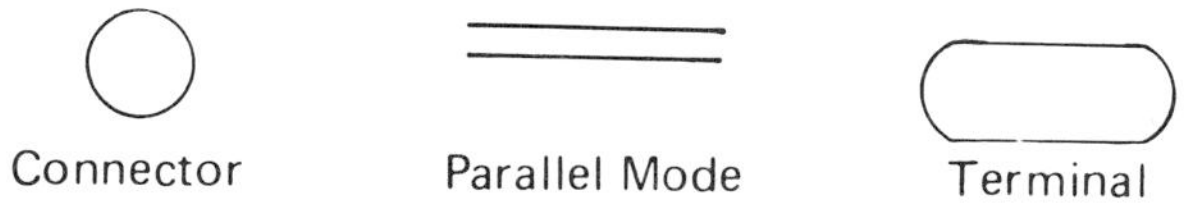

porated into the system, but he rarely prepares the computer flowcharts. Normally, it is not necessary for an accountant to memorize all the computerized flowcharting symbols outlined above, but it is absolutely essential that he have access to a reference work describing them so that he can *read* computer flowcharts whenever the occasion arises. The foregoing computer flowchart symbols have been included in this chapter in order to furnish the accountant with the needed reference material.

FLOWCHARTING SYMBOLS FOR MANUAL SYSTEMS

While the accountant normally need not memorize the symbols for computer flowcharting, it is important for him to be totally imbued with a series of symbols to be used in flowcharting mechanical and manual systems. Symbols for flowcharting manual operations have not been conventionalized and it is up to the individual accountant to select his own personalized symbols. Some accountants use a combination of both abstract and pictorial symbols, incorporating into their flowcharts such items as the following graphics.

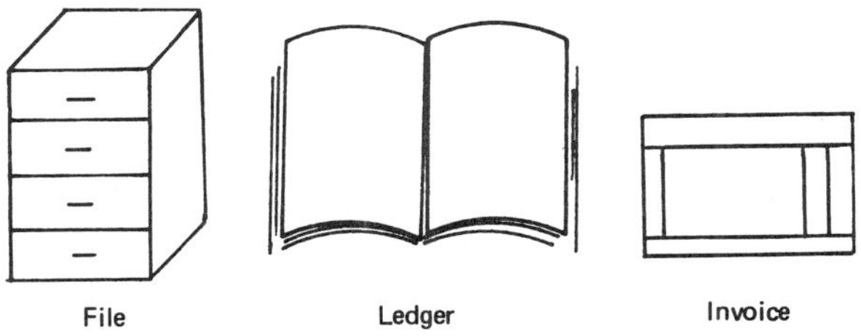

In any logical flowchart, it is essential that the sequence of operations and the linking of symbols be pictured by the conventional use of flowlines and arrowheads promulgated by the ANSI, and described in this chapter. Most accountants, however, have adapted a limited series of conventional computer input/output and processing symbols to flowcharts for manual and mechanical operations.

The symbols described below are used extensively by accountants, are competent to picture any phase of manual operations, and enjoy a limited conventionality by virtue of their general acceptance among accountants.

BASIC SYMBOLS

INPUT/OUTPUT SYMBOLS

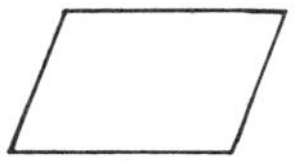

Input/output

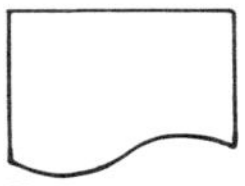

Document

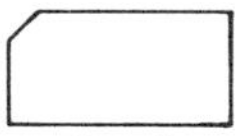

Card

Tape

These input/output symbols should be used to represent either information that is available for processing (input) or information that has been recorded by the processing function (output).

The input/output parallelogram can be used to represent any medium on which the information is recorded. However, it is usually restricted to represent journals, lists, pages, etc.

The symbols for documents, cards, and tapes are generally used when the recording media are various detachable documents, ledger cards, and adding machine tapes, respectively.

PROCESSING SYMBOLS

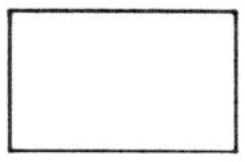

Process

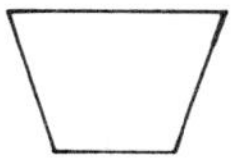

Manual Operation

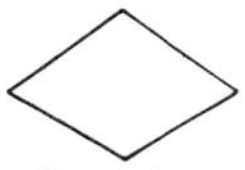

Decision

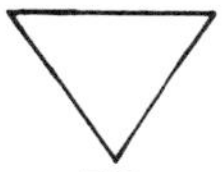

File

The process symbols should be used to represent the processing function. The processing rectangle may be used to represent any operation resulting in a change in value, form, or location of information. However, the manual operation trapezoid is more widely used in manual systems.

The decision symbol represents a decision that determines which of a number of alternative paths is to be followed.

The file symbol is used to represent either permanent or temporary storing of processed or unprocessed information, regardless of the medium on which it is recorded.

FLOWLINES

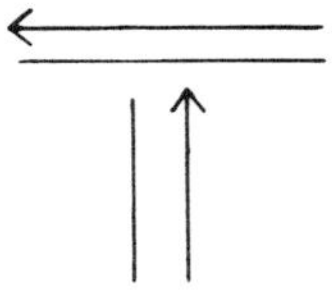

Flowlines

Flowlines represent the basic function of linking symbols in flowcharts. They delineate the direction of flow and indicate the sequence of operations. Normal flow is from left to right and top to bottom. Open arrowheads should be used to indicate flow that is other than normal.

ANNOTATION SYMBOL

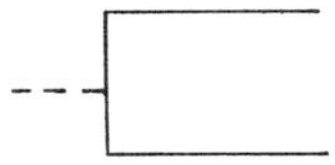

Annotation

The annotation symbol represents the annotation function in flowcharts. It is designed to permit addition of comments, instructions for processing, or explanatory notes. The broken line is connected to any symbol to which the annotation applies.

OTHER SYMBOLS

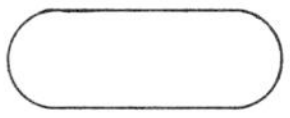

Terminal

TERMINAL SYMBOL

The terminal symbol represents a terminal point in a flowchart such as, for example, start, stop, interrupt, delay.

Connector

CONNECTOR SYMBOL

The connector symbol represents an exit or an entry from another part of the flowchart. It is a junction in the line of flow.

SPECIAL USES OF SYMBOLS IN FLOWCHARTING

Some special applications of symbols in flowcharting are shown below.

<u>Flowlines</u>

1. Open arrowheads may be used on normal direction flowlines in circumstances where the arrowheads would facilitate reading of the chart.
2. Connector symbols should be used where flowlines end on one page and begin on another page.
3. The ANSI standards provide that flowlines may cross where they have no logical interrelation. However, in manual systems the crossing of unrelated flowlines should be indicated by a semicircular hump in one of the lines.
4. When flowlines enter or leave a junction they should have arrowheads near the junction point.

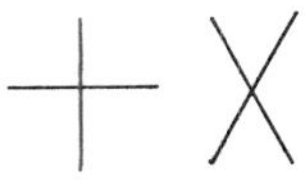

Unrelated Flowlines—Computer

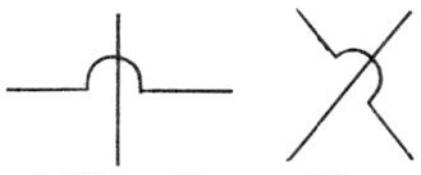

Unrelated Flowlines—Manual System

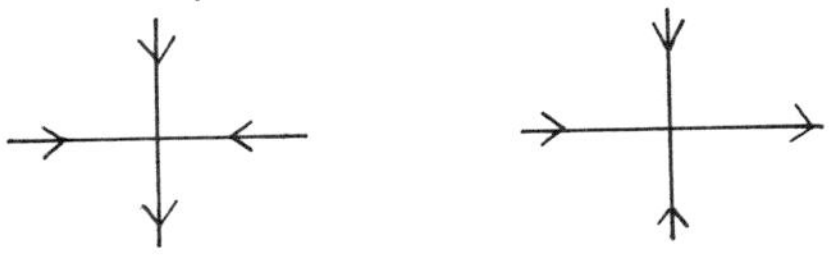

Flowlines at Junction

<u>Striping</u>

Striping a processing symbol provides a means of indicating who performed the processing operation.

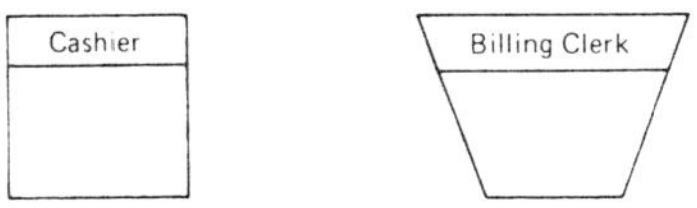

Connector Referencing

Connectors may be used for the following purposes:

1. To associate an input/output document with a processing symbol.
2. To reference pages when flowlines are broken due to page limitations.
3. To cross reference associated symbols.

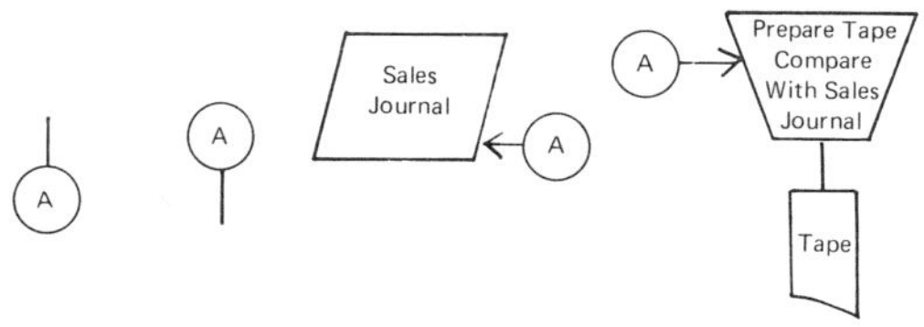

Multiple Exits

Multiple exits from a symbol may be shown by several flowlines from the symbol to other symbols or by a single flowline from the symbol which branches into a number of flowlines.

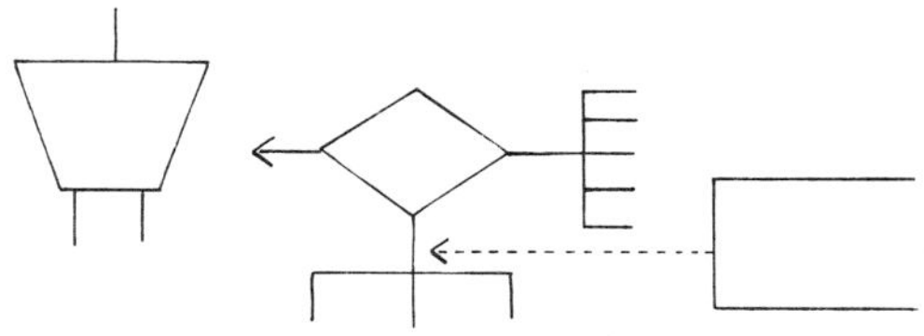

Overlay Patterns

1. Overlay patterns may be drawn to indicate repetitive symbols.
2. When the repetitive symbols are to flow as a unit, flowlines may enter or leave from any point and the sequential order of the multiple symbols is not altered by the point at which the flowline enters or leaves.
3. When repetitive symbols are to flow in individual directions, appropriate flowlines may be drawn to the individual symbols.

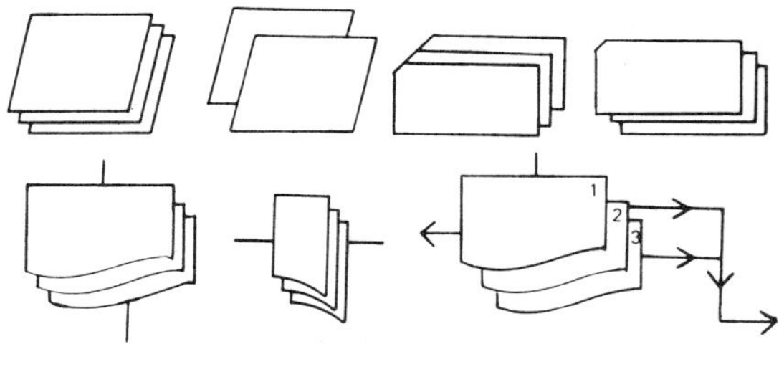

Passage of Time

Dotted flowlines may be used to indicate an operation to be executed at a later time. The length of the lapse of time should be indicated on the flowchart.

SPECIAL FEATURES OF FLOWCHARTING APPLICABLE ONLY TO COMPUTERIZED SYSTEMS

The following flowcharting features are used exclusively in charting computerized systems:

Father Tape — The father tape is the old, or input, tape and is the basis for an updated tape.

Son Tape— A son tape is the updated version of the father tape.

Looping — A series of repeated processing steps that performs computations by modifying a variable with each repetition. The looping is terminated when a processing test indicates that all applicable variations of the variable have been computed.

Endless Loop — A looping process that does not have a processing test that will terminate the looping. In preparing a flowchart of looping processes, precaution should be taken to ensure that a means of terminating the operation is built into the program.

BASIC RULES OF FLOWCHARTING

The fundamental rules of flowcharting are:

1. Standardized (conventional) symbols should be used.
2. Each chart must begin with an input and end with an output.
3. Each input document must be filed or destroyed.
4. All inputs into a system must end with an output.
5. Input and output symbols must be separated by a processing symbol.
6. Normal flow is from left to right and from top to bottom. Arrowheads must be used to indicate both bidirectional flow and any flow that is contrary to normal.

The art of flowcharting has so few inflexible rules that it allows for an expression of personal esthetic values as well as an individualistic approach to documenting a program or system. Consequently, two persons charting the same system could produce quite different flowcharts. However, adherence to the basic rules by both persons would make the system easily understood by reference to either chart, no matter how the general appearance might differ.

CLASSIFICATION OF FLOWCHARTS

Flowcharts are classified into two general types—systems flowcharts and program flowcharts. The two types are described below and are illustrated in detail at the end of this section.

Systems Flowchart

Systems flowcharts are comprehensive charts picturing *what* is to be accomplished rather than *how* it is to be done. They give an overview of the flow of data through all segments of the system. For example, a systems chart would indicate that an invoice had to be prepared, but would not denote each step in the preparation.

Program Flowcharts

Program flowcharts are detailed charts or layouts showing each operation performed within a particular segment of a business system. These charts are usually quite explicit and sometimes require a series of subsidiary flowcharts having a high level of detail.

INTERNAL ACCOUNTING CONTROL

A major benefit provided by the use of flowcharts is derived from the fact that a carefully prepared chart can graphically indicate deficiencies in internal accounting control. However, unless the chart is orientated in the direction of disclosing internal control features, it will not necessarily disclose weaknesses in the internal control system and cannot be relied on to detect flaws in the procedures provided for control and accountability.

However, when projection of internal control procedures is one of the desired objectives of flowcharting, there are devices that can be used to highlight the control features incorporated into the system. Two such devices are described below.

Striping Processing Symbols

The use of striped processing symbols can indicate the person performing the processing operation, and thus disclose a deficiency in proper segregation of functional responsibilities.

For example, consider the simple program flowchart on page 209.

It must be obvious to the reader that without the names shown in. the striping on the processing symbols it would be impossible to determine that there was proper segregation of functional responsibilities among the individuals involved in processing the data.

Departmentalized Flowcharts

In many cases the flow of data through a system can be routed through departments on the program flowcharts. When this is done, interdepartmental checks and controls, or lack of them, will be evident from the charts, and the accountant may be able to evaluate the adequacy of internal accounting control by reference to the flowcharts.

The flowchart on pages 210-211 shows the flow of data through departments and depicts the processing operations in each.

A chart prepared in this manner can enable the accountant to observe what departmental controls are in operation, and may help him evaluate the adequacy of the internal control system.

These flowcharts were prepared for the sole purpose of illustrating the mechanics of flowchart preparation. They do not purport to indicate recommended procedures either for processing or for internal accounting control.

SYSTEMS FLOWCHART

All of the flowcharts illustrated in this chapter have been program flowcharts except for the one on page 212, which is a systems flowchart showing the routine for updating a manual perpetual inventory record.

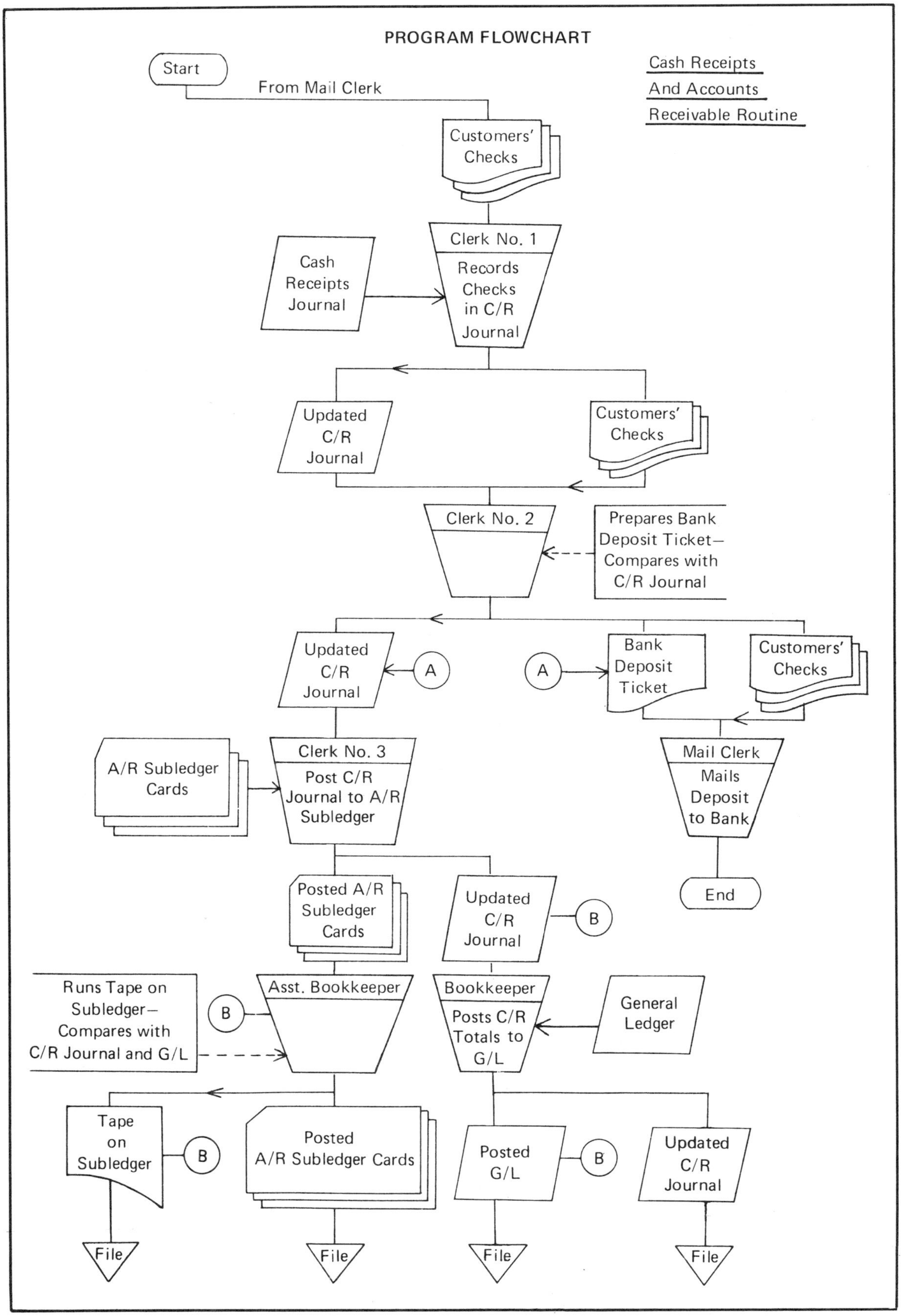
PROGRAM FLOWCHART
Cash Receipts
And Accounts
Receivable Routine
Start
From Mail Clerk
Customers' Checks
Cash Receipts Journal
Clerk No. 1
Records Checks in C/R Journal
Updated C/R Journal
Customers' Checks
Clerk No. 2
Prepares Bank Deposit Ticket— Compares with C/R Journal
Updated C/R Journal
A
A
Bank Deposit Ticket
Customers' Checks
A/R Subledger Cards
Clerk No. 3
Post C/R Journal to A/R Subledger
Mail Clerk
Mails Deposit to Bank
End
Posted A/R Subledger Cards
Updated C/R Journal
B
Runs Tape on Subledger— Compares with C/R Journal and G/L
B
Asst. Bookkeeper
Bookkeeper
Posts C/R Totals to G/L
General Ledger
Tape on Subledger
B
Posted A/R Subledger Cards
Posted G/L
B
Updated C/R Journal
File
File
File
File

DEPARTMENTAL FLOWCHART—PURCHASES PROGRAM

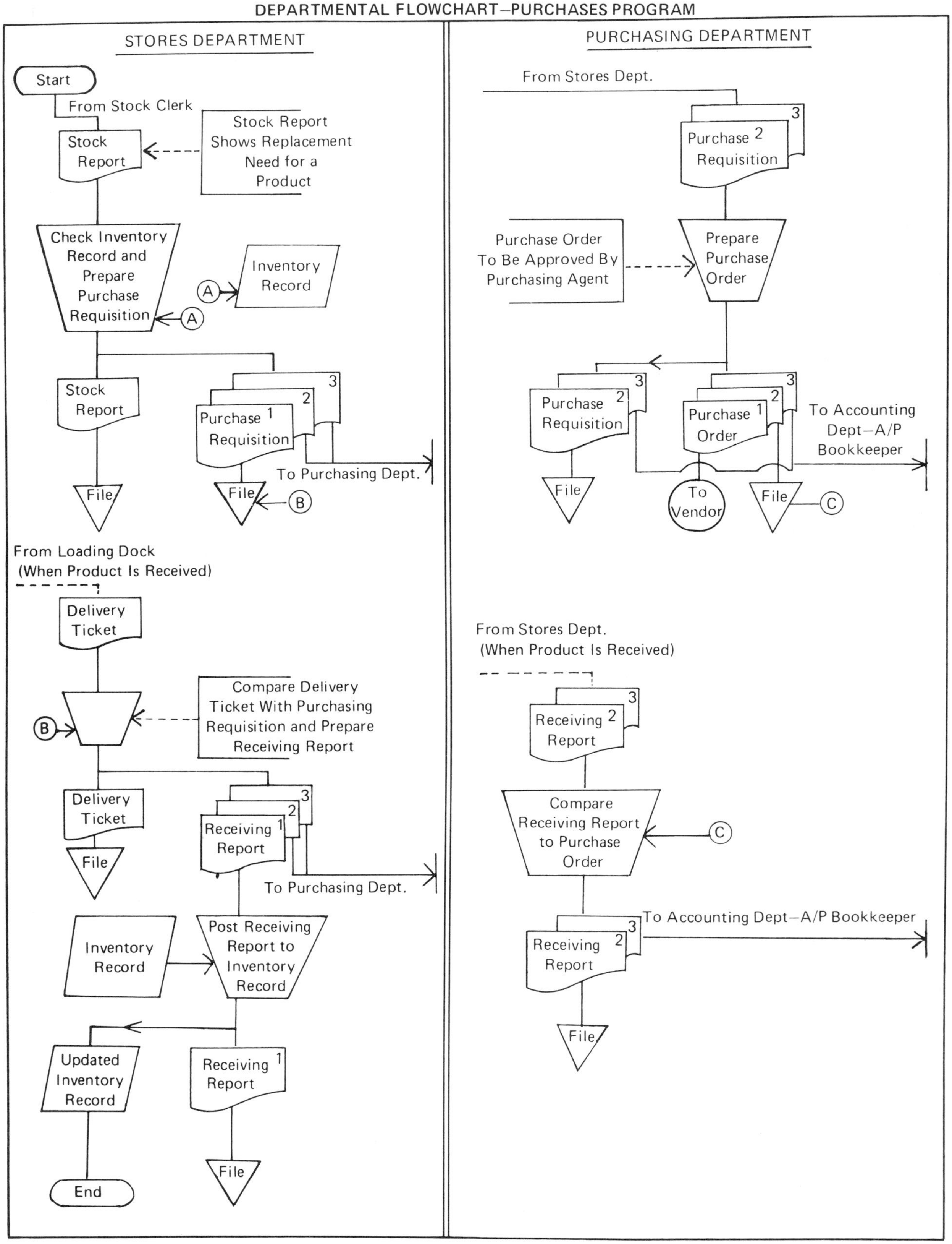

DEPARTMENTAL FLOWCHART—PURCHASES PROGRAM

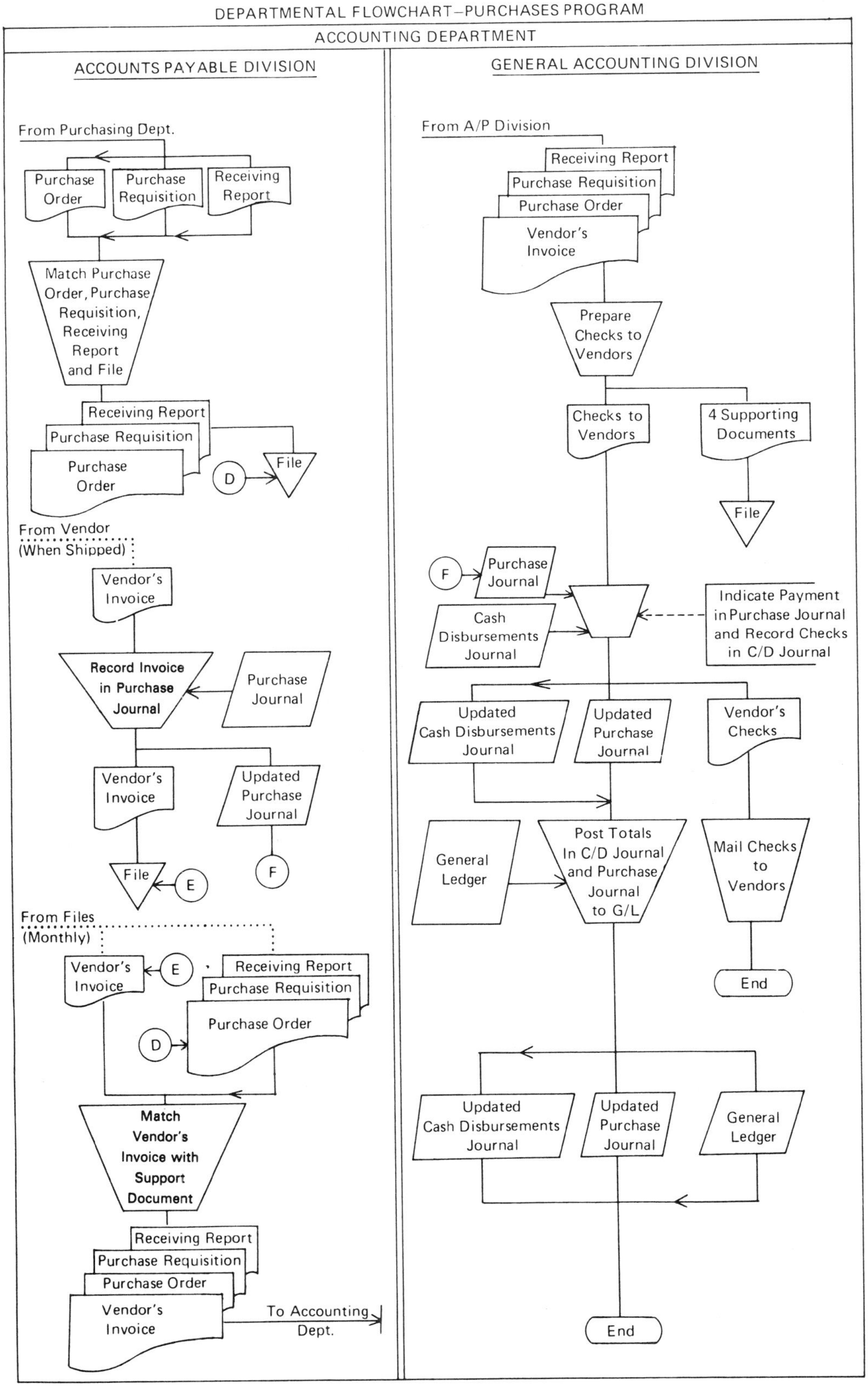

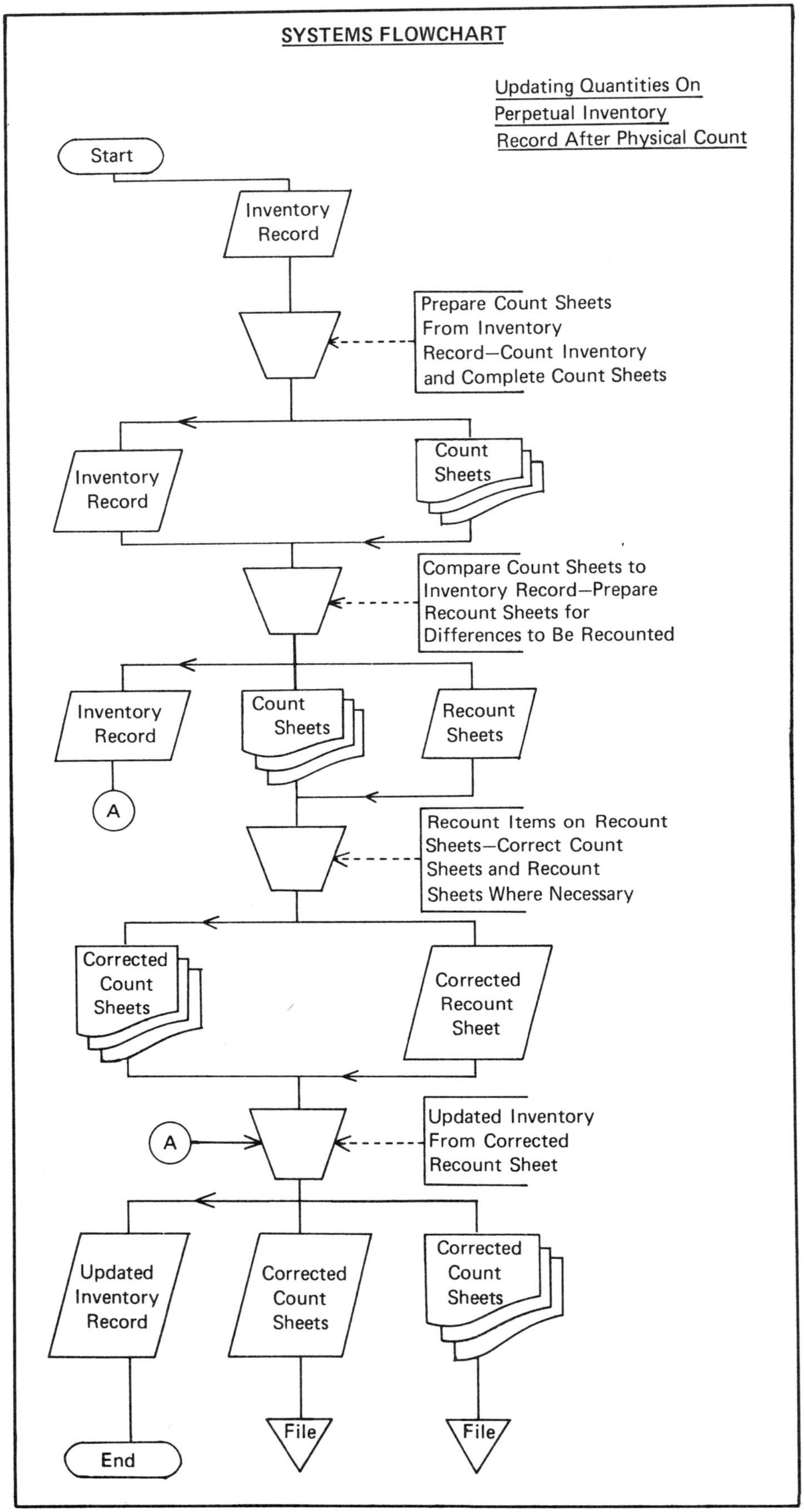
SYSTEMS FLOWCHART
Updating Quantities On
Perpetual Inventory
Record After Physical Count
Start
Inventory Record
Prepare Count Sheets From Inventory Record—Count Inventory and Complete Count Sheets
Inventory Record
Count Sheets
Compare Count Sheets to Inventory Record—Prepare Recount Sheets for Differences to Be Recounted
Inventory Record
Count Sheets
Recount Sheets
A
Recount Items on Recount Sheets—Correct Count Sheets and Recount Sheets Where Necessary
Corrected Count Sheets
Corrected Recount Sheet
A
Updated Inventory From Corrected Recount Sheet
Updated Inventory Record
Corrected Count Sheets
Corrected Count Sheets
End
File
File

DECISION TABLES

Decision tables are decision-making devices that can be used by accountants in seeking solutions to complex procedural problems. A decision table is a tabular form that displays decision logic for conditional propositions by specifying a course of action for each condition, or any combination of conditions, contained in the proposition. The tables are so constructed that one section names and describes the conditions surrounding the problem, another section lists courses of action to be taken where a particular condition appertains, and a grid section denotes whether or not a particular condition is present and, if so, what action to take. The conditions represent *if* statements, while the actions denote *then* statements. The "if this, then that" relationship established by the table precisely defines the elements of the decision.

Decision tables were developed as an alternative to flowcharts for the description of problem logic in connection with electronic computer processing. It was discovered that the tabular form is superior because it can chart conditions and actions explicitly and clearly, requires a minimum of space, and is highly readable. On the other hand, a flowchart depicting decision logic with alternative processing paths usually is hard to construct and difficult to read. The introduction of a decision symbol into a flowchart results in a switching operation that sometimes requires charting of an explosion of the processing blocks, and often requires offpage connectors that are repeated on another page, where they become the entry point for the flowchart depicting the next step in the processing routine.

Decision tables originated as design tools for computer programers and systems analysts. However, in the course of their auditing activities, accountants became exposed to decision table techniques and soon became aware that such techniques could be adapted to accounting and clerical problems and procedures in a variety of ways. Without changing the format, accountants began using the tables not only as aids in the solution of problem logic, but also as tabular descriptions of processes and procedures. Nevertheless, the use of decision tables has not become widespread in the profession and remains a neglected accounting tool. This is probably due to the fact that practically all literature on decision tables is contained in publications devoted to electronic processing techniques.

This chapter is designed to give the reader a working knowledge of decision tables and their use in accounting and clerical procedures. It will describe the structure of single tables, illustrate the construction and referencing of multiple tables, and provide examples of the tables at work.

ILLUSTRATION OF A SIMPLE DECISION TABLE

Table 1 is an illustration of a simple decision table.

Without ever having seen a decision table, or even knowing what a decision table is, the reader, nevertheless, will instantly comprehend Table 1. The Y's in the top section represent the presence of indicated conditions, and the X's in the lower section indicate the related action to be taken. However, in order to use decision tables as an accounting tool, the reader should be able to design and construct them, and apply them to practical problems. This chapter is intended to assist the reader in developing a working knowledge of decision table techniques.

STRUCTURE OF DECISION TABLES

A decision table consists of four basic sections and three annotation sections. A double horizontal line divides the table into two major sections; the upper portion is reserved for *conditions* and the lower portion for *actions.* A double vertical line divides the table into two other major sections: the right portion is the *stub,* and the left portion is the *entry.* Horizontal lines, called *rows,* run across the entire table and may be assigned numbers or letters for identification purposes. The entry portion is further divided by vertical lines to form columns called *rules,* which also may be assigned identifying numbers. The structure of a simple decision table is shown in Table 2.

Oliver Company deals in custom-made machine parts, manufactured to meet certain specifications. Inspectors on the receiving dock are supplied with the following tabular form to aid in the disposition of shipments arriving at the dock.

	SHIPMENT INSPECTION—RECEIVING DOCK	1	2	3	4	5
A	Product Meets Specifications	Y	N	N	N	N
B	Insignificant Variance from Specifications		Y	N	N	N
C	Significant Variance from Specifications			Y	Y	Y
D	Special Clearance Received				N	Y
E	Accept Shipment	X	X			X
F	Reject Shipment			X	X	

Table 1

	TABLE HEADER—IDENTIFICATION	1	2	3	4 (Rules)	5	6	7	8
A									
B	Conditions Stub				Conditions Entry				
C									
D									
E	Actions Stub				Actions Entry				
F									
Comments									

Table 2

	STATUS TO BE ASSIGNED SUCCESSFUL CANDIDATES FOR POSITIONS ON STAFF	1	2	3	4	5
A	Educational Qualification	CPA	CPA	Bachelor Degree	Bachelor Degree	Under-graduate
B	Years of Experience	< 10	> 10	< 5		
C	Test Rating	< 4		< 4	> 4	
D	Status Assigned	Manager	Senior	In Charge	Assistant	Assistant

Table 3

The condition stub lists all pertinent conditions surrounding the problem; the condition entry specifies the condition, or combination of conditions, which we wish to consider. The action stub lists the actions we consider we might take; the action entry specifies the action that *must* be taken. The action taken for a particular condition, or combination of conditions, forms a rule, which may be read as an "if this, then that" statement. The rules are usually numbered in a horizontal row at the top of the entry section of the table.

CLASSIFICATION OF DECISION TABLES

Decision tables are classified according to the type of entries made in the table.

Limited Entry Table

In a limited entry table the condition listed in the stub must be either present, absent, or immaterial. Consequently, the entry is limited to indicating presence, absence, or irrelevancy of a condition by Y's, N's, or blanks. Limited entry tables are used by accountants more extensively than are any other type because each condition is either present or absent and each action is either taken or not taken. Table 1 is an example of a limited entry table.

Extended Entry Table

In an extended entry table the statements in the stub portion are *extended* into the entry portion. The stub portion describes the variables while the entry portion specifies the assigned values. This type of table is generally used where the variables in the problem can have many values.

In the illustration of the extended entry table, an accounting firm tests applicants for positions on the staff and determines the status to be assigned successful candidates, as follows:

Manager — CPA with 10 years experience and test rating in excess of 4.
Senior — CPA with less than 10 years experience, regardless of test rating.
In Charge — Bachelor degree with 5 years experience and test rating in excess of 4.
Assistant — Bachelor degree and test rating less than 4, regardless of experience; and all undergraduates.

The classification of candidates could be charted in the manner shown in Table 3.

Mixed Entry Tables

Mixed entry tables are made up of both single entry rows and extended entry rows. While the table consists of both types of rows, each individual row must be entirely limited or entirely extended.

In the illustration, Black Company, wholesalers of machinery parts and supplies, is taking an annual physical inventory and has decided to write down the carrying value of all slow-moving merchandise except products that have been purchased for special projects. The rate of write-down is as follows:

No sales in 6 months—10%
No sales in 12 months—25%
No sales in 18 months—50%

The inventory cost reduction procedure could be charted as shown by Table 4.

ELSE RULE

In some cases the process of stating a problem may be shortened by providing an "Else Rule" column in the entry section of the decision table. This method permits listing in the stub only those conditions and alternative courses of action that are pertinent to the problem. For each pertinent condition, or combination of conditions, appropriate action is indicated in the entry section. All other sets of conditions are handled by the else rule, which indicates what action is to be taken when none of the listed conditions are present in the problem. The else rule does not indicate conditions; it only specifies the actions to be taken in cases where none of the stated conditions apply.

To illustrate the else rule, we can refer to the illustration of an extended entry table shown in Table 3 and change the conditions for assigning status to successful candidates for positions on the accountant's staff to conditions for *hiring* new staff members, as well as for classifying their status. A decision table to chart the process could be prepared as in Table 5.

MULTIPLE TABLES

In some situations decision patterns are so com-

Table 4

	REDUCTION IN BASIS OF INVENTORY FOR SLOW-MOVING PRODUCTS	1	2	3	4
A	Product Reserved for Special Projects	N	N	N	Y
B	Months Elapsed Since Last Sale	6	12	18	
C	Reduce Cost Basis By	10%	25%	50%	
D	Do Not Reduce Cost Basis				X

Table 5

	PROCEDURE FOR HIRING AND CLASSIFYING NEW STAFF MEMBERS	1	2	3	4	5	6
A	CPA—Experience > 10 Years Test Result > 4	Y	N	N	N	N	
B	CPA—Experience < 10 Years		Y	N	N	N	
C	Bachelor Degree—Experience >10 Years—Test Result >4			Y	N	N	ELSE
D	Bachelor Degree—Test Result > 4				Y	N	
E	Undergraduate Student					Y	
F	Hire as Manager	X					
G	Hire a Senior		X				
H	Hire as In-charge Accountant			X			
I	Hire as Assistant Accountant				X	X	
J	Do not Hire						X

Table 6

	BEGIN TABLE
A	Open vault when time lock goes off.
B	Transfer tellers' carts from vault to tellers' cages.
C	Open on-line computer switch.
D	Instruct tellers to transfer money from carts to operating fund drawers.
E	Admit customers.
F	Go to Table B-1.

plex, or procedures so extensive, that they cannot be described in a single table. In such cases it may be possible to divide the problem into logical segments, prepare tables for each segment, and link the tables by appropriate referencing. It is imperative, however, that the linking and referencing be accomplished in a manner that will control the user's progress from table to table and indicate to him where to proceed when he has completed an action.

A series of multiple tables can consist of open tables, closed tables, and action tables. These tables are described below, and open and closed tables are illustrated in Tables 9, 10, and 11. An action table is illustrated in Table 6.

Open Tables

An open table is one that contains an action which is a directive to go to another table.

Closed Tables

In a closed table the action indicated is complete, and there is no directive to go to any other table.

Action Tables

In some cases a series of actions are required regardless of conditions. In such cases the actions should be removed and put in a separate table. An action table is generally a closed table, and since its function is only to specify a pattern of action there is no need for conditions. An example of an action table is shown in Table 6, which gives the opening routine for a savings and loan association.

USING DECISION TABLES

Decision tables are an efficient and effective means of solving problems, describing procedures, and detailing instructions. Accountants can use them in many ways and for a variety of purposes. The decision tables that follow were designed, respectively, to solve the problem encountered in a feasibility study, describe internal control procedures, and display detailed instructions for completing a self-employment tax form. If the reader will study the construction of the tables presented here and practice constructing tables of his own, in a short time he will be able to apply decision table techniques to solve many of his procedural problems.

Problems in Feasibility Study

Table 7 assumes that a preliminary review has been made in connection with a feasibility study for converting a manual accounting system to electronic processing, and before continuing with the study it is necessary to select a course of action of certain conditions revealed in the preliminary review.

Internal Control Procedures

In this illustration it is assumed that a wholesale machinery and parts distributor has three accounting clerks in a section of the accounting department that is responsible for customer billings, posting subsidiary accounts receivable ledger, posting the sales journal and cash receipts summaries to the general ledger, and performing all cash receipts operations. The workload is no problem; but the auditor is requested to set up a procedure that will segregate the functional responsibilities of the three clerks so as to provide a maximum of internal control. To accomplish this, the auditor used the decision table shown in Table 8 to classify the document-processing functions into nine separate conditions, and the posting functions into five separate actions. He assigned document-processing responsibilities and posting responsibilities to each respective clerk as shown in the chart. His purpose was to assign duties in such a matter that no one clerk had a posting function that resulted from his own document-processing activities.

Instructions for Completing Tax Form

The multiple decision tables shown in Tables 9, 10, and 11 give detailed instructions for completing the self-employment tax return on form 1040SE. The conditions set forth on the form precede the illustrations.

	FEASIBILITY STUDY GUIDE	1	2	3	4	5	6	7	8		
A	Top management support is available	N	Y	Y	Y	Y	Y	Y	Y		
B	Potential savings large		Y	N	Y	Y	Y	Y	Y		
C	Potential increase in efficiency		N	N	Y	Y	Y	Y	Y		
D	Present personnel competent to operate new system				Y	N	N	N	Y		
E	Present Personnel can be shifted to new positions				Y	N	N	N	Y		
F	Trained operators are available					Y	Y	Y			
G	Time for study short						Y	Y	N		
H	Consultants acceptable						Y	N	Y		
I	Additional personnel required					Y	Y	Y	N		
J	Abandon study	X	X	X							
K	Train present employees				X				X		
L	Hire trained operators					X	X	X			
M	Shift present employees				X				X		
N	Hire consultants						X		X		
O	Prepare systems analysis only							X			
P	Prepare detailed program analysis								X		

Table 7

	INTERNAL CONTROL–SEGREGATION OF C/R AND A/R FUNCTIONAL RESPONSIBILITIES	1	2	3		
A	Prepares customer billing	Y	N	N		
B	Records invoices in Sales Journal	Y	N	N		
C	Receives customers' checks	N	Y	N		
D	Records checks in C/R Journal	N	Y	N		
E	Makes bank deposit from C/R Journal	N	N	Y		
F	Follows up delinquent accounts	N	N	Y		
G	Approves allowances and write-offs	N	N	Y		
H	Receives collection on deliquent accounts	N	Y	N		
I	Controls accounts written off	Y	N	N		
J	Post accounts receivable sub. ledger from C/R Journal	X				
K	Post accounts receivable sub. ledger from Sales Journal		X			
L	Post accounts receivable sub. ledger from Sales Allowance Journal			X		
M	Take A/R sub. ledger trial balances			X		
N	Post all journals to General Ledger			X		

Table 8

Conditions

If you had wages, including tips, of $15,300 or more that were subject to Social Security taxes, do not fill in this form.

If you have only farm income, complete Parts I and III.

If you have only nonfarm income, complete Parts II and III.

If you have both farm and nonfarm income, complete Parts I, II, and III.

Farm Optional Method May be Used

If gross profits are not more than $2,400.

If gross profits are more than $2,400 and net profits less than $1,600.

Nonfarm Optional Method May be Used

If adjusted net earnings from nonfarm self-employment is less than $1,600.

If adjusted net earnings from nonfarm self-employment is less than 2/3 of nonfarm profits.

If you had net earnings from self-employment of $400 for at least two of the three previous years.

If you have not used the nonfarm optional method for more than four years.

TABLE I—ELIGIBILITY		1	2	3	4		
A	Wages subject to S/S exceeds $15,300	Y	N	N	N		
B	Nonfarm income only		Y	N	N		
C	Farm income only		N	Y	N		
D	Both farm and nonfarm income		N	N	Y		
E	Do not file Form 1040SE	X					
F	Go to Table II		X				
G	Go to Table III			X	X		

Table 9

	TABLE II—NONFARM INCOME	1	2	3	4	5	6	7	8	9	10
A	Nonfarm income only	Y	Y	Y	Y	Y	Y	Y	Y	Y	Y
B	Adjusted net earnings from nonfarm self-employment less than $1,600	Y	Y	Y	Y	N	Y	Y	Y	Y	N
C	Adjusted net earnings from nonfarm self-employment less than 2/3 of gross nonfarm profit	Y	Y	Y	N		Y	Y	Y	N	
D	Net earnings from self-employment of $400 or more in at least 2 of the last 3 previous years	Y	Y	N			Y	Y	N		
E	Optional method not used more than a total of 5 years	Y	N				Y	N			
F	Total earnings in Part III less than $400	Y	Y	Y	Y	Y	N	N	N	N	N
G	Complete Parts II and III	X	X	X	X	X	X	X	X	X	X
H	May elect optional method	X					X				
I	Not subject to self-employment tax—do not complete rest of form	X	X	X	X	X					
J	Complete form 1040SE						X	X	X	X	X
K	Enter amount of self-employment tax on form 1040						X	X	X	X	X
L	Attach form 1040SE to form 1040	X	X	X	X	X	X	X	X	X	X

Table 10

	TABLE III—FARM INCOME	1	2	3	4	5	6	7	8	9	10	11	12
A	Farm income only	Y	Y	Y	Y	Y	Y	N	N	N	N	N	N
B	Both farm and nonfarm income	N	N	N	N	N	N	Y	Y	Y	Y	Y	Y
C	Gross income under $2,401	Y	Y	N	N	N	N	Y	Y	N	N	N	N
D	Gross income more than $2,400 but net profit less than $1,600	N	N	Y	Y	N	N	N	N	Y	Y	N	N
E	Total earnings in Part III less than	Y	N	Y	N	Y	N	Y	N	Y	N	Y	N
F	Complete Part I	X	X	X	X	X	X	X	X	X	X	X	X
G	Complete Part II							X	X	X	X	X	X
H	Complete Part III	X	X	X	X	X	X	X	X	X	X	X	X
I	May elect optional method	X	X	X	X			X	X	X	X		
J	Not subject to self-employment tax—do not fill in rest of form	X		X		X		X		X		X	
K	Complete form 1040SE		X		X		X		X		X		X
L	Enter amount of self-employment tax on form 1040		X		X		X		X		X		X
M	Attach form 1040SE to form 1040	X	X	X	X	X	X	X	X	X	X	X	X

Table 11

Appendix I
TABLES OF COMPOUND INTEREST AND ANNUITIES

TABLE 1
AMOUNT OF 1 AT COMPOUND INTEREST
$(1 + i)^n$

N	PERCENTAGES 1	2	4	5	6	8	8.75	N
1	1.01000	1.02000	1.04000	1.05000	1.06000	1.08000	1.08750	1
2	1.02010	1.04040	1.08160	1.10250	1.12360	1.16640	1.18266	2
3	1.03030	1.06121	1.12486	1.15763	1.19102	1.25971	1.28614	3
4	1.04060	1.08243	1.16986	1.21551	1.26248	1.36049	1.39868	4
5	1.05101	1.10408	1.21665	1.27628	1.33823	1.46933	1.52106	5
6	1.06152	1.12616	1.26532	1.34010	1.41852	1.58687	1.65415	6
7	1.07214	1.14869	1.31593	1.40710	1.50363	1.71382	1.79889	7
8	1.08286	1.17166	1.36857	1.47746	1.59385	1.85093	1.95629	8
9	1.09369	1.19509	1.42331	1.55133	1.68948	1.99900	2.12747	9
10	1.10462	1.21899	1.48024	1.62889	1.79085	2.15892	2.31362	10
11	1.11567	1.24337	1.53945	1.71034	1.89830	2.33164	2.51607	11
12	1.12683	1.26824	1.60103	1.79586	2.01220	2.51817	2.73622	12
13	1.13809	1.29361	1.66507	1.88565	2.13293	2.71962	2.97564	13
14	1.14947	1.31948	1.73168	1.97993	2.26090	2.93719	3.23601	14
15	1.16097	1.34587	1.80094	2.07893	2.39656	3.17217	3.51916	15
16	1.17258	1.37279	1.87298	2.18287	2.54035	3.42594	3.82709	16
17	1.18430	1.40024	1.94790	2.29202	2.69277	3.70002	4.16196	17
18	1.19615	1.42825	2.02582	2.40662	2.85434	3.99602	4.52613	18
19	1.20811	1.45681	2.10685	2.52695	3.02560	4.31570	4.92216	19
20	1.22019	1.48595	2.19112	2.65330	3.20714	4.66096	5.35285	20
21	1.23239	1.51567	2.27877	2.78596	3.39956	5.03383	5.82123	21
22	1.24472	1.54598	2.36992	2.92526	3.60354	5.43654	6.33058	22
23	1.25716	1.57690	2.46472	3.07152	3.81975	5.87146	6.88451	23
24	1.26973	1.60844	2.56330	3.22510	4.04893	6.34118	7.48691	24
25	1.28243	1.64061	2.66584	3.38635	4.29187	6.84848	8.14201	25
26	1.29526	1.67342	2.77247	3.55567	4.54938	7.39635	8.85444	26
27	1.30821	1.70689	2.88337	3.73346	4.82235	7.98806	9.62920	27
28	1.32129	1.74102	2.99870	3.92013	5.11169	8.62711	10.47175	28
29	1.33450	1.77584	3.11865	4.11614	5.41839	9.31727	11.38803	29
30	1.34785	1.81136	3.24340	4.32194	5.74349	10.06266	12.38449	30
31	1.36133	1.84759	3.37313	4.53804	6.08810	10.86767	13.46813	31
32	1.37494	1.88454	3.50806	4.76494	6.45339	11.73708	14.64659	32
33	1.38869	1.92223	3.64838	5.00319	6.84059	12.67605	15.92817	33
34	1.40258	1.96068	3.79432	5.25335	7.25103	13.69013	17.32188	34
35	1.41660	1.99989	3.94609	5.51602	7.68609	14.78534	18.83754	35
36	1.43077	2.03989	4.10393	5.79182	8.14725	15.96817	20.48583	36
37	1.44508	2.08069	4.26809	6.08141	8.63609	17.24563	22.27834	37
38	1.45953	2.12230	4.43881	6.38548	9.15425	18.62528	24.22769	38
39	1.47412	2.16474	4.61637	6.70475	9.70351	20.11530	26.34762	39
40	1.48886	2.20804	4.80102	7.03999	10.28572	21.72452	28.65303	40

TABLE 2
PRESENT VALUE OF 1 AT COMPOUND INTEREST
$(1 + i)^{-n}$

	PERCENTAGES							
N	1	2	4	5	6	8	8.75	N
1	0.99010	0.98039	0.96154	0.95238	0.94340	0.92593	0.91954	1
2	0.98030	0.96117	0.92456	0.90703	0.89000	0.85734	0.84555	2
3	0.97059	0.94232	0.88900	0.86384	0.83962	0.79383	0.77752	3
4	0.96098	0.92385	0.85480	0.82270	0.79209	0.73503	0.71496	4
5	0.95147	0.90573	0.82193	0.78353	0.74726	0.68058	0.65744	5
6	0.94205	0.88797	0.79031	0.74622	0.70496	0.63017	0.60454	6
7	0.93272	0.87056	0.75992	0.71068	0.66506	0.58349	0.55590	7
8	0.92348	0.85349	0.73069	0.67684	0.62741	0.54027	0.51117	8
9	0.91434	0.83676	0.70259	0.64461	0.59190	0.50025	0.47004	9
10	0.90529	0.82035	0.67556	0.61391	0.55839	0.46319	0.43222	10
11	0.89632	0.80426	0.64958	0.58468	0.52679	0.42888	0.39745	11
12	0.88745	0.78849	0.62460	0.55684	0.49697	0.39711	0.36547	12
13	0.87866	0.77303	0.60057	0.53032	0.46884	0.36770	0.33606	13
14	0.86996	0.75788	0.57748	0.50507	0.44230	0.34046	0.30902	14
15	0.86135	0.74301	0.55526	0.48102	0.41727	0.31524	0.28416	15
16	0.85282	0.72845	0.53391	0.45811	0.39365	0.29189	0.26130	16
17	0.84438	0.71416	0.51337	0.43630	0.37136	0.27027	0.24027	17
18	0.83602	0.70016	0.49363	0.41552	0.35034	0.25025	0.22094	18
19	0.82774	0.68643	0.47464	0.39573	0.33051	0.23171	0.20316	19
20	0.81954	0.67297	0.45639	0.37689	0.31180	0.21455	0.18682	20
21	0.81143	0.65978	0.43883	0.35894	0.29416	0.19866	0.17179	21
22	0.80340	0.64684	0.42196	0.34185	0.27751	0.18394	0.15796	22
23	0.79544	0.63416	0.40573	0.32557	0.26180	0.17032	0.14525	23
24	0.78757	0.62172	0.39012	0.31007	0.24698	0.15770	0.13357	24
25	0.77977	0.60953	0.37512	0.29530	0.23300	0.14602	0.12282	25
26	0.77205	0.59758	0.36069	0.28124	0.21981	0.13520	0.11294	26
27	0.76440	0.58586	0.34682	0.26785	0.20737	0.12519	0.10385	27
28	0.75684	0.57437	0.33348	0.25509	0.19563	0.11591	0.09549	28
29	0.74934	0.56311	0.32065	0.24295	0.18456	0.10733	0.08781	29
30	0.74192	0.55207	0.30832	0.23138	0.17411	0.09938	0.08075	30
31	0.73458	0.54125	0.29646	0.22036	0.16425	0.09202	0.07425	31
32	0.72730	0.53063	0.28506	0.20987	0.15496	0.08520	0.06828	32
33	0.72010	0.52023	0.27409	0.19987	0.14619	0.07889	0.06278	33
34	0.71297	0.51003	0.26355	0.19035	0.13791	0.07305	0.05773	34
35	0.70591	0.50003	0.25342	0.18129	0.13011	0.06763	0.05309	35
36	0.69892	0.49022	0.24367	0.17266	0.12274	0.06262	0.04881	36
37	0.69200	0.48061	0.23430	0.16444	0.11579	0.05799	0.04489	37
38	0.68515	0.47119	0.22529	0.15661	0.10924	0.05369	0.04128	38
39	0.67837	0.46195	0.21662	0.14915	0.10306	0.04971	0.03795	39
40	0.67165	0.45289	0.20829	0.14205	0.09722	0.04603	0.03490	40

TABLE 3
AMOUNT OF ANNUITY OF 1 PER PERIOD

$$\frac{(1+i)^n - 1}{i}$$

	PERCENTAGES							
N	1	2	4	5	6	8	8.75	N
1	1.00000	1.00000	1.00000	1.00000	1.00000	1.00000	1.00000	1
2	2.01000	2.02000	2.04000	2.05000	2.06000	2.08000	2.08750	2
3	3.03010	3.06040	3.12160	3.15250	3.18360	3.24640	3.27016	3
4	4.06040	4.12161	4.24646	4.31013	4.37462	4.50611	4.55629	4
5	5.10101	5.20404	5.41632	5.52563	5.63709	5.86660	5.95497	5
6	6.15202	6.30812	6.63298	6.80191	6.97532	7.33593	7.47603	6
7	7.21354	7.43428	7.89829	8.14201	8.39384	8.92280	9.13018	7
8	8.28567	8.58297	9.21423	9.54911	9.89747	10.63663	10.92907	8
9	9.36853	9.75463	10.58280	11.02656	11.49132	12.48756	12.88537	9
10	10.46221	10.94972	12.00611	12.57789	13.18079	14.48656	15.01284	10
11	11.56683	12.16872	13.48635	14.20679	14.97164	16.64549	17.32646	11
12	12.68250	13.41209	15.02581	15.91713	16.86994	18.97713	19.84253	12
13	13.80933	14.68033	16.62684	17.71298	18.88214	21.49530	22.57875	13
14	14.94742	15.97394	18.29191	19.59863	21.01507	24.21492	25.55439	14
15	16.09690	17.29342	20.02359	21.57856	23.27597	27.15211	28.79040	15
16	17.25786	18.63929	21.82453	23.65749	25.67253	30.32428	32.30956	16
17	18.43044	20.01207	23.69751	25.84037	28.21288	33.75023	36.13664	17
18	19.61475	21.41231	25.64541	28.13238	30.90565	37.45024	40.29860	18
19	20.81090	22.84056	27.67123	30.53900	33.75999	41.44626	44.82473	19
20	22.01900	24.29737	29.77808	33.06595	36.78559	45.76196	49.74689	20
21	23.23919	25.78332	31.96920	35.71925	39.99273	50.42292	55.09974	21
22	24.47159	27.29898	34.24797	38.50521	43.39229	55.45676	60.92097	22
23	25.71630	28.84496	36.61789	41.43048	46.99583	60.89330	67.25156	23
24	26.97346	30.42186	39.08260	44.50200	50.81558	66.76476	74.13607	24
25	28.24320	32.03030	41.64591	47.72710	54.86451	73.10594	81.62297	25
26	29.52563	33.67091	44.31174	51.11345	59.15638	79.95442	89.76498	26
27	30.82089	35.34432	47.08421	54.66913	63.70577	87.35077	98.61942	27
28	32.12910	37.05121	49.96758	58.40258	68.52811	95.33883	108.24862	28
29	33.45039	38.79223	52.96629	62.32271	73.63980	103.96594	118.72037	29
30	34.78489	40.56808	56.08494	66.43885	79.05819	113.28321	130.10841	30
31	36.13274	42.37944	59.32834	70.76079	84.80168	123.34587	142.49289	31
32	37.49407	44.22703	62.70147	75.29883	90.88978	134.21354	155.96102	32
33	38.86901	46.11157	66.20953	80.06377	97.34316	145.95062	170.60761	33
34	40.25770	48.03380	69.85791	85.06696	104.18375	158.62667	186.53577	34
35	41.66028	49.99448	73.65222	90.32031	111.43478	172.31680	203.85765	35
36	43.07688	51.99437	77.59831	95.83632	119.12087	187.10215	222.69520	36
37	44.50765	54.03425	81.70225	101.62814	127.26812	203.07032	243.18103	37
38	45.95272	56.11494	85.97034	107.70955	135.90421	220.31595	265.45937	38
39	47.41225	58.23724	90.40915	114.09502	145.05846	238.94122	289.68706	39
40	48.88637	60.40198	95.02552	120.79977	154.76197	259.05652	316.03468	40

TABLE 4
PRESENT VALUE OF ANNUITY OF 1 PER PERIOD

$$\frac{1-(1+i)^{-n}}{i}$$

PERCENTAGES

N	1	2	4	5	6	8	8.75	N
1	0.99010	0.98039	0.96154	0.95238	0.94340	0.92593	0.91954	1
2	1.97040	1.94156	1.88609	1.85941	1.83339	1.78326	1.76509	2
3	2.94099	2.88388	2.77509	2.72325	2.67301	2.57710	2.54262	3
4	3.90197	3.80773	3.62990	3.54595	3.46511	3.31213	3.25758	4
5	4.85343	4.71346	4.45182	4.32948	4.21236	3.99271	3.91501	5
6	5.79548	5.60143	5.24214	5.07569	4.91732	4.62288	4.51955	6
7	6.72819	6.47199	6.00205	5.78637	5.58238	5.20637	5.07545	7
8	7.65168	7.32548	6.73274	6.46321	6.20979	5.74664	5.58662	8
9	8.56602	8.16224	7.43533	7.10782	6.80169	6.24689	6.05666	9
10	9.47130	8.98259	8.11090	7.72173	7.36009	6.71008	6.48889	10
11	10.36763	9.78685	8.76048	8.30641	7.88687	7.13896	6.88633	11
12	11.25508	10.57534	9.38507	8.86325	8.38384	7.53608	7.25180	12
13	12.13374	11.34837	9.98565	9.39357	8.85268	7.90378	7.58786	13
14	13.00370	12.10625	10.56312	9.89864	9.29498	8.24424	7.89688	14
15	13.86505	12.84926	11.11839	10.37966	9.71225	8.55948	8.18104	15
16	14.71787	13.57771	11.65230	10.83777	10.10590	8.85137	8.44234	16
17	15.56225	14.29187	12.16567	11.27407	10.47726	9.12164	8.68261	17
18	16.39827	14.99203	12.65930	11.68959	10.82760	9.37189	8.90355	18
19	17.22601	15.67846	13.13394	12.08532	11.15812	9.60360	9.10671	19
20	18.04555	16.35143	13.59033	12.46221	11.46992	9.81815	9.29353	20
21	18.85698	17.01121	14.02916	12.82115	11.76408	10.01680	9.46531	21
22	19.66038	17.65805	14.45112	13.16300	12.04158	10.20074	9.62328	22
23	20.45582	18.29220	14.85684	13.48857	12.30338	10.37106	9.76853	23
24	21.24339	18.91393	15.24696	13.79864	12.55036	10.52876	9.90210	24
25	22.02316	19.52346	15.62208	14.09394	12.78336	10.67478	10.02492	25
26	22.79520	20.12104	15.98277	14.37519	13.00317	10.80998	10.13785	26
27	23.55961	20.70690	16.32959	14.64303	13.21053	10.93516	10.24171	27
28	24.31644	21.28127	16.66306	14.89813	13.40616	11.05108	10.33720	28
29	25.06579	21.84438	16.98371	15.14107	13.59072	11.15841	10.42501	29
30	25.80771	22.39646	17.29203	15.37245	13.76483	11.25778	10.50576	30
31	26.54229	22.93770	17.58849	15.59281	13.92909	11.34980	10.58001	31
32	27.26959	23.46833	17.87355	15.80268	14.08404	11.43500	10.64828	32
33	27.98969	23.98856	18.14765	16.00255	14.23023	11.51389	10.71106	33
34	28.70267	24.49859	18.41120	16.19290	14.36814	11.58693	10.76879	34
35	29.40858	24.99862	18.66461	16.37419	14.49825	11.65457	10.82188	35
36	30.10751	25.48884	18.90828	16.54685	14.62099	11.71719	10.87069	36
37	30.79951	25.96945	19.14258	16.71129	14.73678	11.77518	10.91558	37
38	31.48466	26.44064	19.36786	16.86789	14.84602	11.82887	10.95686	38
39	32.16303	26.90259	19.58448	17.01704	14.94907	11.87858	10.99481	39
40	32.83469	27.35548	19.79277	17.15909	15.04630	11.92461	11.02971	40

Appendix II
STATISTICAL SAMPLING TABLES

TABLE 1
DETERMINATION OF SAMPLE SIZE
CONFIDENCE LEVEL—99%
Percentage of Occurrences in Sample

Sample Size	Precision (Upper Limit) Percentage																				
	1	2	3	4	5	6	7	8	9	10	12	14	16	18	20	25	30	35	40	45	50
50									0	0	0	2.0	4.0	4.0	6.0	10.0	14.0	18.0	22.0	26.0	32.0
60								0	0	0	1.7	3.3	5.0	5.0	6.7	11.7	15.0	20.0	23.3	28.3	33.3
70							0	0	0	1.4	2.9	4.3	5.7	7.1	8.6	12.9	15.7	20.0	25.7	30.0	34.3
80						0	0	0	1.2			5.0	6.2	7.5	8.8		17.5	21.2	26.2	31.2	36.2
90					0	0	0	1.1		2.2	3.3	5.6	6.7	7.8	10.0	13.3	17.8	22.2	26.7	32.2	36.7
120				0	0	.8	1.7	1.7	2.5	3.3	5.0	6.7	7.5	9.2	10.8	15.0	20.0	24.2	29.2	33.3	38.3
160			0	0	.6	1.2	1.9	3.1	3.8	4.4	5.6	7.5	8.8	10.6	12.5	16.9	21.2	25.6	30.6	35.0	40.0
240		0	.4	.8	1.7	2.5	2.9	3.8	4.6	5.4	7.1	8.8	10.4	12.1	13.8	18.3	22.9	27.5	32.5	37.1	42.1
340		.3	.9	1.5	2.1	2.9	3.8	4.4	5.3	6.2	7.6	9.4	11.2	12.9	14.7	19.4	24.1	28.8	33.5	38.5	43.5
460	0	.4	1.1	1.7	2.6	3.3	4.1	5.0	5.9	6.7	8.5	10.2	12.0	13.7	15.7	20.2	24.8	29.6	34.6	39.3	44.3
1000	.2	.9	1.7	2.5	3.4	4.2	5.1	6.0	6.9	7.8	9.6	11.4	13.3	15.1	17.0	21.8	26.6	31.4	36.3	41.2	46.2

TABLE 2
DETERMINATION OF SAMPLE SIZE
CONFIDENCE LEVEL—95%
Percentage of Occurrences in Sample

Sample Size	Precision (Upper Limit) Percentage																				
	1	2	3	4	5	6	7	8	9	10	12	14	16	18	20	25	30	35	40	45	50
50						0	0	0	0	2.0		4.0	6.0	8.0	10.0	14.0	18.0	22.0	26.0	32.0	36.0
60					0	0	0	1.7	1.7		3.3	5.0	6.7	8.3	10.0	15.0	18.3	23.3	28.3	33.3	38.3
70					0	0	1.4		2.9	2.9	4.3	5.7	7.1	10.0	11.4	15.7	20.0	24.3	28.6	34.3	38.6
80				0	0	1.2		2.5		3.8	5.0	6.2	8.8	10.0		16.2	20.0	25.0	30.0	35.0	40.0
90				0	0		2.2		3.3	4.4	5.6	6.7	8.9	10.0	12.2	16.7	21.1	25.6	30.0	35.6	40.0
120			0	.8	.8	1.7	2.5	3.3	4.2	5.0	6.7	8.3	10.0	11.7	13.3	17.5	22.5	27.5	31.7	36.7	41.7
160		0	.6	1.2	1.9	2.5	3.1	3.8	5.0	5.6	7.5	8.8	10.6	12.5	14.4	18.8	23.8	28.1	33.1	38.1	43.1
240		.4	.8	1.7	2.5	3.3	4.2	5.0	5.8	6.7	8.3	10.0	11.7	13.8	15.4	20.0	24.6	29.6	34.6	39.2	44.2
340	0	.6	1.2	2.1	2.9	3.5	4.4	5.3	6.2	7.1	8.8	10.6	12.4	14.4	16.2	20.9	25.6	30.6	35.3	40.3	45.3
460	0	.9	1.5	2.4	3.3	3.9	4.8	5.7	6.7	7.6	9.3	11.1	13.0	14.8	16.7	21.5	26.3	31.1	36.1	40.9	45.9
1000	.4	1.2	2.0	2.9	3.8	4.7	5.6	6.5	7.4	8.4	10.2	12.1	14.0	15.9	17.8	22.7	27.5	32.4	37.4	42.3	47.5

TABLE 3
DETERMINATION OF SAMPLE SIZE
CONFIDENCE LEVEL—90%
Percentage of Occurrences in Sample

Sample Size	Precision (Upper Limit) Percentage																				
	1	2	3	4	5	6	7	8	9	10	12	14	16	18	20	25	30	35	40	45	50
50					0	0	0	2.0	2.0		4.0	6.0	8.0	10.0	10.0	16.0	20.0	24.0	30.0	34.0	38.0
60				0	0	0	1.7		3.3	3.3	5.0	6.7	8.3	10.0	11.7	16.7	21.7	25.0	30.0	35.0	40.0
70				0	0	1.4		2.9		4.3	5.7	7.1	8.6	11.4	12.9	17.1	21.4	25.7	31.4	35.7	41.4
80			0	0	1.2		2.5		3.8	5.0	6.2	7.5	10.0			17.5	22.5	27.5		36.2	
90			0	0		2.2		3.3	4.4		6.7	7.8	10.0	12.2	13.3	17.8	22.2	27.8	32.2	36.7	42.2
120		0	0	.8	1.7	2.5	3.3	4.2	5.0	5.9	7.5	9.2	10.8	12.5	14.2	19.2	24.2	28.3	33.3	38.3	43.3
160		0	.6	1.2	2.5	3.1	3.8	5.0	5.6	6.2	8.1	10.0	11.9	13.8	15.6	20.0	25.0	29.4	34.4	39.4	44.4
240	0	.4	1.2	2.1	2.9	3.8	4.6	5.4	6.2	7.1	8.8	10.8	12.5	14.6	16.2	20.8	25.8	30.8	35.4	40.4	45.4
340	0	.9	1.5	2.4	3.2	4.1	5.0	5.9	6.8	7.6	9.4	11.2	13.2	15.0	17.1	21.8	26.5	31.5	36.2	41.2	46.2
460	.2	.9	1.7	2.6	3.5	4.3	5.2	6.1	7.2	8.0	9.8	11.7	13.7	15.4	17.4	22.2	27.0	32.0	37.0	41.7	46.7
1000	.5	1.3	2.2	3.1	4.0	4.9	5.9	6.8	7.7	8.7	10.6	12.5	14.4	16.4	18.3	23.2	28.0	33.0	37.9	42.9	47.9

TABLE 4

DETERMINATION OF SAMPLE SIZE

CONFIDENCE LEVEL—85%

Percentage of Occurrences in Sample

Sample Size	Precision (Upper Limit) Percentage																				
	1	2	3	4	5	6	7	8	9	10	12	14	16	18	20	25	30	35	40	45	50
50				0	0	0	2.0	2.0	2.0	4.0	6.0	6.0	8.0	10.0	12.0	16.0	22.0	26.0	30.0	34.0	40.0
60				0	0	1.7		3.3	3.3	5.0	6.7	8.3	10.0	11.7	13.3	18.3		26.7	31.7	36.7	41.7
70			0	0	1.4		2.9		4.3		7.1	8.6	10.0		14.3	18.6	22.9	27.1	32.9	37.1	42.9
80			0	0		2.5		3.8	5.0	5.0	7.5	8.8	10.0	12.5		18.8	23.8	28.8		37.5	
90			0	1.1			3.3	4.4		5.6	7.8	8.9	11.1		14.4	18.9	24.4	28.9	33.3	38.9	43.3
120		0	.8	1.7	2.5	3.3	4.2	5.0	5.8	6.7	8.3	10.0	11.7	13.3	15.0	20.0	25.0	30.0	34.2	39.2	44.2
160		0	1.3	1.9	2.5	3.8	4.4	5.0	6.3	6.9	8.8	10.6	12.5	14.4	16.3	20.6	25.6	30.6	35.6	40.0	45.0
240	0	.8	1.3	2.1	3.3	4.2	5.0	5.8	6.7	7.5	9.6	11.3	13.3	15.0	17.1	21.7	26.7	31.3	36.3	41.3	46.3
340	.3	.9	1.8	2.6	3.5	4.4	5.3	6.2	7.1	7.9	10.0	11.8	13.5	15.6	17.4	22.4	27.1	32.1	37.1	41.8	46.8
460		1.1	2.0	2.8	3.7	4.6	5.7	6.5	7.4	8.3	10.2	12.2	13.9	15.9	17.8	22.6	27.6	32.4	37.4	42.4	47.1
1000	.6	1.4	2.3	3.3	4.2	5.1	6.1	7.0	8.0	8.9	10.8	12.8	14.7	16.6	18.6	23.5	28.4	33.3	38.3	43.3	48.3

TABLE 5
DETERMINATION OF SAMPLE SIZE
CONFIDENCE LEVEL—80%
Percentage of Occurrences in Sample

Sample Size	Precision (Upper Limit) Percentage																				
	1	2	3	4	5	6	7	8	9	10	12	14	16	18	20	25	30	35	40	45	50
50				0	0	2.0	2.0	2.0	4.0	4.0	6.0	8.0	10.0	12.0	14.0	18.0	22.0	28.0	32.0	38.0	42.0
60			0	0	1.7		3.3	3.3	5.0	5.0	6.7	8.3	10.0			18.3	23.3	28.3	33.3	38.3	43.3
70			0	0				4.3		5.7	7.1	8.6	11.4	12.9	14.3	18.6	24.3	28.6	34.3	38.6	
80		0	0	1.3		2.5	3.8		5.0	6.3	7.5	10.0			15.0	20.0	25.0	28.8		38.8	43.8
90		0	0		2.2			4.4	5.6	6.7	7.8	10.0		13.3	15.6	20.0		30.0	34.4	40.0	44.4
120		0	.8	1.7	2.5	3.3	4.2	5.0	5.8	6.7	8.3	10.8	12.5	14.2	15.8	20.8	25.8	30.8	35.0	40.0	45.0
160		.6	1.3	1.9	3.1	3.8	4.4	5.6	6.3	7.5	9.4	11.3	13.1	15.0	16.9	21.3	26.3	31.3	36.3	41.3	46.3
240	0	.8	1.7	2.5	3.3	4.2	5.0	6.3	7.1	7.9	10.0	11.7	13.8	15.4	17.5	22.1	27.1	32.1	37.1	42.1	46.7
340	.3	1.2	2.1	2.9	3.8	4.7	5.6	6.5	7.4	8.2	10.3	12.1	14.1	15.9	17.9	22.6	27.6	32.6	37.3	42.4	47.4
460	.4	1.3	2.2	3.0	3.9	4.8	5.9	6.7	7.6	8.7	10.4	12.4	14.3	16.3	18.3	23.0	28.0	32.8	37.8	42.8	47.8
1000	.6	1.5	2.4	3.4	4.3	5.3	6.2	7.2	8.1	9.1	11.0	13.0	14.9	16.9	18.8	23.7	28.7	33.6	38.6	43.6	48.6

TABLE 6
EVALUATION OF RESULTS
CONFIDENCE LEVEL—99%
Number of Occurrences in Sample

Sample Size	Precision (Upper Limit) Percentage																				
	1	2	3	4	5	6	7	8	9	10	12	14	16	18	20	25	30	35	40	45	50
50									0			1	2		3	5	7	9	11	13	16
60								0			1	2	3		4	7	9	12	14	17	20
70							0			1	2	3	4	5	6	9	11	14	18	21	24
80						0			1		2	4	5	6	7	10	14	17	21	25	29
90					0			1		2	3	5	6	7	9	12	16	20	24	29	33
120				0		1	2		3	4	6	8	9	11	13	18	24	29	35	40	46
160			0		1	2	3	5	6	7	9	12	14	17	20	27	34	41	49	56	64
240		0	1	2	4	6	7	9	11	13	17	21	25	29	33	44	55	66	78	89	101
340		1	3	5	7	10	13	15	18	21	26	32	38	44	50	66	82	98	114	131	148
460	0	2	5	8	12	15	19	23	27	31	39	47	55	63	72	93	114	136	159	181	204
1000	2	9	17	25	34	42	51	60	69	78	96	114	133	151	170	218	266	314	363	412	462

TABLE 7
EVALUATION OF RESULTS
CONFIDENCE LEVEL—95%
Number of Occurrences in Sample

Sample Size	Precision (Upper Limit) Percentage																				
	1	2	3	4	5	6	7	8	9	10	12	14	16	18	20	25	30	35	40	45	50
50						0				1		2	3	4	5	7	9	11	13	16	18
60					0			1			2	3	4	5	6	9	11	14	17	20	23
70					0		1		2		3	4	5	7	8	11	14	17	20	24	27
80				0		1		2		3	4	5	7	8	9	13	16	20	24	28	32
90				0		1	2		3	4	5	6	8	9	11	15	19	23	27	32	36
120			0	1		2	3	4	5	6	8	10	12	14	16	21	27	33	38	44	50
160		0	1	2	3	4	5	6	8	9	12	14	17	20	23	30	38	45	53	61	69
240		1	2	4	6	8	10	12	14	16	20	24	28	33	37	48	59	71	83	94	106
340	0	2	4	7	10	12	15	18	21	24	30	36	42	49	55	71	87	104	120	137	154
460	0	4	7	11	15	18	22	26	31	35	43	51	60	68	77	99	121	143	166	188	211
1000	4	12	20	29	38	47	56	65	74	84	102	121	140	159	178	227	275	324	374	423	473

TABLE 8
EVALUATION OF RESULTS
CONFIDENCE LEVEL—90%
Number of Occurrences in Sample

Sample Size	Precision (Upper Limit) Percentage																				
	1	2	3	4	5	6	7	8	9	10	12	14	16	18	20	25	30	35	40	45	50
50					0			1			2	3	4	5		8	10	12	15	17	19
60				0			1		2		3	4	5	6	7	10	13	15	18	21	24
70				0		1		2		3	4	5	6	8	9	12	15	18	22	25	29
80			0		1		2		3	4	5	6	8	9	10	14	18	22	25	29	33
90			0		1	2		3	4		6	7	9	11	12	16	20	25	29	33	38
120		0		1	2	3	4	5	6	7	9	11	13	15	17	23	29	34	40	46	52
160		0	1	2	4	5	6	8	9	10	13	16	19	22	25	32	40	47	55	63	71
240	0	1	3	5	7	9	11	13	15	17	21	26	30	35	39	50	62	74	85	97	109
340	0	3	5	8	11	14	17	20	23	26	32	38	45	51	58	74	90	107	123	140	157
460	1	4	8	12	16	20	24	28	33	37	45	54	63	71	80	102	124	147	170	192	215
1000	5	13	22	31	40	49	59	68	77	87	106	125	144	164	183	232	280	330	379	429	479

TABLE 9
EVALUATION OF RESULTS
CONFIDENCE LEVEL—85%
Number of Occurrences in Sample

Sample Size	Precision (Upper Limit) Percentage																				
	1	2	3	4	5	6	7	8	9	10	12	14	16	18	20	25	30	35	40	45	50
50				0			1			2	3		4	5	6	8	11	13	15	18	20
60				0		1		2		3	4	5	6	7	8	11	13	16	19	22	25
70			0		1		2		3		5	6	7	8	10	13	16	19	23	26	30
80			0		1	2		3	4		6	7	8	10	11	15	19	23	26	30	34
90			0	1		2	3	4		5	7	8	10	11	13	17	22	26	30	35	39
120		0	1	2	3	4	5	6	7	8	10	12	14	16	18	24	30	36	41	47	53
160		0	2	3	4	6	7	8	10	11	14	17	20	23	26	33	41	49	57	64	72
240	0	2	3	5	8	10	12	14	16	18	23	27	32	36	41	52	64	75	87	99	111
340	1	3	6	9	12	15	18	21	24	27	34	40	46	53	59	76	92	109	126	142	159
460	1	5	9	13	17	21	26	30	34	38	47	56	64	73	82	104	127	149	172	195	218
1000	6	14	23	33	42	51	61	70	80	89	108	128	147	166	186	235	284	333	383	433	483

TABLE 10
EVALUATION OF RESULTS
CONFIDENCE LEVEL—80%
Number of Occurrences in Sample

Sample Size	Precision (Upper Limit) Percentage																				
	1	2	3	4	5	6	7	8	9	10	12	14	16	18	20	25	30	35	40	45	50
50				0		1			2		3	4	5	6	7	9	11	14	16	19	21
60			0		1		2		3		4	5	6	7	8	11	14	17	20	23	26
70			0		1		2	3		4	5	6	8	9	10	13	17	20	24	27	30
80		0		1		2	3		4	5	6	8	9	10	12	16	20	23	27	31	35
90		0		1	2		3	4	5	6	7	9	10	12	14	18	22	27	31	36	40
120		0	1	2	3	4	5	6	7	8	10	13	15	17	19	25	31	37	42	48	54
160		1	2	3	5	6	7	9	10	12	15	18	21	24	27	34	42	50	58	66	74
240	0	2	4	6	8	10	12	15	17	19	24	28	33	37	42	53	65	77	89	101	112
340	1	4	7	10	13	16	19	22	25	28	35	41	48	54	61	77	94	111	127	144	161
460	2	6	10	14	18	22	27	31	35	40	48	57	66	75	84	106	129	151	174	197	220
1000	6	15	24	34	43	53	62	72	81	91	110	130	149	169	188	237	287	336	386	436	486

TABLE 11
PROBABILITY IN PERCENT OF INCLUDING AT LEAST ONE OCCURRENCE IN A SAMPLE
For Populations Over 10,000

Sample Size	If the True Population Rate of Occurrence is: .01%	.05%	.1%	.2%	.3%	.5%	1%	2%
	The Probability of Including at Least One Occurrence in the Sample is:							
50		2%	5%	9%	14%	22%	39%	64%
60	1%	3	6	11	16	26	45	70
70	1	3	7	13	19	30	51	76
80	1	4	8	15	21	33	55	80
90	1	4	9	16	24	36	60	84
100	1	5	10	18	26	39	63	87
120	1	6	11	21	30	45	70	91
140	1	7	13	24	34	50	76	94
160	2	8	15	27	38	55	80	96
200	2	10	18	33	45	63	87	98
240	2	11	21	38	51	70	91	99
300	3	14	26	45	59	78	95	99+
340	3	16	29	49	64	82	97	99+
400	4	18	33	55	70	87	98	99+
460	5	21	37	60	75	90	99	99+
500	5	22	39	63	78	92	99	99+
600	6	26	45	70	84	95	99+	99+
700	7	30	50	75	88	97	99+	99+
800	8	33	55	80	91	98	99+	99+
900	9	36	59	83	93	99	99+	99+
1,000	10	39	63	86	95	99	99+	99+
1,500	14	53	78	95	99	99+	99+	99+
2,000	18	63	86	98	99+	99+	99+	99+
2,500	22	71	92	99	99+	99+	99+	99+
3,000	26	78	95	99+	99+	99+	99+	99+

TABLE 12
PROBABILITY IN PERCENT OF INCLUDING AT LEAST ONE OCCURRENCE IN A SAMPLE
For Populations Between 5,000 and 10,000

If the True Population Rate of Occurrence is:

Sample Size	.1%	.2%	.3%	.4%	.5%	.75%	1%	2%
	The Probability of Including at Least One Occurrence in the Sample is:							
50	5%	10%	14%	18%	22%	31%	40%	64%
60	6	11	17	21	26	36	45	70
70	7	13	19	25	30	41	51	76
80	8	15	21	28	33	45	55	80
90	9	17	24	30	36	49	60	84
100	10	18	26	33	40	53	64	87
120	11	21	30	38	45	60	70	91
140	13	25	35	43	51	65	76	94
160	15	28	38	48	55	70	80	96
200	18	33	45	56	64	78	87	98
240	22	39	52	62	70	84	91	99
300	26	46	60	70	78	90	95	99+
340	29	50	65	75	82	93	97	99+
400	34	56	71	81	87	95	98	99+
460	38	61	76	85	91	97	99	99+
500	40	64	79	87	92	98	99	99+
600	46	71	84	92	96	99	99+	99+
700	52	77	89	95	97	99+	99+	99+
800	57	81	92	96	98	99+	99+	99+
900	61	85	94	98	99	99+	99+	99+
1,000	65	88	96	99	99	99+	99+	99+
1,500	80	96	99	99+	99+	99+	99+	99+
2,000	89	99	99+	99+	99+	99+	99+	99+

TABLE 13
PROBABILITY IN PERCENT OF INCLUDING AT LEAST ONE OCCURRENCE IN A SAMPLE
For Populations Between 2,000 and 5,000

	If the True Population Rate of Occurrence is:							
Sample Size	.3%	.4%	.5%	.6%	.8%	1%	1.5%	2%
	The Probability of Including at Least One Occurrence in the Sample is:							
50	14%	18%	22%	26%	33%	40%	53%	64%
60	17	21	26	30	38	45	60	70
70	19	25	30	35	43	51	66	76
80	22	28	33	38	48	56	70	80
90	24	31	37	42	52	60	75	84
100	26	33	40	46	56	64	78	87
120	31	39	46	52	62	70	84	91
140	35	43	51	57	68	76	88	94
160	39	48	56	62	73	80	91	96
200	46	56	64	71	81	87	95	98
240	52	63	71	77	86	92	98	99
300	61	71	79	84	92	96	99	99+
340	65	76	83	88	94	97	99+	99+
400	71	81	88	92	96	98	99+	99+
460	77	86	91	95	98	99	99+	99+
500	79	88	93	96	99	99	99+	99+
600	85	92	96	98	99	99+	99+	99+
700	90	95	98	99	99+	99+	99+	99+
800	93	97	99	99	99+	99+	99+	99+
900	95	98	99	99+	99+	99+	99+	99+
1,000	97	99	99+	99+	99+	99+	99+	99+

TABLE 14
CONVERSION OF CONFIDENCE LEVELS TO U VALUES
(Confidence Coefficients)

Confidence Levels	U Values
65%	.93
70%	1.04
75%	1.15
80%	1.28
85%	1.44
90%	1.64
95%	1.96
99%	2.58

TABLE 15
CONVERSION OF U VALUES TO CONFIDENCE LEVELS

U Values	Confidence Levels	U Values	Confidence Levels	U Values	Confidence Levels
.5	38%	1.35	82%	1.95	94%
.6	45%	1.40	83%	2.00	95%
.7	51%	1.45	86%	2.05	95%
.8	56%	1.50	86%	2.10	96%
.9	63%	1.55	87%	2.15	96%
1.00	68%	1.60	89%	2.20	97%
1.05	70%	1.65	90%	2.25	97%
1.10	72%	1.70	91%	2.30	97%
1.15	74%	1.75	91%	2.35	98%
1.20	76%	1.80	92%	2.40	98%
1.25	78%	1.85	93%	2.45	98%
1.30	80%	1.90	94%	2.56	99%

Note: All U values represent plus or minus values.

TABLE 16
RANDOM NUMBER TABLE

	(1)	(2)	(3)	(4)	(5)	(6)	(7)	(8)	(9)	(10)	(11)	(12)	(13)	(14)
1416	47405	97469	90403	49420	45421	08755	98228	34796	88746	66820	26942	20890	93616	12668
1417	43258	95534	87336	44598	21812	47574	37461	71134	51379	02560	59287	18163	32017	34079
1418	78054	38053	76625	40189	85260	15936	19764	06393	52717	26632	03845	84789	57660	06534
1419	98009	48697	99745	57271	27845	89662	97060	34924	74216	40330	62163	84100	03510	87018
1420	89539	20545	01572	80160	99113	60898	15979	21744	31802	00506	70014	34224	24303	60213
1421	50971	68414	12747	98328	01385	03650	28584	46795	61672	18108	53097	98729	74866	73116
1422	08985	78498	12409	90670	70068	44249	86142	58168	49415	81671	40515	47715	14092	65155
1423	56387	98581	50840	43657	79899	79340	56881	39843	73894	04555	17874	01733	77115	24638
1424	95291	50890	88317	18046	23068	10820	87401	91948	77129	11243	71657	03462	75057	05700
1425	48269	12957	89398	73619	77078	38993	52967	80016	64932	44532	18121	93764	49174	82724
1426	30129	45255	61883	86928	40119	10822	81133	28040	49345	19326	81373	61492	45306	82317
1427	60384	92751	24437	92878	41118	45281	95549	34677	50057	11832	95817	72517	29479	09776
1428	90697	21527	45677	01301	32776	90315	24528	24802	44516	96779	92902	60511	33634	52737
1429	69348	59490	41924	15472	63892	04948	54391	86001	21344	19270	71069	18425	29397	24754
1430	31541	95745	00621	81689	34455	81882	85116	57733	55992	50017	69765	09465	52352	30175
1431	07365	84787	80609	25283	43880	74610	57662	59244	24173	03354	79635	76874	22007	15860
1432	32863	12770	71142	62515	68375	82877	56590	32717	83166	75115	57813	88814	40352	80827
1433	41459	65791	87317	31296	21168	07674	03736	96448	44439	32621	21884	41834	09015	86305
1434	70246	16564	57312	07083	91043	80663	33807	91347	09334	14579	22283	25043	51437	21623
1435	81769	34679	87801	46900	19251	48485	98608	68556	71292	63616	23231	96106	74890	98186
1436	58710	07935	41379	88812	98238	51991	27332	16278	22901	83504	91681	99962	95007	67523
1437	93137	62174	33395	37878	94351	38641	42854	62566	31140	73489	51051	44116	71495	49005
1438	92028	33566	76951	38293	59501	26781	35827	91719	09878	42461	06902	65924	35159	77071
1439	77643	97236	96376	43223	94208	43244	21477	64603	07954	96465	86425	04285	59298	94413
1440	48743	03178	22000	40815	29181	80767	27226	27128	35260	56008	03457	79998	23686	51235
1441	94061	44835	98120	78478	95414	08809	49294	85821	42752	70197	41772	01040	37368	53650
1442	43017	28338	32308	95011	44996	58065	14245	38794	96652	13214	79685	49385	08327	55004
1443	99631	98431	76974	63349	87461	39090	18052	66650	96938	68938	96831	33274	12612	62788
1444	88846	58974	93606	11833	28431	42696	49063	37026	04726	54248	44787	20724	91378	08937
1445	62332	76895	13101	41226	11923	94970	16685	23620	11918	86257	11694	43880	24531	27272
1446	26084	74818	49139	99047	02534	87700	27332	08393	39222	23943	91980	85104	07614	16278
1447	85785	03962	98057	67638	92405	44683	82124	07060	87337	09739	60577	36052	40571	56199
1448	08537	80929	66352	83924	21331	79310	93710	60398	74570	91901	94755	55198	11729	49801
1449	61985	45155	39295	67906	49594	08100	64610	68547	43692	80002	63518	31691	05598	66601
1450	92834	25766	03415	86498	18061	78501	20573	85081	77480	41572	36330	71213	68582	32234
1451	12066	40826	41486	23853	91969	03168	30629	50804	67753	08584	19882	23713	81435	90352
1452	57442	56762	76110	24363	72447	34084	80879	10938	91391	25386	36962	51084	90753	23549
1453	72078	39251	50886	46430	53994	56049	36030	71580	10161	70116	16556	95669	62817	05335
1454	63675	45810	44199	84436	13081	31652	36509	10949	05446	30913	60149	66850	89498	07155
1455	60595	74791	23267	37039	84875	87192	93298	46426	39072	98984	17404	28804	99841	61663
1456	45204	01095	86043	30604	28361	63342	48430	41094	64356	01440	86840	33363	12019	49913
1457	39994	25083	60371	97716	52655	58508	50026	50928	20567	17379	96141	06955	69389	92222
1458	06909	70912	30714	90653	83792	38309	42841	39378	16075	50103	15226	71790	42099	51455
1459	54780	92942	41783	68934	98006	71249	98263	59085	19490	59014	78394	92519	32837	33379
1460	34355	05525	52357	80287	89998	89576	11541	62443	17505	02287	58373	28620	70154	40433
1461	44229	68964	76398	97736	29356	19720	30957	40275	55062	07333	94037	64528	45791	95969
1462	79210	48613	03454	95486	70690	82321	21989	52789	88459	40665	98123	90591	43018	52535
1463	79746	45302	92695	80348	90693	32522	98359	82507	29368	74058	82667	05911	64996	69916
1464	41917	70277	95306	28321	40298	83054	80470	38497	41582	40297	10731	21011	76868	76451
1465	81682	67920	71356	90892	73481	32239	75242	22339	27678	21353	18881	51285	26395	76095
1466	03662	33387	37376	28181	10523	94005	06120	42216	15987	81374	19623	03216	33089	39776
1467	44950	55990	23779	93362	46063	58980	84151	09106	62520	65630	41521	27747	23516	97984
1468	19099	87872	79283	53751	80925	24221	74310	16851	21678	65600	78803	32680	75685	43132
1469	60213	68931	09542	71109	12758	25464	82318	08841	21851	19698	11087	71475	20908	85700
1470	58554	88248	81547	61101	13373	31787	17293	86404	54460	03941	62491	64924	13200	71641

INDEX